Greenhill Books

GUDERIAN
PANZER GENERAL

Kenneth Macksey

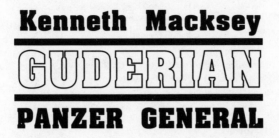

GUDERIAN

PANZER GENERAL

Greenhill Books, London
Presidio Press, California

Greenhill Books

This edition of *Guderian: Panzer General* first published 1992
by Greenhill Books, Lionel Leventhal Limited, Park House,
1 Russell Gardens, London NW11 9NN
and
Presidio Press
P.O. Box 1764, Novato, Ca.94948, U.S.A.

British Library Cataloguing in Publication Data
Macksey, Kenneth, *1923–*
Guderian: Panzer General
1. Germany. Heer. Tank units. Guderian, Heinz – Biographies
I. Title
358'.18'0924

ISBN 1-85367-059-6

Library of Congress Cataloging-in-Publication Data
Macksey, Kenneth.
Guderian, Panzer general / by Kenneth Macksey: with a new introduction
by Kenneth Macksey.
p. cm.
Revised ed. of: Guderian, creator of the blitzkrieg. 1975.
Includes bibliographical references and index.
ISBN 1-85367-059-6
1. Guderian, Heinz, 1888–1954. 2. Generals – Germany – Biography.
3. Germany. Heer – Biography. 4. Germany. Heer – Armored troops – History.
5. Tank warfare – History. 6. Lightning war – History.
I. Macksey, Kenneth. Guderian, creator of the blitzkrieg.
II. Title.
U55.G8M3 1992
358'.18'092 – dc20   91–40278
[B]   CIP

Publishing History
Guderian: Panzer General was first published in 1975 (Macdonald and Jane's)
and is reproduced now exactly as the original edition, complete and unabridged,
with the addition of a new Introduction by the author.

Quality printing and binding by Biddles Ltd.,
Guildford and King's Lynn, England.

Contents

Comparative Table of Officers' Ranks in the German, British and American Armies

German	British	American
Generalfeldmarschall	Field-Marshal	General of the Army
Generaloberst	General	General
General der (Arm)	Lt-General	Lt General
Generalleutnant	Major-General	Major General
Generalmajor	Brigadier	Brigadier General
Oberst	Colonel	Colonel
Oberstleutnant	Lt-Colonel	Lt Colonel
Major	Major	Major
Hauptmann	Captain	Captain
Oberleutnant	Lieutenant	1st Lieutenant
Leutnant	2nd Lieutenant	2nd Lieutenant
Oberfähnrich	Senior Officer Cadet	Senior Officer Cadet
Fähnrich	Officer Cadet	Officer Cadet

ILLUSTRATIONS
Between pages 130 and 131

MAPS   *Facing page*

Preface

Of the organisations that were the target for hatred and prosecution for their role in the Second World War, none among the acquitted was more roundly condemned by the Nürnberg International Military Tribunal than the German General Staff. The judges felt bound to add, with characteristically high moral tone, 'They have been a disgrace to the honourable profession of arms. Without their military guidance the aggressive ambitions of Hitler and his fellow Nazis would have been academic and sterile'. The strictures related, of course, to a small minority only, to the ruling clique of the General Staff who had occupied posts of the highest responsibility. This included several senior commanders and staff officers who were absent from the dock at Nürnberg but who, in due course, would stand trial on their own account. Yet the most celebrated of this group, the creator of the *Panzertruppe* which, of all the elements in the German *Wehrmacht*, had made conquest swift and thus economically feasible, and whose battlecraft was most feared in the days of mastery, was never arraigned.

Generaloberst Heinz Wilhelm Guderian remains an enigma who frightened the armies of Europe to death and who deeply disturbed the conservative, disciplined circle of the German military profession. On the one hand he rejected the conduct of anonymity demanded of a member of the General Staff by becoming an arch publicist of radical ideas, one who was in the forefront of a furious debate which introduced schisms into the political, as well as the military sphere. To the world at large he came to personify the archetypal, single-minded Prussian bent upon war. To the German people, however, in his heyday, he was a hero – and worshipped by the soldiers too. On the other hand, powerful adversaries within the *Wehrmacht* regarded him as a threat to the sanctity of their caste, while to influential members of the Nazi hierarchy he represented much that was repugnant to them about Army officers, even though, at times, he seemed closer to their way of thinking than most of the General Staff. And of them all, nobody seemed more confused in his relationship with Guderian than Adolf Hitler himself.

The recording of Guderian's activities has been warped by the prejudices that were generated by his impulsive and persuasive maverick spirit. Inevitably the predispositions of orthodox people were hostile to him and jealousy was nursed by the casualties of a fierce internecine struggle that took place within a revolutionary German hierarchy. In the aftermath of an epoch of violence and hatred, what sort of convincing personal defence could be made by a general who had been kept behind bars, without trial, for three years?

In the pages of *Erinnerungen eines Soldaten* (hereafter called by its English title of *Panzer Leader*), Guderian wrote what was, in effect, an account of the raising of the *Panzertruppe* interwoven with a defence of his activities in the years that followed. Since its publication it has become a standard reference work in connection with the *Panzertruppe* and Guderian, though it is wide open to criticism as all autobiography must be. Apart from its omissions it measures up well by standards of accuracy because the complete Guderian family archives were preserved. As a balanced description of the man, however, it is strangely deficient. Partly this is explained by the non-availability, at the time of composition, of official records from which he could refresh and widen his knowledge, and partly the lack of other men's memoirs. But to some extent Guderian proved his own worst advocate in that he denied the reader insight into his background and a sight of the fundamental evidence which displayed the man in the making and in his true colours. He chose to reduce the story of his first thirty-five years to a mere couple of pages and thus concealed the cause of so much that came to pass. The reasons for this are not entirely obscure. There seems to have been a certain presumption on his part of an unchallengeable integrity – a reasonable notion, as it happens, but one that, at times, makes him sound almost too good to be true. Although family documents lend support to a strong case in his favour, he rarely bothered to produce them and, in explaining a few contentious matters, such as various accusations against him or the circumstances of certain intrigues, relapsed into oblique or even devious replies instead of giving blunt retorts such as were characteristic. Even to his tormentors he extended an almost exaggerated generosity that weakened his own case.

However, it must be realised that Guderian assembled the memoirs under conditions of peculiar stress. Largely the material was collected while he was a prisoner of the Americans, by whom he was interrogated in the search for evidence against both himself and his old comrades. The early days of his incarceration were spent in discomfort, sometimes in humiliating circumstances, and always in the expectation of indictment. Even when the Americans and British absolved him the Poles endeavoured to bring him to trial in connection with the Battle for Warsaw in 1944. Later he became involved in a legal wrangle with Fabian von Schlabrendorff whose book, *Offiziere gegen Hitler*, had appeared in Switzerland in 1946 and was, in 1948, to be serialised in a West German newspaper. Sections of that book were harmful to Guderian: they not only stimulated the distaste of those who already detested him but drove Guderian to defend himself at law. Although Schlabrendorff was induced to recant publicly in 1948, the damage had been done. Schlabrendorff's first edition was quoted – and still is. Despite the appearance of a second edition in 1951 with all references to Guderian deleted, and his *The Secret War against Hitler* (published in 1956, long after Guderian's death) in which Guderian is hardly mentioned at all, Schlabrendorff is still read with a strong measure of credibility. In *Panzer Leader* Guderian denied everything that Schlabrendorff had written in connection with his activities concerning the anti-Hitler plotters, though he by no means clarified the story to complete satisfaction as he so easily could with considerable credit.

Family documents, particularly the correspondence with his wife, help sharpen blurred passages in *Panzer Leader* and fill some of the gaps. One begins to discern the man's basic loyalties, his humanity and brimming patriotism – and here, too, a professed honesty of purpose is made apparent, for sometimes he expressed himself with startlingly dangerous clarity. These contemporary letters – so at variance in many respects to the hindsighted memoirs of so many German generals – render a service to history and provide an essential understanding of the circumstances and the factors which conditioned and confused the Germans. It is well to know about urgent people of creative ability at moments of sudden change and to understand the idealists of vision and power, men who, in days of disaster, may infer, as Guderian quoted in 1919 at the depths of a shattering revolution: 'May the day be dark, may the sun shine bright. I am a Prussian and a Prussian I will be', adding 'Everything now depends upon keeping the oath. Germany would go under if everybody were to say: "Not I, others can do it". Everybody who has the smallest sense must say instead, "I will help".'

This, in fact, is the story of a Prussian who was inclined sometimes to be more Prussian in outlook than the Prussians, one who mixed clear vision with precise honour and subtle flexibility in the execution of modern ideas that were the antithesis of rigidity.

I am deeply indebted to *Generalmajor* Heinz-Günther Guderian for making available family papers, which appear here for the first time, and for reading my drafts in his father's spirit – that is by arguing a case with good-humoured patience, rising nobly to each challenge and, like his father, being absolutely frank when the occasion demanded. Guderian's one-time Chief of Staff, Walther Nehring, once remarked to me that if you know the son you obtain a good impression of the father. As time went by and I came to know Heinz-Günther Guderian, I found the experience stimulatingly enjoyable.

To the German generals who contributed I am immensely grateful too – to Walther Nehring, the doyen of Guderian's staff officers and a celebrated historian of the *Panzerwaffe*; to Hermann Balck, one of the staunchest and most combatant of Guderian's old comrades who not only warned me that 'to understand Guderian you have to understand Prussian discipline', but wrote an essay on the subject; to Wilfred Strikfeld, Generals Chales de Beaulieu and Walter Warlimont who answered certain important questions. As on previous occasions Dr Kurt Peball of the Austrian Kriegsarchiv gave help and so, too, did Mr Dermot Bradley. I am also indebted to *Generalleutnant* G. Engel, *Oberst* H.W. Frank, *Oberst* G. von Below, Paul Dierichs and *Major* H. Wolf for memoirs about Guderian and to *Generalmajors* Kurt von Liebenstein, and K H von Barsewisch for the use of their war diaries.

Naturally it was vitally important that I should be in possession of sound translations of many German books and documents. In this respect I was extremely fortunate to have the help and advice of Helga Ashworth, Reinhold Drepper, and Simon and Ursula Williams who spent long hours deciphering letters and documents.

The photographs of A German Pz IV tank in action in Poland, The Command Group in operation: orders on the march, The Command Group in operation: Guderian reads an incoming message, Action in France, Products of the *Panzertruppe*, and Guderian with von Rundstedt after the French campaign, are from the Bundesarchiv; those of the Tiger and Panther tanks are from the Imperial War Museum. All the other pictures came from the Guderian family albums by kind permission of *Generalmajor* Heinz-Günther Guderian. I am grateful to Peter Chamberlain and Brian Davis for their help with picture research.

To the staff of the various museums and libraries, who provided me with so many essential documents and books, go my boundless thanks and admiration for their endless patience. I refer in particular to the Royal Armoured Corps Museum, the Royal Signals Museum, the Imperial War Museum, the Library of the British Ministry of Defence and the Office of the US National Archives. Finally, as so often before, I thank Margaret Dunn for her typing and criticism, Michael Haine for preparing the maps, and my wife for her constant support and encouragement.

Introduction

It is a pleasure to record the publication by Greenhill Books of this third English language edition of a biography about General Guderian which has achieved three major editions in his own country. Not simply because of the opportunity to draw new attention to this great German General but also to explain a matter which was played down deliberately in previous editions. I refer, of course, to the dubious influence of Captain Basil Liddell Hart referred to on pages 40 and 41.

My doubts about Guderian's admission of indebtedness to Liddell Hart, on page 20 of the English version of *Panzer Leader*, were established long before 1973 when I met his elder son, *Generalmajor* Heinz Günther Guderian, while engaged in research for this biography. Almost at once he pointed out that the vital paragraph ending 'So I owe many suggestions of our further development to Captain Liddell Hart' was not in the original *Erinnerungen eines Soldaten*. He then showed me the complete correspondence between the two men, that included two vital letters which I already knew were missing from Liddell Hart's own meticulously kept files. Letters in which Liddell Hart emphasised his help in arranging publication of the *Erinnerungen* in English and writing the Foreword, and asking if Guderian might consider adding a piece to reinforce Liddell Hart's claim to have contributed significantly to the formulation of German armoured doctrine. He even obligingly submitted a draft paragraph which Guderian, no doubt feeling under an obligation, virtually copied.

None of this would have mattered if it had been true or if Guderian had been the only target for this kind of deception by Liddell Hart. But as Professor John Mearsheimer has recently demonstrated in his admirably documented *Liddell Hart and the Weight of History*, General von Manstein and the Rommel family also were singled out to lend testimony to Liddell Hart's ambitious claims of prescience for having correctly envisaged the shape and dominating nature of offensive armoured warfare before 1939. When in fact, for reasons and with effects explained by Mearsheimer, since 1935 he had been expounding in Government circles and in public the concept that Defence would be superior to Offence and the tank would be neutralised and therefore out-moded by the latest anti-tank weapons. This indeed was part of a most effective propaganda campaign by Liddell Hart (who was foremost a journalist of great vanity) to restore his faulted pre-war reputation.

Guderian's son and I were in agreement that, while reference to the discrepancy on page 20 was essential, no purpose would be served by mentioning Liddell Hart's 'missing' letters. Now that the whole dismal business is public knowledge it merely has to be asked why Guderian agreed to co-operate (as von Manstein would not) and what effect this has on his reputation. Beyond much doubt Guderian wrote the paragraph out of kindness of heart and gratitude for Liddell Hart's friendship and help – such was the man. He could also afford to be generous since nothing Liddell Hart might claim could detract from Guderian's mighty achievements. But he might not have been so compliant had he lived to witness Liddell Hart's blatant trading upon that paragraph. Whether or not he perceived that, if a true disciple of Liddell Hart, he logically should in 1939 have rejected Panzer Divisions, we will never know. Because he did not is proof that Guderian, always his own man, was never, with the exception of General Fuller, anybody's disciple.

KM
1992

1 A Peculiar Fellow

On 21st May 1940 a travel-stained German general, short in stature but powerful in enthusiasm, drove into Abbeville and gazed out across the English Channel. At the end of 'this remarkable day', as he described it, he basked momentarily in the realisation of a dream because, in and around the precincts of the town, the army corps of his creation, strong in armoured vehicles, held undisputed possession by right of conquest at the culmination of a performance which was unique in military history. With scarcely a pause the German tank force had fought its way through the intricate Ardennes, breached a fortified river-line and defeated a major portion of the enemy's best troops as it cut a swathe through France. Still quite fresh, it had taken Abbeville practically unopposed because, at the end of an advance of nearly 220 miles in eleven days, it had, by the sheer speed of its progress, left the opposing forces far behind. The Anglo-French and Belgian armies, which the Germans had so comprehensively outpaced, lay broken in their trail: the rest of the Channel ports stood virtually undefended, ripe for seizing, and those out-manoeuvred allied forces which still retained a measure of cohesion could only look on, aghast in the realisation that they were on the verge of total envelopment.

General der Panzertruppe Heinz Wilhelm Guderian had arrived at the zenith of his career. At negligible cost and by the employment of a mere three divisions, with occasional assistance from others helped spasmodically by air power, he had thrown the Anglo-French allies into chaos and accomplished in a matter of days what the entire German Army had failed to achieve at unprecedented cost in the four years of war preceding 1918. In the process this General Officer had elevated himself to the eminence of Gustavus Adolphus by creating a truly revolutionary concept and weapon in time of peace and pursuing the idea to a successful conclusion in war: the difference in authority between a monarch and a quite junior officer, however, made his achievement all the more outstanding. The force he had created was motivated by speed allied to armoured protection for the fighting men, and the panzer divisions he commanded were dominated by the tank, a weapon which had barely demonstrated its potentiality before 1918. Yet on 21st May 1940 the sheer pace of Guderian's advance, which had stricken the Anglo-French

1

armies by its dash and discreet selection of objectives, also baffled the conventionally minded strategists and tacticians of the Great German General Staff when they watched the unbelievable unfolding before them on their maps and heard the reports flooding back by radio from the panzer spearhead.

Let it not be imagined that the officers of the General Staff were laggard in their search for military improvements; for generations their preoccupation had been the harnessing of the latest technology and techniques to the acquisition of swift decision in battle in pursuit of the aim of resolving political problems by means of short wars. Yet with the prospect of a short war in sight the finishing touches to the design etched by the panzer force were bedevilled by paradox. Cautious leaders restrained Guderian for fear of his becoming over-extended at a moment when one more quick advance would have completed the envelopment of the enemy. The Allies were allowed, eventually, to escape via Dunkirk. At the same time the reaction of the German hierarchy to Guderian's success was euphoric. *Generaloberst* Alfred Jodl, the *Chef des Oberkommandos der Wehrmacht* (OKW) Operations Staff, recorded how the Head of State and Supreme Commander, Adolf Hitler, was '. . . beside himself with joy and he already foresaw victory and peace'. France, it was true, would fall, but the triumph was incomplete. For the British, encouraged by their army's escape, declined to give up the struggle: tanks could not easily cross the Channel and aircraft, unlike armies, would not bring a decision on their own. Guderian's triumph of method now acted as a spur to disaster. With the seizure of such immense gains by the application of comparatively minimal force, Hitler and the uplifted members of his entourage came to believe that nothing was beyond the power of their tank and air forces. In due course German tanks would stamp their track marks across the rest of Europe, deep into Russia and along the North African shores. But never again would they wholly bring about the destruction of an entire major nation along with its army. The lessons which Guderian had learnt by studying the tactics employed against Germany in 1918 could themselves be copied. A colossal and unexpected military imbalance which had been revealed on the battlefield in 1940 was to be corrected.

The road which led Guderian to Abbeville stretched back far beyond the point at which he joined it. As a Prussian he was identified with the tribe which, in medieval times, located itself between the Rivers Vistula and lower Niemen and whose gradual expansion after 1462 reflected the natural reaction of a people who for long had been under harsh Polish rule. Nevertheless, while the family of Guderian may well be either of Dutch or, far less likely, of Scottish descent, it is certain that it had little experience of military professionalism: they were landowners and professional people who, like the vast majority of Junkers, lacked great wealth. Such military ancestors as Guderian could claim came from the family of his grandmother, Emma Hiller von Gaertringen. The Hillers had produced a crop of Prussian generals who had fought under Frederick the Great and in the Revolutionary Wars against France. Rudolf Freiherr Hiller von Gaertringen had been a cavalry captain involved in the débacle of 1806 though later, as Commander of the Neumark *Landwehr*, he had served with distinction against the French in the campaign of 1813 and in the conclusive fight against Napoleon at Waterloo in 1815; and in 1861 a Hiller von Gaertringen had been a cavalry captain told to plan a march on Berlin in support of the General Staff against the Diet.

The Guderian family found its early role as civilian supporters of burgeoning Prussian militarism, the cult which flourished as a modern Sparta under the urging of the saviour of the Army after 1806, Gerhard Scharnhorst, and his notable successors, Carl von Clausewitz, Albrecht von Roon and Helmuth von Moltke the Elder. These men dwelt amid the relative poverty of the Junker aristocracy and recognised military preparations alongside what a future Chief of Staff, Paul von Hindenburg, described as 'wantlessness'. They felt a binding patriotism which traditionally permitted them, for example, to carry out a *coup d'état* against the government providing the monarch did not object.

Heinz Guderian's father, Friedrich, had recognised wantlessness only too well. His father had died young leaving a widow with six children and the widow had felt compelled to sell the family estate at Hansdorf Netz in the Warthegau in order to spend more time on the children (Guderians to this day form a closely knit family group) as part of a rationalisation of frugal effort for their well-being. But it was at his own wish that young Friedrich went to the Kadet Korps in 1872, though this was helpful to the family exchequer. He arrived there in the aftermath of Moltke's greatest victorious campaign, at a moment when Prussian armed might was supreme and Moltke was engaged upon extending its technical innovations. This the old nobility had opposed and so Friedrich Guderian fitted neatly into Moltke's scheme of diluting the army nobility with healthy infusions of the middle classes to fill vacancies in the technical arms. By 1872 only two-thirds of the General Staff was titled and the proportion of middle class officers throughout the Army was steadily rising – particularly among the most technical branches, including the Engineers, of whom it was quipped, 'A man sinks from step to step until he becomes an Engineer'.

Yet Friedrich Guderian became a light infantryman, a *Leutnant* of the 9th *Jäger* Battalion in an army which rated the cavalry uppermost in social favour, followed by the Guards infantry, the light infantry and then the artillery. Light infantry, like cavalry, were the swiftest moving elements

3

of a fighting force which was thoroughly imbued with von Moltke's insistence that victory in war should be sought as a natural outcome through high mobility and offensive action. Coming fresh to the Army, untrammelled by traditional notions of how everything should be done, Friedrich welcomed each breath of change without rancour and was far from shocked by such typically Moltkesian dicta as 'Build no more fortifications, build railways'. This sense of radical openmindedness he, in due course, passed on to his soldier sons.

The year 1888 was of intrinsic importance to Friedrich Guderian, and to Germany too. In October 1887 he had married and on 17th June 1888 he and his wife Clara were blessed with the birth of their first son, Heinz. Two days before, on the 15th, a new monarch, Kaiser Wilhelm II, had come to the throne and soon he was to sponsor the brash *Weltpolitik* which was to replace the shrewd statesmanship of Chancellor Bismarck.

It would be wrong to suggest that Germany lived in a war atmosphere in the 1890s even though France longed for revenge after 1871 and even though the attempt to challenge British naval supremacy was being formulated in the shipyards. Germany's trade was expanding and busy industrial zones and outward signs of prosperity in the principal cities, along with advances in mass education, were beginning to replace the old austerity. Changes in government policy had scant effect upon the Guderians who indulged in routine garrison life in the manner of all newly wed couples who occupy a place in a privileged society. Fritz, a brother for Heinz, was born in October 1890 and the following year they moved to Colmar in Alsace, staying there until 1900 when they were posted to St Avold in Lorraine.

By this time both Heinz and Fritz had determined to become army officers, a choice fully endorsed by their father whose wishes in the matter can hardly ever have been in doubt since necessity also made demands. At St Avold there were inadequate boarding school facilities whereas the cadet schools in Germany, like the *Real Gymnasium*, taught modern subjects (including French, English, Mathematics and History). From 1901 to 1903 Heinz and Fritz attended the Karlsruhe Cadet School at Baden and in 1903 Heinz was transferred to the Principal Cadet School at Gross-Lichterfelde, Berlin, whence he was later followed by Fritz.

Here they came under the spell of Prussian discipline in its most insistent and sophisticated form. In contrast to the absurdities of the external manifestations of its military regime – the rigid minutiae of drill, dress and formality – there was an inculcation of a definitive philosophy and attitude, a flexibility which is unfathomed by those who visualise Prussianism only in its unbending form. In parallel with uniformity of application went – chiefly for the officers' benefit – a recognition of the right and desirability of expressing uncompromising opinions up to the moment of an order's delivery. Thus a cadet's mental processes were schooled to acknowledging ultimate authority, but only after argument had been exhausted. It may be remarked that this is not so very different from the methods employed in most other armies. Quite: most other armies had copied the Prussian system the difference between them being merely that of degree. It was the meticulous thoroughness applied by the Germans that caused their embarrassed enemies to fear and hate a superior type of execution. Outwardly, at first, Guderian acquiesced to the system: his reservations as to the spirit if not its letter would appear much later to suit the convenience of difficult situations.Flexibility of response was for ever close to his thoughts and actions. He did not immediately rebel and his reports improved as he progressed and began to develop the essential enthusiasm for those subjects which were for ever to enthral him. Usually he attained a good position in class. In *Panzer Leader* he recalled his instructors and teachers at Gross-Lichterfelde '. . . with emotions of deep gratitude and respect'. However, it was not so of the instructors at the War School in Metz: of them, in 1907, he wrote: 'The system is not for ambitious people – only for average persons. It is tedious', and added that he found his seniors unsympathetic. Yet, from what was written of him at the end of the course, it would seem the seniors were rather impressed by a cadet whom, they said, was serious-minded and looked ahead; was ambitious, honourable, a good rider, a strong character with charm, one who was, 'Intensely interested in his profession and very earnest'. Ironically, in the light of the future, he did poorly in his final examination on tactics by adopting a posture of defence instead of the prescribed solution of attack.

To his immense satisfaction Guderian had been sent in February 1907 to Bitche as a *Fähnrich* to join the 10th *Hannoverian Jäger* Battalion, at that time under his father – a commander who was both loved and feared by family and battalion alike. In January 1908 he became a *Leutnant* and immersed himself in the normal life of a typical young officer who liked animals, rode well, enjoyed hunting and shooting; and he also developed a delight in architecture and the countryside, and appreciated the theatre and dancing. But music defied him: he was dismally tone deaf and had to be dropped from a cadet choir when it was found that he sang different tunes from the others. There was perhaps something significant about this. Certainly his diary illustrates an awakening criticism of the system which possessed him and a healthy scepticism such as was shared by only a very small proportion of his contemporaries. It speaks of the study of military history: with an outstandingly good memory he could quote from the classical and military works by heart. It also tells of profitable battalion exercises under his father's direction, from whom he learnt so much: 'I try to copy him', he wrote.

There is, too, within the pages of a diary which records passing thoughts, the suggestion of an obsession with the meaning of enduring friendship. In July 1908 at a moment of loneliness he wrote: 'Friends demand that I should spend more time with them. If they had been more careful there need not have been a rift. Now it is difficult to repair the damage. They have lost my respect. They accuse me of being an intro-vert . . . but to run with the mob is nothing to be proud of.' And in November 1909: 'If only I could find a real friend. My comrades are very good, but there is not one I can depend upon wholly . . . Everywhere mistrust reigns.' A year later he finds a glimmer of hope when some new officers joined the battalion and he was no longer the most junior member: 'Good friendships are developing . . . Our youngest officers, including [Bodewin] Keitel, are very pleasant. The most promising with the most aptitude as a soldier and in other ways is Keitel, I think.' Already it was apparent that he was better with his juniors than with his seniors, another recurrent theme in later life. There were thus distinct similarities between Guderian and the men who, in many respects, were to play an equivalent role in the development of British armoured methods – Percy Hobart and J.F.C. Fuller. Hobart had an even keener appreciation of the arts and was quite as earnest in his professional dedication and bubbling sense of criticism – but much rougher and ruder in emphasising a point. Yet Hobart spent his early career in fairly tolerant agreement with the professional standards of his fellow officers; but *he* belonged to the Engineers, a corps d'élite in the British Army. Guderian, on the other hand, regarded many of his brother infantry officers as insufficiently interested in their profession. So, in this respect he echoed J.F.C. Fuller, a light infantry man too, who also found himself mentally isolated from his fellow officers, '. . . a monk in a Trappist monastery, because when everyone round you is talking about the same things (foxes, duck and trout) morning, noon and night, they might just as well be saying nothing at all.' Fuller's invective was thus as acid as Guderian's was to become, their way of escape from mediocrity alike – by an application for a place at the Staff College.

In October 1909 the 10th *Jägers* were transferred to Goslar in the Harz Mountains, one of the loveliest parts of Germany, and there Heinz Guderian met and fell in love with Margarete Goerne. Difficulties arose, however, when in December 1911 they decided to marry. Gretel, as he called her, was only eighteen, and her father felt she was too young. Heinz was persuaded to agree to a cooling off period of two years, although they became officially engaged in February 1912. He concluded that it was unfair for him to remain in Goslar. Moreover he felt the need to under-take some sort of technical training to broaden the basis of his profes-sional knowledge. Two courses of attachment were available, either to learn about machine-guns or about signal communications. Friedrich, who had just been promoted *Generalmajor* in command of the 35th Infantry Brigade, advised against machine-guns '. . . because they have little future', but he saw prospects in signalling, particularly the brand new wireless systems which had come to prominence at the turn of the century and with which German technology took a lead. His son was in accord. On 1st October Heinz joined the radio company of the 3rd Telegraph Battalion at Koblenz and there began the work which was to lead him to the peak of his achievements.

The year to come – indeed the next decade – was packed tight with activity for Guderian. Time passed quickly because the new work taxed him hard. As he describes it himself:

'Having had no previous experience with radio communications and being in addition in charge of recruit training for some time, I was heavily burdened by my military duties. According to directives issued by the Chief of Staff, VIII Corps . . . officers from the Koblenz garrison conducted the preparatory course for the *Kriegsakademie* [War Academy]. Preparation was very intensive . . . Moreover the instructors enlivened the class rooms with a spirit of comradeship, thus making our social relations also very pleasant. The curriculum covered tactics up to the level of a reinforced infantry brigade, field craft, engineering and instruction in arms . . . It was left to our discretion to choose our own method of studying languages, geography and history.'

In due course Guderian would qualify as an interpreter in French and he also became fluent in English. By frenetic application he passed the Academy exam at the first attempt and was thus the youngest at twenty-five of the 168 officers selected to attend the three years' course starting at the War Academy in Berlin on 5th October 1913. This was a clear indication of his maturity. But first there was another matter of high priority to be settled. Parents bowed before Guderian's wave of success and consented to an early marriage. On 1st October he wedded Margarete. Not for nothing in the years to come was he to earn the nick-name *Schnelle Heinz* (Quick Heinz). Nor by chance did he adhere to one of Moltke's dicta he liked to quote: 'First reckon, then risk'. He would win renown for his contradictory juxtaposition of methods, a compound of studied contemplation on the one hand with sudden impulse on the other. But his marriage was a deeply contemplated step and of fundamental importance. Margarete, with her peaceful soothing nature, adapted herself to his moods and aspirations and provided the perfect foil for the young officer who had already won a reputation for bursting energy and frightening impetuosity. Of her he wrote that she was a 'perfect helpmate' and their first son was to tell the author that she was absolutely essential to her husband. In fact this need of his for a cool partner and chief of staff was to become an absolute necessity to the German Army, too, as his career progressed. Of still greater importance were the evolving ambitions of Margarete who, as time went by, came to believe in her husband's great destiny and whose influence upon him, as will be seen, was not only designed to encourage but to guide his footsteps along safer paths when, in tempestuous moments, he threatened to throw everything away. And the wedding itself held pointers to the future: in attendance was the admired Bodewin Keitel (a second cousin of Margarete) whose brother, Wilhelm, would one day become Adolf Hitler's principal staff officer: both Keitels were destined to have their impact on Guderian's destiny in the years to come.

At the War Academy still more strong characters in the drama of Guderian's life began to assemble. Among his contemporaries was Erich von Manstein who, of them all, came closest to understanding the philosophy and methods that, later, were to be preached and practised by Guderian. The senior member of the board of directors was *Oberst Graf* Rüdiger von der Goltz who, according to Guderian, exerted even pro-founder educational influence upon the younger officers than the director himself: six years later von der Goltz was to have a direct effect upon his erstwhile student. The first year at the college concentrated chiefly upon improving the general knowledge of the students. Guderian says that tactics were the main subject along with military history '. . . with special emphasis on the opening of the campaign in 1757, with the advance into Bohemia in separate groups and their juncture for the Battle of Prague. The campaign of 1805 was discussed subsequently'.

Study of the past was terminated sharply when the assassination of Archduke Franz Ferdinand of Austria at Sarajevo on 28th June threw the future into turmoil and uncertainty. At that moment Guderian, with the other infantry and cavalry members of the course, was serving an attachment with the field artillery for a period 'long enough to guarantee that the students gained a real insight'. The German Army always had been a protagonist of practical work in the absence of a war of its own, despite its delight in the developing of theories. Now the war which Kaiser Wilhelm II had provoked was upon them and the theories would be put to the test.

On 1st August mobilisation was declared, the course at the War Academy was dissolved before Guderian could complete his attachment and he was ordered to join the unit with which he was to go into battle. It was not, however, the parent regiment to which his heart belonged – the 10th *Jägers*. Because he had last served with 3rd Telegraph Battalion, his place in the mobilisation plan was in charge of Heavy Wireless Station No. 3, attached to the 5th Cavalry Division in I Cavalry Corps which was part of the Second Army. War came at a bad moment for the Guderians. The political tensions which had raised Europe to fever pitch throughout the preceding decade were as nothing to the strain imposed by the knowledge that Margarete was expecting their first child within the month.

Although the officer of twenty-six who went to war that August may not have been fully prepared for his task and had a backward look at his home, it is doubtful if many of his age were any better trained at that time. He had formulated a philosophy to which he had generally adhered since analysing himself prior to joining the battalion. In the diary, which was reserved more for reflections than a day-by-day record, he had written in 1908:

'I am a peculiar fellow. Sometimes I feel uplifted and believe that everything must go right and nothing wrong. The longer one lives the more one comes to realise that these are illusions. Sometimes little things cause despondency. Perhaps I will manage to discover the source of wisdom so that everything becomes easy. Yet I do not believe it is good to acquire too much equanimity otherwise one would become careless.'

Absorbed as he was in the essential disciplines of the good soldier – high patriotism, a strict sense of duty and honour besides the basic tricks of his trade – he had not in the process, particularly when on field exercises, reduced an acute and fearless critical sense which he exposed both in manner and writing. To disguise personal feelings was almost an impossibility for Guderian, though the cutting edge of his temperament was frequently sheathed in banter.

During the manoeuvres of spring 1913 he had been involved in one of the earliest trials of a wireless detachment working with cavalry and, in co-operation with the 5th Cavalry Division under *Generalmajor* von Ilsemann, had gained valuable experience but also a feeling of disquiet at the way the exercises had proceeded. Often he was left out of touch with the division because insufficient thought was given to the Section's part in projected operations. As a result the wireless detachment usually lacked orders and frequently was out of touch. He wrote a strongly critical report which reached the general but, as Guderian remarked, '. . . it disappeared into his desk'. The fact remained that Guderian's detachment had failed to give the service of which it was capable and, due to excessive and unnecessary movement, its horses and the men (in that order of priority since, without the horses, the heavy radio and its batteries could not be moved) had become exhausted. This was the general under whom he was to serve in his first campaign.

The difficulties of co-operation between signal detachments and their parent headquarters were by no means restricted to Guderian's level, however, or to this particular commander. A failure to resolve basic misunderstandings between an infant technological weapon system (as wireless undoubtedly was, even if not recognised as such) and the General Staff's established practices lay at the heart of the trouble; yet it was merely typical of the problems normally associated with initiating any new and powerful weapon to best effect in the teeth of reactionary and entrenched practice and opinion.

In 1914 the newly created wireless arm had neither the confidence nor the sympathy of the General Staff and consequently was deprived of

9

information about strategic intentions and denied its full potential. Moreover its Chief was not a man to press his claims too heavily. In consequence forward planning of signal services to match operational requirements went by default. The equipment, which was heavy, incapable of operation on the move and none too easy to tune, was given little chance of achieving its best performance by a procedure which demanded that 'out-stations', such as Guderian's, had the responsibility of establishing contact with the central control set. This was far too time-consuming for units which were in contact with the enemy. The ether became jammed by competing out-stations struggling to break through to Control which, in turn, complained that there was insufficient time to pass a mass of information and orders to stations which switched off as they pleased. The Control Station did not command the networks; breakdowns occurred more frequently as the intensity of operations increased. There was chaos and waste on a vast scale and so fighting formations were delayed in reaching the critical points at the right moment and in good order.

These things Guderian witnessed as part of his induction to war, at a moment when he was malleable to sharp impressions.

2 Factors for the Future

To understand the reasoning which prompted the arguments that Guderian was one day to use in support of mechanised armies one has only to follow his career throughout the First World War, and in its immediate aftermath on the eastern frontier of Germany. Fate was to carry him to almost every front where the definitive actions took place. Thus he was able to witness and, in comparatively remote circumstances, register and store away acute personal memories, particularly concerning the atrophy of mobile warfare and the consequent onset of the stalemate which was to kill all hope of a quick end to the conflict.

The German Army went to war in 1914 under the direction of Helmuth von Moltke the Younger – a Chief of Staff who, though the nephew of his great namesake, was a paler character by far. Likewise the plan of campaign which he adopted was a thinner version of the one created by his predecessor, *Graf* Alfred von Schlieffen, an officer whose commitment to the study of war was such that he thought of nothing else. The army of Schlieffen's design was modern and contained two weapons which, it was hoped, would give a margin of technical advantage sufficient to overcome the enormous defensive fire power and élan of its enemies. Heavy mobile artillery was intended to crush all kinds of fortifications and demoralise armies in the field; radio communications would enable information and orders to pass swiftly to and from command posts to the extremities of the battlefield and thus enable commanders to exert detailed control of the battle from remote locations. The sort of initiatives at the lower levels of command, which Moltke the Elder had found it essential to encourage, were being stifled. At the same time all-embracing envelopments in the quest for a modern Cannae, such as Moltke had accomplished at Sedan in 1870, was Schlieffen's aim, the mobility to be achieved by an even more extensive use of railways than Moltke had dreamed of. By a strange omission the method which might most extensively have increased the flexibility of the German Army's mobility was largely omitted from Schlieffen's plans and those of Moltke the Younger. Motor vehicles, fast becoming popular and in greater supply, were provided in some quantity but even so were neither sufficient in number nor efficient in performance. In 1923 *Generaloberst* von Kluck, who commanded the First Army in the march on Paris, and whose army was the principal sufferer from logistic failure, was to write that these systems needed to undergo a further test. In due course a young officer in 3rd Wireless Section would see to that.

The German plan of attack into northern France, via Belgium and the Ardennes, committed the four principal armies involved to long marches in trying conditions of summer heat and dust. Once they had departed from the railheads adjacent to the frontiers it was the endurance of men on their feet and horses on their hooves which would decide whether or not the momentum of the marching masses could be sustained. *General-leutnant* von Richthofen's I Cavalry Corps, of which 5th Cavalry Division was a part, and Guderian's 3rd Wireless Section the tentacle for its vital communications, was to have an almost unique opportunity to tour the battlefields leading to the River Marne. For it began its progress into France within the boundaries of the Third Army, having marched to Dinant through the Ardennes in the first fortnight of August, and was then to pass across the rear of von Bülow's Second Army to enter the battle at the junction between Bülow's force and the strongly reinforced mass of manoeuvre, residual in von Kluck's First Army on the right wing, where it bore down past Mons towards Le Cateau and Paris. The arrows marked across the maps indicate that I Cavalry Corps marched 160 miles before it began to come seriously into action on 31st August, and that therefore it may already have travelled well over 200 miles when allowance is made for diversions. Guderian stayed with 5th Cavalry Division at Dinant between the 17th and 20th and thus was witness to the mass of horsemen, marching men, guns and transport columns passing smoothly in well-regulated columns of march through the intricate lanes and across the River Meuse – a spectacle which would have excited the least responsive military mind but which, upon him, was to leave indelible impressions of the logistic feasibility of moving such numbers through this notably difficult terrain. His detachment had to move greater distances than the rest of the division because, due to its unique nature, it was in constant demand and therefore switched from one division to another besides the 5th Cavalry. Frequently it was wastefully employed through lack of forward planning: either it was without clear orders or it was sent on tasks from which it might have been spared. More than most elements of First and Second Armies, which soon began to suffer from exhaustion, the horses and men of 3rd Wireless Section, dragging their heavy long-range set (with its transmission range of 150 miles), were in dire straits.

German cavalry as a whole ran into trouble. II Cavalry Corps, pushing ahead as flank guard of First Army into Belgium, had soon complained of a fodder shortage and suffered a severe rebuff at Haelen on 12th August when they had been mown down by machine-gun and rifle fire from weak Belgian detachments. Never again would German cavalry advance with the supreme and gallant confidence of arrogance as that with which they began the war, though for a little longer the fascination of cavalry power held good. On 31st August, when the Fifth French Army stood its ground to the south of the River Serre and the British Expeditionary Force continued in withdrawal, a gap opened between the two armies. Richthofen was directed by radio from Second Army into the gap and told to turn east in order to seize ground between Soissons and Vauxaillon, thus cutting off the French Fifth Army's retreat. It was due to the contribution made by radio communication that the French were almost as quickly aware of this order as was Richthofen: most German radio traffic was either in 'clear' or in code and the French had broken the German code within forty-eight hours of the outbreak of war. Thus Guderian was unwittingly wielding a double-edged weapon, for little thought had been given to signal intelligence's manifestations.

A grim race ensued on the French part to despatch infantry by rail and cavalry by road to block the German thrust before it reached its objective. German progress was monitored as their radio reports from the leading troops came in. There was rising panic when the British failed at once to send a division to head off the German spearhead. But the Germans were advancing fast because there was no opposition, yet beginning, as they got deeper into the 'gap' (so precious to cavalry in the implementation of its power), to complain bitterly that their horseshoes were worn out: a radio message (duly monitored by the French) asked for four lorry loads of shoes and, above all, nails to be sent to Noyon, at the starting point of their sweep. This habit of exposed forces in mobile operations to find excuses that might save them from further exertion was a psychological mannerism which Guderian would remember. In fact the whole Corps safely reached the area north of Soissons, well in the French rear, but then was pulled back; ostensibly because the higher command wished it to continue the advance to the south and maintain contact with First Army which was well ahead on the right; partly because enemy forces threatened and compelled the cavalry to dismount in order to fight; largely because they did not recognise the opportunity. The only material aid they gave to their own side was cursory information about enemy forces in Soissons.

Richthofen, a commander who understood mobility, had actually created the opportunity dreamed of by cavalry men and so outpaced the enemy that they were unable to devise defensive measures fast enough to bar his way. But since he allowed himself to become divorced from radio, his advantageous position was unknown to those above him. In any case, he lacked an instrument that was capable of survival on the modern battlefield. His regiments, unprotected against fire, simply could not press home the advantages which his generalship had gained. When Guderian came to write *Achtung! Panzer!* in 1937 he quoted from the Reichsarchiv in its conclusions that '. . . nowhere had they [cavalry] managed to penetrate and gain insight into activities behind the enemy lines'. The judgment was sweeping and, as the action at Soissons suggests, perhaps a little unfair, but it was duly recorded as a precedent for use in shaping the future as horsemen began to pass into the shades of war.

The series of command vacillations which produced a German crisis at the Battle of the Marne could not be solved by Moltke from Luxembourg where he sat at the centre of a network of overloaded communications. Radio and telephone messages failed to compensate for close personal contact near the front – and that Moltke eschewed until the battle was lost. But personal contact was frequently at a premium everywhere. On 5th September, I Cavalry Corps was leading Second Army deep into another gap which had opened between the British and French and had pushed its leading elements across the Grand Morin '. . . continuing in its efforts to take the initiative', as the Reichsarchiv says. Guderian was with them and, had he known it, at the head of a formation which had completely broken through an Anglo-French line – the last time that was to happen until he personally repeated the performance twenty-six years later. But again nobody on the German side recognised the opportunity and for the reason, as usual, of Richthofen's isolation from Second Army. Meanwhile his men, faced with the lightest opposition, were invariably compelled to forfeit momentum while they took dismounted action. On the following day First Army's readjustment to curb the threat of the French, taking them in flank from the west, brought to Guderian's notice, for the first time, a feeling that things were going wrong.

He had been noting with interest the neglected French villages as a sign that French power was on the wane, and he had glorified in the buildings of Soissons and the beautiful Marne valley. Suddenly everything changed. Overnight the cavalry ceased to be a spearhead and reverted to flankguard, first at the halt and then as a rearguard in retreat, filling the gap which had opened between First and Second Armies and which was about to be entered by both British and French troops.

About 6th September Guderian recorded, in a letter to Gretel, that he was back with 5th Cavalry Division and under artillery fire at Cerneux – which was hardly surprising since at that moment this village was in no-man's-land! Next day he was at Bois Martin: 'Due to over-exertion three horses died. Horses and men extremely exhausted, added to the uncomfortable feeling of retreat'. On the 8th: 'The station under shrapnel fire for 3 km. Very uncomfortable situation.' And on the 9th, when 5th Cavalry Division alone filled the gap between First and Second Armies: 'Continuation of march at first without event, quite alone. In the afternoon when we reached the division, suddenly shrapnel fire into the column, again fortunately no losses . . . Horses and men pretty well done in.' Finally on the 11th, after being verbally ordered to march to Chéry via

Cohan (no written orders were ever received), two horses fell and had to be replaced by requisitioning. But the delay was fatal. All at once the French were upon them, the station captured and with it all his personal belongings and a few of the less fortunate men. Guderian escaped by the skin of his teeth to finish up only with those clothes in which he stood at Béthenville, north-west of Reims. It was here that, at last, he received a letter saying that Margarete had also passed her crisis, for in his reply on the 16th he was to write:

'My dearly beloved, sweet wife,

'To-day I received the first anxiously awaited news of your well being from your father . . . He told me about the happy birth of our beloved son. With deep thanks to God who protected you in this difficult hour, I extend you my dearest wife my deepest congratulations, my thanks for your love and kindness towards me. My thoughts are with you and our child all the time. Stay healthy and fresh and if God grants me a return from this terrible war may he then bestow upon us a happy reunion.

'But now I know that you came through this difficult time in good health a weight has been lifted from my heart and I shall approach the serious task which still awaits us here in a calmer way.'

A few days later the tenderness had dispersed and he was angry, writing to Gretel: 'The newspapers I have read make too much noise . . . It is cheap to joke about a brave enemy . . . Also that which is written about breach of promises . . . everybody looks after himself and might is right. I therefore consider that scribbling about treason and the Tsar and the English is ridiculous. It simply happens that it is our world position and state of existence which is inconvenient to others. In some ways it gives me satisfaction to have foreseen this development.'

He was angry, too, with the apparent failure of *General* von Ilsemann who seemed to have failed to meet the highest standards he expected of him; but of his comrades in 5th Cavalry Division he had nothing but praise. These were traits which would shape his career – an unbending expectation of excellence from those set above him and a compassionate feeling, blended with hard demands, for those below.

The war called him again almost at once, and once more to the crucial front – to Flanders with Fourth Army under the Duke of Württemberg. Here he was to be made aware of the fate that must almost always overtake infantry when pitted against a determined and unshaken defence, armed with what Fuller was to call 'a nerveless weapon' – the machine-gun. Fresh German formations were thrown against Ypres in the attempt to roll up the Allied flank and seize the Channel ports. Of the advance on 20th October, of which he was well informed since he had been appointed to 14th Wireless Section at HQ Fourth Army (where his knowledge of communications and languages was invaluable), he was to write of '. . . the young regiments, the German National Anthem on their lips', and go on to describe in *Achtung! Panzer!* '. . . their losses were very heavy, the results encouraging'. Then, 'The young troops renewed their attack after the artillery had supposedly done its work of destruction. The reserves pressed forward, filling out the depleted lines – and increased the losses . . . Sacrifices rose to immeasurable heights while offensive power declined . . . They had to dig in and call for entrenching tools.' Mobility was at an end; trench warfare behind barbed wire had begun on the Western Front.

Once more it was Guderian's destiny to observe closely the most important experiments, those of trench warfare. His sense of enthusiasm instantly welcomed the value of aerial reconnaissance and he was among the few who flew as observer in the search for information. He was on the Ypres front still when the Germans made their badly prepared, half-hearted attempt at a breakthrough using gas on 22nd April 1915 – a classic example of the premature use of a 'secret weapon' before its potential value was assessed and a proper drill for its use worked out. On 27th January 1916, as Intelligence Officer, he was sent to join the Headquarters of the Fifth Army under the Crown Prince at Verdun where, for the ensuing six months, he helped synthesize the results of the first great attempt at reaching a decision by the brute application of force to the total exclusion of mobility. Later his conclusions were those of every thinking soldier, a condemnation of the artillery's inability '. . . to break down enemy defences quickly and thoroughly enough to secure more than a simple incision – the prolonged time one needed to allow the guns to become effective'. Yet in the early days of the offensive he wrote to Gretel, perhaps by way of encouragement but more likely in tune with a current and general feeling of optimism, that the offensive was 'going well'. Guderian of course always was an optimist – his survival otherwise was inconceivable.

One important event Guderian missed. In July he was sent back to Flanders to become Intelligence Officer at HQ Fourth Army. Therefore he was not present when British tanks made their début on the Somme on 15th September. But even had he been there it is unlikely that he would have been any more impressed than his contemporaries. A mere 32 machines had caused only local terror where they had appeared in twos and threes, but the artillery had quickly destroyed those which persisted and the integrity of the trench front had never been seriously threatened. Along with the rest of the deeper thinkers in the German Army he largely ignored the reports of front line soldiers who called the tanks 'cruel as effective', and looked for more subtle combinations of proven weapons to unlock the fronts for the restoration of mobility. Nor, for that matter, did the possessors of this new weapon have much hope for its prospects. Major J.F.C. Fuller was frankly sceptical of their value at the time of his appointment as senior Staff Officer to the newly formed British

Tank Corps at the end of 1916. He, like Guderian, was forever seeking new methods for infantry and in 1914 had published a perceptive article called 'The Tactics of Penetration'. Unlike Guderian, however, he pronounced (perhaps with tongue in cheek as might Guderian too when challenging the sanctity of official doctrine) that '. . . tactics are based on weapon-power and not on the experiences of military history' and that 'The commander who first grasps the true trend of any new, or improved, weapon will be in a position to surprise the adversary who has not'. Nevertheless, it was the British and, later, the French, who were to thrust the tank idea to the fore and largely because they placed officers of imagination and drive in charge of their new weapon. Though the Germans were to begin preliminary efforts to build a tank, starting in January 1917, there was negligible impulse because technicians and mediocrities were placed in charge and the General Staff withheld serious interest.

Several crucial turning points of the war were rounded in 1917 – the outbreak of the Russian Revolution, the entry of the USA into the war and the final demonstration by the British of the abortive nature of an offensive based mainly upon artillery attack. For the Germans it was a year out of character. The exertions of the first two years' combat had so reduced their army that a period of recuperation on the defensive was obligatory. The logical conclusions of Moltke's dictum that because '. . . the defender has decided advantage during action under fire, the Prussian Army has all the more reason to use defensive methods' was put into practice by the construction of costly and intricate fortified zones, in addition to railways to serve them, guarding the Western Front. As a result a relatively limited industrial capacity was diverted from making primarily offensive weapons. To the concern of conventional General Staff officers, the morale of the men was undermined. More pernicious still, in the view of those who came to denigrate this development in hindsight (Guderian among them), the tactical doctrine of the 'delaying defensive' was virtuously adopted as a measure of economy in inherently wasteful attritional warfare – a method of defence in depth with an attendant wastage of life and material conducted by both sides with the intention of gradually inducing exhaustion. This was the inverse corollary of the Verdun type of offensive which, as Guderian put it '. . . converted the beautiful countryside into a moonscape'. Development of a method such as this, in the view of its critics, was the antithesis of a search for worthwhile conclusions in any war.

Of immediate importance to the Germans, in the aftermath of 1916's destruction, was replacement of the wastage which had been incurred since 1914. The old army had not only bled to death; it had been denied infusions of new blood by a policy which had been based upon a short war and had not sufficiently come to grips with the demands of a long one. Promotions among the officers had been made at the peacetime rate and

17

were insufficient to replace losses; the training of a new generation, including new members for the General Staff, had been minimal. As part of the process of reconstruction, fresh staff officers were created by taking, among others, those, like Guderian, who had been at the War Academy when it was dissolved in 1914 and putting them through a modified but strictly practical course that covered every aspect of staff duties. It included attachments of a month's duration at all levels from Army Group to Division, plus short spells with an artillery unit and, finally, a month in command of an infantry battalion in the line.

Throughout April Guderian was with formations along the River Aisne and thus present when the French used tanks – with barely recognisable results – for the first time. Then, starting in January 1918, he spent two months as a student in a General Staff Officers' Course at Sedan where, no doubt, in the intervals between intensive study, he took the opportunity to visit the scene of Moltke's 'Cannae' of 1870 and fixed in his memory the nature of the ground where, twenty-two years later, he was to play his own great gambit. The short detachments he deplored as unsettling, but the training he received called only for praise. It was, he claimed, '. . . comprehensive and thorough. After finishing my studies in Sedan I felt capable of mastering any tasks which the future might hold in store for me. On 28th February 1918 I was appointed a regular member of the General Staff Corps.' It was among the proudest moments of his life. Of its performance in the First World War he was to say that: '[Germany's] position as a world power . . . called forth a military self-confidence which found perhaps its most graphic expression in the very top intellectual ranks of the officer corps, hence in the General Staff'. Not that his final judgement on the General Staff would be uncritical – far from it: on reflection he considered it 'too narrow a concept', though there was no such pronouncement when first he took the carmine stripe.

Undoubtedly the General Staff's failure to maintain fully the principles of Moltke, which Guderian claimed it tried to do, led to its lack of technical awareness in perceiving the tank's potentiality. The events of 20th November 1917 when Guderian was working at the Headquarters of Army Group C and therefore remote from Cambrai and the first victory by massed tanks, exposed the General Staff's deficiency of foresight. That event, Guderian was to rate the moment when '. . . the tank force provided the real dynamic punch [*Stosskraft*] of the Entente armies since they broke through the Siegfried [Hindenburg] Line, regarded as impenetrable at Cambrai, in one morning'. Cambrai was the brain-child of Fuller, though it was hardly his fault that an initial victory should have been turned abruptly against the British within a matter of days by an equally shattering German counter-offensive which also employed new methods. Crucial to the future of warfare, as 1917 drew to its end, was the disclosure by both sides of methods which, when used in conjunction in a later decade, would revive mobility as the key to the swift decision of a campaign.

At last the Germans were made aware that the tank posed a deadly threat and one to which they had no immediate answer due to their neglect of technology. At the same time they had proof that the new tactical methods which they had been developing since *Generaloberst* August von Mackensen and his Chief of Staff, *Oberst* Hans von Seeckt, had defeated the Russians in Gorlice in 1917, gave them the chance of a victory before tanks (and millions of Americans) appeared in sufficient numbers to make utter defeat unavoidable. Mackensen and Seeckt had achieved deep penetration of the Russian front in 1915 by superior organisation. They fed reserves through the breach in a narrow front and then maintained the logistic momentum of their pursuit in depth. The Russians had collapsed but it had to be admitted that they were already weakened by serious deficiencies in equipment and organisation. Again, at the end of 1915, the same German command team broke a weakened Serbian Army and practically eliminated that nation from the war. To Seeckt's joy an infantry mass made cavalry exploitation possible and convinced him that horsemen still had a future on the battlefield; it was a false lesson but of importance to the unfolding history of Germany. For Seeckt, too, was a man of the future.

German experiments into the restoration of open warfare continued in 1917 while the tactics of defence in depth stood prominent as the expression of their strategy. In September of that year another enfeebled Russian army received a paralysing blow when an army under *Generaloberst* Oskar von Hutier struck hard at Riga. This time the technique of infantry penetration had been advanced a stage further. Following a surprise bombardment which was short and sharp (not in the least like those which had rolled on for days at Verdun and were at that moment pulverising the Ypres salient) the assault was spearheaded into the enemy lines by a hardened tip of specially picked and trained 'storm troopers' who infiltrated the Russian defences, bypassing opposition that could not at once be eliminated, and plunged ever deeper into the undefended enemy rear, creating chaos and uncertainty by their mere presence. Later the isolated strong points which held out would be destroyed by yet another new combination – *ad hoc* teams of infantry, machine-gunners and light artillery combined in the forefront of the battle under a nominated local commander who made best use of whatever was locally available to him. With this there emerged a flexible devolution of the command function: the man at the front, who best understood the situation, was again given local control within an overall design laid down quite loosely from above. Flexibility of method depended heavily upon far better signal communications than those which had failed in the 1914 campaign. The Germans had industriously made use of every possible new technical device and had so reorganised that the Signal Officers were closely associated at all levels of command so that they could exert a profound influence upon operations. German communication methods had acquired recognition as the weapon system it was, but it was still technically defective, as Albert Praun, one of its most able practitioners, points out: 'The technical problems of adequate permanent communications systems for strategic and tactical purposes during movements, of telephone connections over long distances and of the use of multiple-channel telephone cables and of wireless transmission without interference still remained unsolved.'

Even so the elder Moltke's cloak was once more laid upon the battlefield and at once inspired outstanding results. The Russians were routed at Riga. A month later, at Caporetto, when the same treatment was meted out to the Italians, Italy might have been thrown out of the war if only the offensive's momentum could have been maintained. Here were the weakest links. Logistical failure, the exhaustion of the leading troops, and an inability to keep control at the point of action and to feed in fresh reserves, brought things to a standstill as they had at the Marne. The methods of infiltration by storm troops and battlegroups that were employed at Cambrai in effective retaliation to the British tank, worked smoothly enough, but there a deep penetration was not sought and logistics went untested. They would not be tried again on a vast scale until 21st March when the Germans under Hindenburg and the direction of *Generaloberst* Eric Ludendorff launched what was intended to be the final, crushing offensive in the West, designed to complete the task of defeating the British and the French now that Russia was out of the war and immersed in the turmoil of the Bolshevik phase of the Revolution.

The methods studied by Guderian and his contemporaries at Sedan in the winter of 1918 were those to be used in the Ludendorff offensive. They were intended to fit the students for any task that the attacking formations demanded. But so far as tanks were concerned there were less than 20 of their own manufacture available to the Germans, plus a few captured machines, and so they were hardly worth study. For his part Guderian was to find himself divorced from tactics because, in May, he became quartermaster of XXXVIII Reserve Corps and thus immersed in the world of logistics – admirable experience for one who, in the years ahead, was to tax the capabilities of logisticians to the limit. To him fell the responsibility of arranging the supplies for his corps as it provided flank protection for a subsidiary offensive across the River Aisne. It began with complete surprise on 27th May, and achieved the longest advance (14 miles) so far accomplished since trench warfare began in 1914. On that occasion his task was limited. It was tougher the next time when XXXVIII Reserve Corps was made to attack under the redoubtable Hutier on the left flank of the so-called 'Matz' offensive which was launched on 9th June with the intention of widening the scope of its failing predecessor on the left and expanding the threat to Paris. Unhappily this offensive lacked the surprise factor enjoyed by its predecessor. Moreover it was met by Frenchmen who kept their nerve and who retaliated with a brusque counterattack which turned the Germans about. Nor was it merely the steadiness of the French which helped them prevail. This time they used tanks with a concentration and strength such as had been absent in all the previous Allied defensive battles of 1918.

Tank soldiers had to learn new lessons like everybody else; learning became swifter when time was cut to the bone. It had taken a year for Allied recognition of the need for concentration of tanks in attack: it took a mere three months for it to be seen that, since the tank was essentially a weapon of offence, its employment in defence must be conditioned by the principles of attack – of the same need for concentration in force instead of dilution by 'penny packets', the acceptance of what was an age-old principle of orthodoxy. Even so, until 144 tanks were used along a broad front by the French on 12th June, the tendency had been for them to be employed in handfuls: the Germans put in five at St Quentin on 21st March (their first use of tanks), the British mostly used them in twos and threes; at Villers-Bretonneux on 24th April 13 German tanks had an encounter with 10 British tanks and the honours in this first tank-versus-tank engagement were about even. Against the French, the Germans scattered 15 machines along the front with scant success at Soissons and Reims on 1st June: they merely copied the French who themselves rarely committed more than six at a time throughout April and May. Not that the first more concentrated use of tanks by the French at the Matz was an enormous triumph. Of the 144, 70 were lost because insufficient care was taken to neutralise German artillery which killed the scattered French machines at will. Nevertheless where tanks were not available or were destroyed the French infantry stuck: when tanks were present they advanced.

These things Guderian may have noticed in spare moments between his normal duties so that, when he came to write of the 1918 tank battles in the course of his crusade for tanks, he was aware of them. But his primary duties came first and nobody pointed him in the tanks' direction at a moment when the claim of the tank upon attention was irresistible. Massed tank counter-attacks became the rule. Sixty went in with the French at Cutry on 28th June; another 60 on 4th July; 471 spread over various sections between 18th and 26th July to reverse irrevocably the final effort by the Germans to break through on the Marne. In this battle there began to appear a degree of mobility unseen for years, for the 'delaying defensive' practised by the Germans stimulated the resurgence of open warfare. Allied tanks and infantry, supported by artillery and aircraft, drove deep among German infantry who were mainly defended by artillery in the anti-tank role. Losses up to 80 per cent were sometimes incurred by the tanks when the guns fought them over open sights, but somehow the attackers kept going and the defending infantry fled once their guns were lost. Into this cauldron was thrown XXXVIII Reserve Corps to stabilise the right flank of the German Army as it fell back in the first week of August. In due course its frontage rested upon the original alignment between Soissons and Vesle. Of this period Guderian significantly records his operations as involved with 'mobile defence Marne-Vesle'. Five days later he, and the rest of the German Army, were shaken by reports of the heaviest tank attack of the war, one which had been launched opposite Amiens and had achieved such concentration that the artillery defence was, in places, saturated by tanks. The infantry had given way and though Ludendorff might attempt to denigrate a tank threat which he could not match, the fact remained that the German Army from this moment onward was jittery whenever these machines were supposed (let alone known) to be present. What the British regarded as a means of destroying machine-guns and barbed wire was looked on by the Germans as a 'Terror Weapon'. The withdrawal that was to become endless until an Armistice was signed in November now began. For Guderian it was a period of endless toil with little rest, made no easier because his commander came in for criticism: 'He makes life very difficult and is pretty demanding compared with good old Hofmann.' But in those days, as he wrote, 'Always there is something to worry about . . . The whole Army is exhausted.' Tersely he traced the battles:

'4th to 16th August. Oise.' (Here XXXVIII Corps fell back under flank leverage caused by the defeat at Amiens and the subsequent pressure exerted against the Germans on an ever widening frontage until the decision was taken to withdraw to their starting point in the Siegfried Line.)

'17th August to 4th September. Aisne.' (XXXVIII Corps was covering the withdrawal in a period when increasing war weariness and obvious disaffection made it all the more apparent that even a delaying defensive was unlikely long to avail and, to Ludendorff, that the war had to be ended.)

'5th to 18th September. Siegfried Line.' (The final 'backing' into the Line in which XXXVIII Corps fought at the hinge of the German manoeuvre, first in Ninth Army and then in Seventh when it took over the Ninth.)

Then he was sent to Italy as Ia (Chief Operations Officer) to the German Military Mission, just in time to be caught in the backwash from the Austrian defeat at Vittorio Veneto which was to put Austria out of the war. Yet the nature of this ephemeral appointment cannot be glossed over in consideration of the development of Guderian's career. It indicates that he had made a considerable impression upon his superiors both before, during and after the Sedan General Staff Course as an eager, imaginative and earnest staff officer who, sometimes, perhaps breached Moltke's rule: 'Accomplish much, remain in the background, be more than you appear to be'. Guderian liked that maxim, however.

Fate ordained that he should experience the Revolution in double measure with a double shock. On 20th September he could not envisage an immediate end to the war, writing to Gretel that 'The peace efforts of the Austrians . . . seem utter nonsense to me. The time chosen was unfortunate – in the middle of a battle which gives only hope to the enemy . . . I believe we will achieve more by dignified waiting and actions than through all this twaddle about peace. Nobody wants the war to last longer than necessary. In my opinion we will not achieve an endurable peace the way it is sought now'. He was ever the supreme optimist and this passage simply illustrates an attitude which was to both buttress and undermine his efforts in two world wars.

Comprehensively he was disabused. On 30th October he found himself the junior member of a two-man German delegation that was sent to Trent to act in negotiations between the Austria-Hungarian Armistice Commission who were dealing with the Italians. They travelled in a railway coach without windows or heating and arrived to find the Commission had already left. Next day they caught up by motor, crossing into the Italian lines under the protection of the White Flag and preceded by a trumpeter. But the Italians at XXVI Corps were not interested in having the Germans present and so Guderian and his companion were returned to their own lines, '. . . with our bright blue eyes blindfolded', there to find scenes of the greatest turmoil.

Indignation poured from Guderian in his letter to Gretel in description of a hair-raising and shameless scene in which Germany's allies behaved 'without honour'. 'The regiments were coming back singing, without weapons but with red flowers in their place. The mob demonstrated in front of the Dante monument. All stores were plundered and burnt. Russian prisoners of war were released and took part. Soon shooting and stabbing began while the population happily joined in.'

He was fortunate to escape and return to a Germany that was in even worse case.

'Our beautiful German Empire is no more. Bismarck's work lies in ruins', he wrote to Gretel from Munich on 14th November. 'Villains have torn everything down to the ground . . . All comprehension of justice and order, duty and decency, seems to have been destroyed. The Soldiers' Council still suffers from teething troubles . . . and makes ridiculous regulations . . . I only regret not having civilian clothing here in order not to expose to the jostling mob the clothes which I have worn with honour for twelve years.'

Almost overnight the highly disciplined Army abandoned its cohesion and ceased to be reliable as Sailors' and Soldiers' Councils took the law into their hands and the old order degenerated into a whirl of putsch and counterputsch. At the end of November Guderian returned to Berlin, to a city of violence and fear, and in the knowledge that the Army no longer counted as a factor of stability in the affairs of the nations. In the knowledge, too, that Germany herself was threatened not only by Communism from within but from the encroachment of Bolshevik and Polish armies approaching the eastern frontier, while the victorious but less predatory powers in the west closed upon the Rhine. In the New Year he was given his next assignment on the staff of Central Headquarters of the newly formed Eastern Frontier Protection Service, the organisation brought into being by Hindenburg as an agency to co-ordinate the emergency defence bands which were to spring into existence to combat the Bolshevik and Polish menace. The General Staff would run it as a symbol of its abiding integrity, but in chaos the Regular Army was of far less account than the freshly raised groups of dedicated fighting men known as the *Freikorps*, the invention of *Major* Kurt von Schleicher. With a mammoth task before it the Eastern Frontier Protection Service would allow none of its staff much time to think about the immediate future, let alone long-term problems connected with tanks. Guderian was committed to the defence of German soil and the very territory in the east from which his family had sprung. At the same time the ugly conditions he had witnessed within Germany prompted a changed attitude of mind – the need to save Germany from herself – which pervaded his political philosophy thereafter. He spoke of Bismarck who had created modern Germany and, by omission, discarded Kaiser Wilhelm II who failed his nation. Subconsciously, perhaps, he began to yearn for a new Bismarck, a strong man who would save Germany.

3 The Blackest Days

From first to last the *Freikorps* saw itself as the sole secure bulwark against Communism. Its advent coincided with revolution, its first role was in the destruction of the Spartacists in January 1919, and its subsequent expansion was arranged in proportion to the size of the Bolshevik threat both from within and from outside Germany. Where *Freikorps'* brutality stained the pages of history there was invariably a foregoing or simultaneous record of excess by their sworn opponents, for these antagonists numbered among their ranks the most deadly killers produced by the armies of the First World War. The prime elements of fanaticism and military professionalism rubbed shoulders and exchanged blows. The Communists were led by fervent ideologists and revolutionaries. The *Freikorps* was largely directed and officered by men for whom the overthrow of the Monarchy and the old system of life appeared outrageous, besides aiming a blow at their own status. They were the core of an essentially patriotic group which was bitterly ashamed at losing the war; at the same time they feared the elimination of their influence and wealth. The soldiers who followed them, to use Guderian's definition, were 'the real fighting men', those who represented 'Germany's last chance'. Few who fought with or against the *Freikorps* would deny their military prowess, but inevitably the ruthless and, at times, depraved nature of their behaviour became a byword even when undeserved.

Excesses, of course, were all the more likely when it is realised that each unit and formation owed direct allegiance to the men who raised and commanded them and that, initially, the Government was compelled to make do with them for want of an alternative. Largest and most efficient of all the *Freikorps* formations was the Iron Brigade. It had been raised by *Major* Joseph Bischoff – 'an old campaigner' – partly from the most determined elements of Eighth Army which had fought Germany's battles in Russia from the start. As that army was brought home under the arrangements made by *Generaloberst* von Seeckt and his Ia, *Major* Freiherr Werner von Fritsch, the belligerent minority who wished to carry on with the fight joined Bischoff and his type. Seeckt also wished to fight. Early in 1919 he had become Chief of Staff of Frontier Protection

Service, North, at Bartenstein – at the same time as *Hauptmann* Guderian was sent as a staff officer to Frontier Protection Service, South, at Breslau. It was in the north where the action was hottest and here that the ablest men began to congregate. Guderian was transferred to Bartenstein in March.

Because the Bolsheviks pressed hardest into the Baltic States and closely threatened the heart of Prussian heritage, tribal sentiments were strongly aroused and the toughest of the *Freikorps* were attracted in that direction. Furthermore they were tempted by promises of free land, and there arose in the minds of some that what could be taken by the sword would be theirs at the peace – that the more Latvians who died the more vacant estates there would be. They did not all think this way: the genuine settler wants to settle in friendly territory. Nevertheless one of the oldest lures in history attracted the fiercest, most predatory agents of a feudal-style warfare. Bischoff's Iron Brigade rapidly raised its strength to 15,000 men, organised into three regiments fully supported by artillery. Soon it had to be renamed the Iron Division and was in need of a properly constituted staff. Unavoidably it became a significant political force, and with redoubled effect in the hands of Guderian's revered pre-war instructor at the War Academy – *Generalmajor* Rüdiger von der Goltz who had won a distinctive reputation for determined leadership in unusual situations during the war. Von der Goltz was a hero – with all the exaggeration and magnetism that invoked.

Seeckt had mixed feelings about von der Goltz and his followers. As stopgaps prior to reconstitution of a new army, they were essential to the defence of Germany against the traditional enemy from the East. On the other hand he had to weigh the *Freikorps*' impact on Germany's internal security: their independence of mind and intention was a constant threat to a weak Government which existed under terrible pressures from all sides, pressures that would soon multiply when the terms of the Peace Treaty became known.

In the spring of 1919 Germany stagnated politically in a fool's paradise. Apart from a handful of politicians and soldiers, her people, short of food, ill-clad and frightened, entertained false hopes (built on propaganda delusions) that her erstwhile enemies would be 'realistically' generous and permit the German Empire to revert to a semblance of its pre-war status: the generous settlement by the British with the defeated Boers earlier in the century gave grounds for this optimism. But Germany's former enemies were the prey of the same hate propaganda which had sustained their war effort, and they regarded the people who had started the war as 'criminal' – particularly the dominant Prussians and their institutions. Some of these things Seeckt already knew (and when he shortly became Military Member of the Peace Commission to Versailles would understand only too well): he grasped at anything that might shore up German morale and which might, at the same time, embarrass the Entente. By April, von der Goltz had repulsed the Red Russians in Lithuania and from the southern part of Latvia. At the same time he delved in politics by appointing a Latvian prime minister of his own nomination, Karlis Ulmanis. His operations were accompanied by a purge, the pitiless execution of Reds, or anybody suspected of Communist sympathies, and plans for the taking of Riga.

Seeckt favoured the Riga operation also because German presence in the Baltic States alongside White Russian troops would provide a bridge with a future Russian government, assuming that the Whites achieved their aim of advancing on Petrograd and unseating the Reds – a nebulous aim which also had the support of the Entente powers. The bridge was desirable since Germany was totally without allies and this she could not afford to be. It was a delicate situation and one demanding an almost impossibly tight supervision over von der Goltz and the Iron Division – the most aggressively German and volatile elements in the polyglot units who were endeavouring to co-operate against the Reds while retaining Entente goodwill.

The German Government, which had no alternative but to comply with the wishes of the Entente, could not overtly support von der Goltz's expansionist schemes. Yet a way round the problem of committing the Iron Division to the attack upon Riga on 21st May was found. To this division on 2nd June went Guderian as 2nd General Staff Officer, an appointment that was clearly intended by Seeckt and Fritsch to reinforce General Staff influence at the most sensitive spot. It was a pointer to the future and their confidence in this young officer of a mere thirty years that they reposed such trust in his judgement at a time of mortal danger when patriotic feelings could so easily overcome circumspection. If he did well his sound prospects would be vastly enhanced: not only was Seeckt the man of the future, so too were Wilhelm Heye (the new Chief of Staff) and Fritsch: those who were selected for high places usually carried their most favoured staff officers along with them.

Within only a few days, on 21st June, in a battle at Lemsal, Guderian displayed, for the first time in a moment of critical importance, that tactical flair for which he was to become famous. The leading column under *Hauptmann* Blankenburg failed after its commander had been wounded. Guderian at once saw the danger but recognised also an opportunity. On his own initiative he alerted a reserve infantry regiment, throwing it into the fray to keep the momentum of the attack rolling. It was not his fault that the attack finally broke down due to insufficient preparation and inadequate resources.

Already, of course, the situation was passing out of German control, and largely they were to blame. The fall of Riga had been followed by massacres to which Bolsheviks, Germans and Latvians had contributed.

Guderian reported in a letter that the Bolsheviks had killed over 4,000 people, but there is enough evidence to show that as many atrocities were committed by their opponents. Standards fall low in times of desperation. A member of the *Freikorps* wrote: 'Where once peaceful villages stood was only soot, ashes and burning embers as we passed. We kindled a funeral pyre, and more than dead material burned there – there burned our hopes . . . the laws and values of the civilised world . . . and so we came back swaggering, drunken, laden with plunder'. They certainly overstepped the bounds of common sense at a time when moderation might have paid. Ulmanis had already complained that the Germans were driving the Latvians towards Communism '. . . the Latvian people have found that the Bolsheviks are less cruel than the Germans' he wrote. Von der Goltz replaced Ulmanis with a new government of his own choice under Andreas Needra and the Allies, who until now had vacillated, recognised at last the implications of von der Goltz's ambitions. Irresistible pressure was at once applied by the Entente to halt the rape of Latvia. In May the terms of the Peace Treaty became public and on 28th June the Tuc treaty of Versailles, in all its severity, was signed. It dealt a shattering blow to Germany, her armed forces and her hopes. The Navy would be forbidden U-boats and great warships; for the Army there were to be no more aircraft, heavy artillery, gas or tanks. Moreover the Army itself was to be reduced to a strength of 100,000 by 3rd March 1920 and those institutions in which Guderian had been educated – the Cadet College at Lichterfelde, the War Academy and the Great General Staff – abolished.

Germany would soon be defenceless, as Hindenburg, Seeckt and the upper hierarchy fully recognised. Optimistic notions of retaining what the Allies now forbade had to be abandoned; only through subterfuge could much be saved. Seeckt, appointed as Chairman of the Preparatory Commission of the Peacetime Army and the Commander-in-Chief designate, had as his primary task the removal of German soldiers from the Baltic States and, as a desirable corollary, the elimination of *Freikorps*' power. It was he who at once persuaded von der Goltz to withdraw from Riga, making it clear how tenuous was the future but also striking a wounding blow at those like Guderian whose loyalties were torn between military obedience and patriotism.

All at once everything Guderian held dear was demolished and emotions, such as can hardly be imagined by anybody with a grain of patriotism who has not suffered the ignominy of sudden defeat, were aroused. Every letter to Gretel tells of a kind of desperation and almost unbearable personal inner tension that is fundamental to an understanding of his subsequent career. On 14th May he had recorded astonishment at what he called the 'beer-calmness' of the East Prussians at the revelation of the peace terms and their apparently supine acceptance of their implications. 'If we accept this peace we are finished as we may be if we don't. Therefore I am for doing nothing. The Entente can then seize by force what it wants. We shall see how far they get for they can do no more than destroy us. If we only still had the army, our proud, beautiful army, such an ignominy would not have been possible'. But already he knew that the existing German forces in the Baltic States, with the notable exception of the Iron Division, were fading away because '. . . they will not fight for the Fatherland, only the land they would be settled on'. He was disgusted. On 6th July he heard they must withdraw from Riga and that same day had received a realistic letter of reproof from a worried Gretel:

'I can understand your rage at this shameful treaty', she wrote, 'and yet a few people cannot alter things, their sacrifice is in vain. The Fatherland will need you later on, the moment has not come . . . nothing can be achieved now that the peace has been signed and the conditions accepted by this criminal government. So you will have no backing for your campaign in the Baltic States . . .'

The letter was intended to calm him but he rarely paid much attention to her political advice – sound though it was on this occasion. On the 12th he passionately replied:

'You write that our work here is hopeless. That may be so. But who can judge whether some small success may yet materialise out of these struggles? . . . The enemy resolves to destroy us. So be it. The English can certainly force us to leave the country and with it cut the only connection we still have with Russia . . . The enemy now has the power to impose his will . . . in spite of that: show strength and never give in . . .

'Salvation can only come from within us. We ourselves have to see to it that the shameful peace cannot be implemented, that our proud army does not disappear and that, at least, an attempt is made to save its honour. We will try to put into practice the solemn promises we carelessly made earlier. You well know the "Wacht am Rhein" and the old Prussian march: "As long as a drop of blood flows, a fist the sword draws . . . May the day be dark, may the sun shine bright, I am a Prussian and Prussian I will be". The day now is gloomy. Everything depends now on keeping the oath . . . Everybody who still has the smallest sense of honour must say: I will help.

'Believe me, my darling, above all I would love to return to you and the children . . . I am not acting recklessly. I have given this step very careful thought.

'An officer can do nothing more in Germany. According to the Peace Treaty the General Staff is to be abandoned. It is questionable whether the next independent German government will, in general, still keep reactionary officers. Nevertheless, one cannot expect an old Prussian officer to serve under criminals. I would therefore resign my commission. Where shall I go? Do we receive a well-earned pension? . . . Shall I perhaps lead, under French control, a so-called "company" of continuously mutineering policemen and adorn my hat with the black, red, golden cockade of shame? You cannot expect that of me – at least not now when all the possibilities have yet to be exhausted and I have not yet become a miserable scoundrel.'

Towards the end of July, Guderian (who for most of this time had acted as 1st Staff Officer of the Iron Division in the absence of the actual Ia) wrote a memorandum for Bischoff. It is difficult to translate into English in all its original force, for Guderian composed with an elaborate – and at times dramatic – style. It began by summarising the deteriorating political situation, reflecting Seeckt's earlier aims, continued with views that were his own and divergent from official policy: 'Germany is then surrounded at her borders by Entente states. Industry and commerce are subject to supervision by the Entente. An upsurge and strengthening of the German Empire is excluded.

'Therefore the question arises, how to keep a way open to Russia through the Baltic?

'The Division has not abandoned the plan to establish a bridge between Germany and Russia, even though the policy with Latvia has been wrecked. It has made contact with [White] Russian units in Mitau in order to achieve an association with the Russians.

'Two political alternatives are offered by the Russians. One sees them joining the Entente as the best and right way. This view is predominant in Lieven's battalion and is, therefore, English orientated. The larger part of this battalion has, in the meantime, been taken to Reval for action on the Northern Front.

'The Regiment of *Graf* Keller, which is led by Bermondt, represents the other view. This Regiment is German orientated. Colonel Bermondt considers the German Empire strong enough to help the Russians in their endeavours, particularly as an alliance with Russia is of the greatest significance and would free Germany from encirclement. Important German authorities, like High Command North and Zegrost, support the Division. Even if they were not convinced of the hope for the plan they nevertheless thought it should be tried.* In this they were supported by the 2nd General Staff officer, *Hauptmann* Guderian, who personally went to High Command North at Bartenstein.

'The German Empire does not suffer pecuniary damage by handing over war material [to the Russians] as, according to the Peace Treaty, the largest part of it has to be given to the Entente for destruction.

'If the Division remains in the Baltic States against the orders of the Government it should naturally make itself recognisable as Russian troops.

*Not all of them, it must be pointed out. Wheeler Bennett, for example, states that Seeckt looked on von der Goltz's schemes as 'pure fantasy'.

'The transfer depends primarily upon its being financed by the Russians . . . The Division has forbidden a preliminary transfer of individual formations. Only through a complete transfer can the rightful demands be met . . . If individual officers and men go over they do so at their own peril . . . The Entente insists on the speediest evacuation of the Baltic States which has been emphasised emphatically at various discussions . . . The English fear a reorganisation of Germany in the Baltic States and, simultaneously, the nullification of the Versailles Treaty. The Higher Command has already issued orders for an evacuation . . .'

This document deeply impressed Bischoff because it represented his own ideas. Yet its bias was hardly that of the dispassionate staff officer sent by Seeckt to restrain the Iron Division. Guderian's personal preferences show through along with the political notions which disturbed so many German officers of his persuasion. Bischoff remarked that he had no desire to ask the 'so-called Weimar Coalition' Government for anything impossible. 'Even if the Government is unable to identify itself openly with us . . . it does not mean that in reality it has to work against us or make our work impossible'. But, Micawber-like, he, Guderian and the rest waited for something to turn up in their favour even after the first orders for a phased withdrawal were received. August 23rd was the day set for the first departures.

'I travelled with *Hauptmann* Guderian', wrote Bischoff, '. . . still hoping that perhaps a counter order might yet arrive. As I stood in front of the troops, and saw misgivings in their eyes whether it really was in earnest and the hope that it was not, all doubts and misgivings fell from me. I was convinced that the whole division would stand behind me.'

He refused to order entrainment and called upon the troops to remain. There was a display of wild enthusiasm and a torchlight procession in celebration.

This was the awful moment of climax after a period of terrible anxiety for Guderian. On 26th July he had replied to a letter in which Gretel had complained of his seeming indifference to her and the children. 'I need peace and quiet in a deep wood – away from work to become calmer, to be rid of these emotional upsets . . . The emotions stir one's nerves until one feels raving mad. You must cure me once more – as I know you will in a few days and twist me round your little finger.' But in the same letter he had asked, 'Where is there a man who dares to commit a single satisfactory deed?' His memorandum and personal pleading had warned those at Bartenstein that he did not wholeheartedly support Seeckt although Seeckt at that moment was suffering a heart attack which, temporarily, put him out of action. On 27th August he had written to Gretel about his feelings on 23rd August. 'My dearest little woman' – and told her again of the torture he was enduring. 'I had to make the most difficult decision of my life and take a step fraught with consequence. May God grant us success. We acted for the best, for our country and our people.' He concluded: 'Matters are on a razor's edge and I am nearly at my wit's ends. It is desperate with us. The morale of the troops is good – almost as in 1914.' He had flung his career into the melting pot and opted to stay with an organisation which did not have first call upon his loyalty. It could have been an irredeemable turning point in his life had not his masters at Bartenstein also been torn by identical conflicts of conscience. The Great German General Staff now demonstrated its compassion and its appreci-ation of a young staff officer whose abilities it valued highly*: it pre-emptorily recalled him to Bartenstein and prevented him from going near the Iron Division again. It – probably *Oberst* Heye, who in a few years would become C-in-C – tried to provide time for Guderian's inner storm to subside and the impulsive facet of his nature – that side which rebelled against injustice and against harm to the interests of the soldiers he respected – to be subjugated once more to the discipline of the Staff Corps. But his involvement with politics and his susceptibility to the lures of extremist factions marked an important stage in his development. Within the rules of the Prussian disciplinary code he had carried an argument up to and then beyond the point of decision: he had disobeyed, had so nearly been destroyed and yet had survived. It had been painful and yet it indicated the feasibility of breaking rules providing the cause seemed just.

The parting of the ways had come between the established army that Seeckt was restoring, and the freebooters of the *Freikorps* who were to prolong their resistance and become transfigured into the forces that are recognisable as the vanguard of the Nazis. In Bartenstein, Guderian obstinately chanced his arm and continued the struggle on behalf of the Iron Division. But its lonely stand in the Baltic was as hopeless as Gretel originally said. Although on the 27th he had written pessimistically that he could not expect to remain in a General Staff which had been reduced to 120 officers or expect a place in the Frontier Force, on the 31st optimism reasserted itself and led him to the bitter end: 'Up to date the movement in Kurland has gone in such a way that it will produce the results desired by the troops. It means, therefore, permission for settlers, fighting Bolshevism and the continuing existence of a national force capable of improvement. It would be welcome if *Graf* Goltz were to remain at the head of the corps. He is an excellent man with good soldiers, has tremendous diplomatic qualities and is of a high-minded disposition.' This letter was just another illustration of a blind spot in his outlook, an inability to foresee or evaluate political factors, which time was not to cure. If on 15th September he could encourage Bischoff on the lines that '. . . the Government, Reichs Defence Ministry and Foreign Office would

---

*Hermann Balck, who was close to Guderian at this time, says that Guderian *had* to be in the 100,000 man army from sheer virtue of strength of character. 'He was like a coiled spring.'

not abandon the Iron Division and the other troops in the Baltic States' that unrealistic persuasion was soon undermined along with his own position. He had believed what he had been told and had failed to examine political forces. *Freikorps'* numbers were dwindling as the disenchanted drifted home and their opponents increased in such strength that military defeat became inevitable. In October the German forces were beaten in battle. Thereafter further official support for the *Freikorps*, even clandestinely given, was pointless.

At the end of September Guderian had been put out of harm's way, or as he wrote to Gretel, '. . . please remember that I am just now plunged into loneliness'. They posted him to a place of relative political innocuity – with *Reichswehr* Brigade 10 in Hanover. Then, in January 1920, he was given what was, maybe, an essential respite from General Staff work and sent to rejoin his old 10th *Jäger* Battalion at Goslar as a company commander. The future he regarded gloomily, recording in *Panzer Leader* that he had left the General Staff '. . . in circumstances not of the happiest'. He was distinctly under a cloud in fact! He had sampled the heady wine of ideological nationalism, found it tempting but then had it dashed from his lips. He had been retained as part of the sober and respectable officer corps whose task it was to restore the stability of an old and trusted order to Germany, and thus he was diverted from the self-destruction upon which the *Freikorps* was bent. This withdrawal from hot political contacts was effective if not absolute. There is little doubt that his removal from the General Staff post inflicted a severe and memorable shock. Under conditions of moderate political pressure in the future he would react like a Pavlovian-conditioned animal and seem to resist positive political commitment by assuming an attitude of military propriety. Yet Guderian always retained a proneness to subversive intervention into matters which he judged to be of overriding importance. This he would justify as the ultimate interpretation of Prussian discipline's inner meaning, but it was a proclivity of which ill-disposed colleagues in the future became increasingly wary. Nor did he quite forgive Seeckt for his part in sanctioning the withdrawal from the Baltic States – even though he paid lip-service to the fundamental tenets of Seecktian political behaviour. Not long after the Second World War Guderian gave the Americans a character sketch of Seeckt which, in one way, was more revealing of himself than it was of the subject. Seeckt, he said, '. . . was alert, reflective, cool and *an almost timid person*'. The italics are mine because it is a judgement, so far as I am aware, which is unique, somewhat different to Guderian's subsequent assessment that Seeckt was 'coldly calculating'. It was at variance with the consensus of opinion among German generals – those like Manstein, Guderian's old classmate at the War Academy who had served under Seeckt in war and peace, when he wrote of '. . . the inner fire that inspired him and the iron will which made him a leader of men'.

Seeckt was the new Commander-in-Chief and faced with the formidable task of rebuilding an army that was deep in politics at a time when a weak Government was threatened with serious internal disorders. He recovered from his heart attack in sufficient time to meet the first major challenge to his intention of steering the Army out of politics, a challenge which came, not unexpectedly, from the remnants of the *Freikorps*, homeward-bound in hostile mood from the Baltic with the ambitious von der Goltz in their midst. Officially they had been abolished though many were still in the Baltic, and for years they were to reappear in various forms. Men such as von der Goltz were not easily denied. In March 1920 the long-feared coup took place when elements of the *Freikorps* converged on Berlin and appeared in several other cities in response to a putsch initiated by a politically inept civil servant called Wolfgang Kapp. Backed by Ludendorff, the *Freikorps*, and those who still looked upon them as the salvation of Germany, put heavy pressure upon the Government and formed a puppet regime of their own in Berlin. Seeckt refused the request of the Government to use the *Reichswehr* against the *Freikorps* saying, 'Would you force a battle at the Brandenburg Tor between troops who a year and a half ago were fighting shoulder to shoulder against the enemy?' Instead he took indefinite leave and thereby emphasised his professed determination to keep the Army out of politics. Into his place Kapp put von der Goltz, but it was all a charade. A General Strike called by the real Government quickly brought about the collapse of Kapp, with his ramshackle organisation, and Seeckt was able to return to the work of reconstruction with a strengthened hand.

There was little bloodshed as a result of the Kapp putsch even though the *Freikorps* marched on Berlin and made its presence felt in various other parts of Germany. The 10th *Jäger* Battalion, Guderian with it, were on stand-by and he was provided with light comic relief when most of his fellow company commanders were captured by rebels in Hildesheim. They managed, however, to seize guns from the rebels. In five days all was over. Commonsense persuaded him to resist the temptation to join with Kapp and von der Goltz in their attempt to set up a military dictatorship. A year later, during the Max Höltz disturbances, and in 1923 at the time of the Hitler putsch in Munich, Guderian remained loyal to Seeckt and the new *Reichswehr* as it grew as a separate instrument of state, controlled by the Chief of the Army High Command, working through and not against the Republic to which they swore their oath of allegiance.

Nevertheless Guderian had railed, on 8th April 1920, against 'lack of energetic action' in the aftermath of the Kapp putsch and '. . . the cowardice, stupidity and weakness of this lamentable Government . . . when at long last will the Saviour come . . . ? I am becoming more and more pessimistic with regard to the hope for peace. We are in the middle of a

Thirty Years' War. It is sad but cannot be altered. Our children will only know the word peace by its name'. Soon he was answered by a ruthless killing of Communists in the Ruhr by units of the Army and the *Freikorps* of Ritter von Epp.

In the reorganisation of the *Reichswehr*, Seeckt's aim encompassed, in addition to political isolation, the creation of a defence force which could be so constructed that it laid the foundation for the resurrection of the German Army when the time was ripe. The 100,000 men it was to recruit, many of whom would be of commissioned or non-commissioned officer calibre, would form a strong foundation of leadership in the event of expansion. Though the General Staff was proscribed, its function and existence were to be preserved in a special *Truppenamt* (Troop Office) with responsibility for defence, organisation, intelligence and training. In addition a civilian department, guided by ex-General Staff officers, carried out research into history and future military developments. In the shadow of defeat the new organisation was dedicated to the analysis of what had gone wrong and to the development of every feasible scheme of modernisation which could be studied or carried out within, or just beyond, the fringes of the Versailles Treaty. The officers of the German Army performed their task in an atmosphere absolutely different from that enjoyed by their predecessors. Guderian stated that 'They had to relinquish many privileges and forego many cherished traditions, and they did so to save their Fatherland from inundation by the flood of Asiatic Bolshevism then already threatening. The Weimar Republic did not succeed in turning this marriage of convenience into a love match.* No genuine attachment evolved between the officer corps and the new State.'

Until the end of 1921 Guderian was committed to a solitary function – lowly but fundamental: that of training a company of infantry. Since this was almost his first spell of duty in command of soldiers since 1914 (apart from the brief month as a temporary battalion commander in September 1917) and a considerable diminution of responsibility, he threw the most terrific energy into the task and drove his men hard. This was his first opportunity to become involved with exercises at the lowest level in consolidating the lessons of 1918. In 1921 there were exploratory manoeuvres with mechanised troops in the Harz near Goslar. The task was dear to his heart since it enabled him to experiment with the closer officer-man relationship that to him was so important – as it was to Seeckt whose policy sought a closing of the gap between the ranks. He could be rough with the men, even rougher with the officers, and his caustic tongue would lash and hurt. Yet he was fair and, as a trainer, systematically progressive, meticulously thorough, and always careful to explain the

---

* A quaint irony when one recalls that, in 1921, the Germans were about to embark on another marriage of convenience – co-operation with Red Russia through the Rapallo Treaty.

reasons for whatever demands he made. Only a company of the finest skill, morale and polish could be the product of such inspired and relentless leadership by a man who believed as much in persuasion as brute compulsion. They never forgot him and always welcomed him back.

When the time came to leave, his men expressed their feelings in a piece of verse which perfectly sums up his impact upon ordinary soldiers:

It is you, *Hauptmann* Guderian
Who not merely saw an instrument in man,
Who taught us the 'why' of such unavoidable toil.
If things were sometimes severe, then duty is harsh!
What fears the Warrior!
The company is grateful.

4 The Search For a Saviour

At the heart of the task of military reconstruction facing Germany, as Hans von Seeckt saw it in 1921, was the restitution of the ancient and traditional codes of honour and obedience and their fusion with a modern, forward-looking outlook in the fields of strategy and tactics as conditioned by burgeoning technology. Seeckt, like so many of his predecessors and contemporaries, was a man of maxims. Concerning the soldier's honour which demanded of an officer, for example, that he defend to the utmost not only his own character but that of his wife also, he was unbending: 'Herein lies the new and serious duty of the commander, the duty of severity for honour's sake', he wrote. The requirement was not so very new but he felt it had to be said over and again. Nor was he pronouncing startling originalities when he wrote:

'The more efficient this [regular] army, the greater its mobility, the more resolute and competent its command, the greater will be the chance of beating the opposing forces' and demanded:

'High mobility, to be attained by the employment of numerous and highly efficient cavalry, by the fullest possible use of motor transport and by the marching capacity of infantry; the most effective armament and continuous replacement of men and material'. He did not actually exclude tanks from his inventory, even though they were not mentioned: these he regarded as 'developing into a "special troop" besides Infantry, Cavalry and Artillery' – an important distinction which was to cause much controversy later on.

In addition to the *Truppenamt* and related central organs of the *Reichswehr*, command Inspectorates were set up to control and probe into matters which Seeckt deemed essential for the future. Among them was the Inspectorate of Transport Troops, under *General* von Tschischwitz, whose wide-ranging task encompassed both their tactical employment and the widespread complexities of their administration – such matters as fuel supply, repair and maintenance and road construction, none of which had been seriously tackled except from the angle of logistic supply of a fixed front prior to 1918. It was to this Inspectorate that Guderian was nominated in 1922. But the manner of his posting clearly, and for sufficient reason, undermined his confidence in what the future held. A vague enquiry by his colonel in the autumn of 1921 as to his feelings about rejoining the Staff, was followed by a long silence until January when he received a telephone call from *Oberstleutnant* Joachim von Stülpnagel of the *Truppenamt*, asking why he had not reported to the 7th (Bavarian) Motorised Transport Battalion at Munich. There had been a breakdown in staff duties. Immediately, however, a suspicious Guderian was demanding explanations. What was going on? How stood his prospects? At a time when promotion was stationary a job in a lonely Bavarian Transport Battalion far from represented a staff appointment with sound prospects. The appointment sounded all too much like a side-track, remote from a place at the centre of things to which Guderian was accustomed and which an ambitious officer required as a springboard for advancement.

Stülpnagel hastened to explain that he was destined to become the General Staff officer to Tschischwitz but that the posting to Munich was to enable him to obtain prior, first-hand experience of transport troops. He followed this with a letter on the 16th January which was a mixture of placation and sound advice:

'. . . your employment with the Inspectorate of Motorised Troops is intended to be a special recognition for your performances up till now. To speak in confidence, you are supposed to transmit the intentions of the General Staff to the motorised troops . . . You can imagine that some specialists will not like your coming. All the more important it is for you to break through with tact and understanding for the larger interests and gain the recognition of the specialists.'

At that time, in every army, there yawned a gulf between specialists and regimental and staff soldiers, a gulf that was exceptionally wide in the German Army due to a common contempt for 'rude mechanicals'. With Guderian no such snobbery existed. His service with the signallers had eliminated any there might have been and so his selection for this task was admirably made. He was, as he wrote, delighted and made happier still by *Major* Oswald Lutz, the battalion commander in Munich, whose task it was to give him all the experience possible in less than three months. Lutz was a railway engineer by training, a man of remarkably clear mental aptitude and thoroughly receptive to new ideas. He also possessed the sort of whimsical humour that was compatible with Guderian's kind of banter: he once ordered the cadets at the training school to climb into the trees and when they returned to the ground explained that he had done so in order to see 'if their platoon leader would go up into the trees for me'. He had!

Guderian was on the threshold of his last years of comparative repose in his military career. Ahead lay a decade of study, the development of revolutionary ideas and the pursuit of knowledge stimulated by the demand that he should teach. It was of small account – in fact it was to his

eventual advantage – when, at the outset in the Inspectorate, Tschischwitz's Chief of Staff, *Major* Petter, insisted upon overruling his general
concerning the sort of work upon which Guderian was employed – as any
Chief of Staff in the German Army was fully entitled to do. Instead of
directing Guderian's energies upon the organisation and employment of
motorised troops in a combat role he was put to work on logistics. The
prospect appalled him. He protested and was overruled: he asked to be
sent back to the 10th *Jägers* and was told quite firmly not to argue and
instead to get on with his job. It could not have been better than if it had
been so arranged. It deflated Guderian's ego and cleared his mind so that
he could tackle a totally new experience from first principles, working for
men who were determined to be masters in their own house. The General
Staff, even in its new, covert guise, was a remarkably tightly knit organisation with a talent for making the best use of its component parts. Seeckt
might desire that its members should conform to a standard code of
conduct in addition to standardised methods of work, but, in the final
analysis, careful attention was given to putting the right men into the most
appropriate employment. It is to be wondered, however, if anybody had
foreseen the outcome of posting young Guderian to a rather out of the
way appointment in 1922, whether they would have held back. For
Guderian was bent on innovation on a scale which would leave the
General Staff and, eventually, the world breathless.

By the application of that dynamic industry which now was second
nature, he mastered the office work and decentralised routine subjects to
the clerks. With mundane things out of the way he could turn his mind to
what Tschischwitz – a hard taskmaster – had always intended he should
do: study motorised troops. He entered an academic world, almost cutting himself off from the political and economic turmoil that went on
outside – the upheavals of putsch and counter-putsch; the effects of allied
reparations on the economy with the attendant French occupation of the
Ruhr in 1923 and the runaway inflation of the Mark which did fearful
damage to stable segments of society and crippled industry; the rise of the
private armies – *Stahlhelms, Sturm Abteilung* and their ilk; the prevalent
wavering of a weakened democracy before the threat of strong men and
vested interests. Political events he carefully watched but studiously
managed to avoid or deflect since his work and income remained fairly
constant. Yet, in anger, he could sympathise with political aspirations and
formulate political alignments even though, as an officer, he was neither
allowed to take part in politics nor cast a vote. At heart he remained a
patriot in search of a Saviour – a new Bismarck – for his country and,
when in 1925, Paul von Hindenburg, a staunch monarchist, became
Reichspresident and inaugurated, in company with Seeckt and Gustav
Stresemann, a period of tranquillity, it seemed possible that the deity he
longed for had been found. In a letter to his mother on 21st September

1925 he described the great ovation Hindenburg received when he visited the annual Army manoeuvres – the enthusiasm of the people for the man, the torchlight processions and the specially composed poems recalling the glories of the past. He rarely mentioned the politician Stresemann whose achievements were, in fact, considerable, but consigned him, as a politician, to a lower place, well beneath the god-head, the President.

But the Army upon which so much glory had been built in the past, was now a feeble specimen armed with material that could have little practical use either in war or for experiments into the future. The tracked transport vehicles in the columns were neither robust nor agile enough to simulate the cross-country movement demanded of fully mobile troops. Moreover they were even more vulnerable than the cavalry and infantry who had been shot down by droves in the course of five years' combat. Some form of protection, a vehicle with armour since men could not be personally armoured, was obviously needed and this Guderian must have realised from the start, even though in *Panzer Leader* he makes awfully heavy weather of describing the evolution of his mental processes. Later he was to complain that the official historical division had failed because it did not issue progressive directives to the Army Archives Office which was working on the history of the First World War, saying: 'The problems of modern warfare, problems arising from air and armoured operations, had deliberately been neglected, the historians not being equal to the task'. Though a trifle unfair (the historians quite reasonably tackled the war in chronological order) his remark that the history 'had not even reached the tank battle of Cambrai by the time the Second World War broke out' was only too true. Nor, for that matter, had the British Official History got that far by 1939. So Guderian was compelled to look elsewhere for precedents from a few German tank survivors, particularly from *Leutnant* Ernst Volkheim (the most experienced of German tank survivors), from a couple of German handbooks, but also from the French and, above all, the British practitioners.

In 1923 the British became unique in establishing a Tank Corps that was detached from the Infantry, Cavalry and Artillery; a separation that was the result of the expression of an independent line of thought by those among them who had built the tank force into a match-winning combination at the end of 1918 and who had devised schemes which bordered upon the suggestion that special Tank Armies ought to be created. The brain behind these ideas was Fuller's, whose talents for analysis, organisation and penetrating expression had marked him out as a staff officer and a reforming military genius of the very first water. Immediately after the war Fuller had written highly perceptive articles expounding the future of armoured mechanised warfare dominated by the tank and by aircraft. At the same time a good book about the Tank Corps by the brothers Williams Ellis, had been published in 1919. Also at that time Captain

Basil Liddell Hart was beginning to make a name for himself by his early lectures and writings on infantry tactical systems which were very similar to those already in use in the German Army. But it was to Fuller who Liddell Hart turned for guidance on tanks and to Fuller who Guderian looked for initial guidance with regard to the development of armoured warfare – notwithstanding the implication in a paragraph on page 20 of *Panzer Leader* that Liddell Hart provided the principal inspiration. In fact, that paragraph appears only in the English editions of *Panzer Leader*, for which Liddell Hart wrote the foreword, and not in the original German language *Erinnerungen eines Soldaten*. Moreover there is no mention of works by Liddell Hart in the bibliography of Guderian's *Achtung! Panzer!* (though he is mentioned in company with Fuller, Martel and de Gaulle in the text of that book) whereas books by Fuller, Martel and de Gaulle do appear in that book's bibliography. Guderian's elder son, in fact, writes: 'As far as I know it was Fuller who made the most suggestions. Once before the war my father visited him. Fuller was almost certainly more competent as an active officer than Captain B.H.Liddell Hart . . . At any rate my father often spoke of him [Fuller] while I cannot remember other names being mentioned at that time [before 1939] . . . The greater emphasis upon Liddell Hart seems to have developed through contacts after the war.'

In the simplest terms Fuller envisaged armoured mechanised armies which had the inherent capability, supported by aircraft and artillery, to breach a fortified line and then achieve deep penetration of enemy territory, mopping up the forward artillery zones, knocking out head-quarters, capturing supply dumps, cutting communications and generally causing such damage and confusion amid the least well defended parts of the enemy hinterland that a total collapse of morale, command and control and resistance could be expected. To sustain operations of this kind Fuller demanded heavy tanks for breaching the line in what, by 1918, was a conventional assault with infantry and artillery. This would be simultaneous with exploitation in depth by lighter and faster tanks that had a speed of 20 mph and a circuit action of 150 to 200 miles. They would be supported by mobile artillery, tractor-drawn infantry and caval-ry 'if [the latter] have sufficient endurance to keep up a pursuit of at least 20 miles per day for a period of 5 to 7 days'. For practical experiments the British possessed, in addition to the clumsy machines with which they had fought in the war, a new family of much more agile heavy, medium and light tanks along with armoured cars, cross-country lorries and troop transports and self-propelled artillery. Mainly these machines existed only in prototype but by the middle 1920s there was a growing number of the Vickers Medium tank – a fighting vehicle which, though so thin of skin as to be nearly pervious to ordinary bullets, achieved new standards in speed and reliability (without saying too much for the latter) along with an improved layout of the fighting compartment which allowed the crew to make best use of their single 47mm quick-firing gun, in its rotating turret, and of several machine-guns. With this sort of equipment, such as no other nation had either in sufficient quantity or quality until the 1930s, the British were able to establish a lead both in theory and practice. In the summer of 1927 they deployed a completely motorised force of all arms on Salisbury Plain and used it to such effect that a conventional horse and foot force was hopelessly outmanoeuvred – despite the motorised force being inferior in number, bereft of an established technique and almost totally devoid of wireless for command and control. The other nations of the world intently watched and eagerly began to emulate what they had seen.

By order of the Versailles Treaty (or *Diktat* in German terminology) the Germans could only listen, take note, study and wait – their every false move observed and squashed by the members of a Control Commission which acted as monitors of good behaviour. But monitors have their blind spots and treaties their loop-holes: the all-demanding sport with the Germans was finding them. The Versailles Treaty did not prohibit Germany from having allies. What more sensible policy that she should look to another 'isolated power' for the alliance that the Entente discouraged? When, in 1921, Lenin made overtures for a German-Russian treaty of co-operation, Seeckt welcomed the new 'bridge', such as he had sought in 1919 in company with different supporters on the Russian side. Moreover Seeckt, as the most powerful man in Germany, carried the political weight to push through the Treaty of Rapallo which was signed on 17th April 1922, which restored collaboration between the signatories and encouraged, among other things, military co-operation, particularly with regard to the projects of more advanced technology such as tanks, gas and aircraft. In due course three experimental training centres were set up in Russia where machines, substances and techniques could be tested and a cadre of specialists trained. Not only were Russian-built tanks (the MS I and the MS II with its 37mm gun) developed and employed for the most part, but also certain German designs. One was a 9 ton light tank (*Leichter Traktor*) armed with a high velocity 37mm gun in a fully rotating turret, produced in secret as agricultural machinery by the firm of Rheinmetall in 1926 or thereabouts and assembled in Russia: it had a remarkable similarity in layout to the British Medium. Another was the heavy, 20 ton *Grosstraktor* which appeared about 1929 and was armed with a short, low velocity 75mm gun in a fully traversing turret mounted on a hull inherited from an experimental tank of 1918 vintage – the A7V(U). Produced secretly in Germany and at once shipped to the tank testing ground on the Kama River, in Russia, the secret existence and quick disappearance of these machines neatly skirted infringement of the Versailles Treaty. Thus small tank design cells were formed within German industry (Krupp and Daimler Benz came in at this stage along with Rheinmetall) to tackle basic design and production problems in connection with optics, armament, armour, power plant, transmission, suspensions and tracks. Also an eye was kept on the Swedish M 21 tank, manufactured by Bofors, who had an arrangement with Krupps. The M 21 was a derivative of the German LK II which had been copied in 1918 from the British Whippet. It was out of date – but at least it was German.

Encouraged by Tschischwitz and Lutz, and kept firmly on the ground by Petter, Guderian approached motorisation with inventive zeal. The constructively critical faculties of his mind, which, up to now, had merely been called upon to modify matters of daily routine in work conditioned by the stress of war and civil strife, were highly responsive to brand-new concepts. War had left him physically unscathed and mentally uninhibited by paralysing experiences of trench warfare. Never had he been wounded, rarely infected by personal involvement with the cramping fears of the circumscribed tactical routines of the trenches. Hence he could scan the future prospects of warfare with an outlook that was untrammelled by indelibly inflexible impressions. He began to envisage himself as a repository for information from which he developed new combat ideas that encroached upon a largely unexplored operational field. The age of thirty-five was perhaps a little late to find original inspirations, but he could hardly have been expected to initiate original schemes before since the war had precluded an opportunity. Be that as it may, he now recognised, with mounting and excited perception, the deficiencies of the current ways of making war and, more important, means to make a fundamental change. As he read more deeply into his subject there began to appear profound conclusions drawn from his study of ancient and contemporary history. This led to the pursuit of a pastime which used to absorb the old Prussian General Staff – prodigious writing in military journals. Encouraged by *General* von Altrock, the Editor of the *Militär-Wochenblatt* (Military Weekly) he composed articles (some of them anonymous?) which crystalised his thoughts and his style and, at the same time, won him a reputation for clear exposition on controversial matters of immediate interest in the contemporary debate surrounding the reasons for Germany losing the last war. But it also won him enemies, for at this early stage the tank enthusiasts proposed converting the cavalry to mechanised divisions.

There were German generals too, among them von Kuhl, who were saying that the tank had won the war for the Allies and that lack of the tank had been crucial in Germany's failure – an exaggeration that was sufficiently emotive to discourage serious denial. Essentially Guderian opened his own mind to the future. Günther Blumentritt was to remark: 'If you suggest revolutionary ideas to Guderian he will say, in 95 per cent of cases, yes, at once'. But that too was an exaggeration.

In exercises which had taken place in the winter of 1923/24 with motorised troops under *Oberstleutnant* Walter von Brauchitsch, the examination of mechanisation had gone further than the earlier Harz exercises in that, in addition to march discipline, command and control, they investigated close co-operation with aircraft. As time went by, before and after theoretical exercises such as these, *Hauptmann* Guderian would be invited to give the tank expert's opinion – a quite essential requirement demanding of imaginative description since German experience was mostly at the receiving end from these machines. Always his precise and convincing explanations, interlaced with witty historical precedents and skilfully angled arguments, made a strong impact upon the audience. He developed into a star turn equipped with keen analysis and bubbling enthusiasm. Once more career prospects were moving ahead: in 1924 it was suggested that he should be employed as an instructor in tactics and military history – a shrewd placing of a man who had worked himself out of the pit into which he had fallen. Moreover his new master was to be an old commander, von Tschischwitz, whose open-mindedness guaranteed Guderian ample room for the expansion of ideas.

Prior to 1914, von Schlieffen had sought historical precedents to substantiate the basis of his military theory of attack. Of him Guderian once wrote that he was clever, cold and sarcastic, a general who '... through clarity and firmness in military planning ... sought to compensate for the aimlessness and indecisiveness of politicians'. Guderian also searched for precedents to justify the creation of a new theory of attack, one which could swiftly overcome the barriers erected by current defensive practices. But it was revealing that, as a supreme optimist, he took to examining examples of failure in history in order to justify his arguments for change, whereas Schlieffen had pinned his hopes on successes, on the Prussian victory at Leuthen and, later, on Hannibal's masterpiece at Cannae as illustrating how a battle could be won by total envelopment – forgetting to mention that neither of these victories had actually decided a war. Guderian looked to defeats for enlightenment and enlivened his lectures and papers with remarks and quotations which were more sardonic than sarcastic, with a delivery that was as direct as it was pointed. Standing in front of a class, eyes sparkling with enthusiasm, and using the minimum of demonstrative posturing, he would drive home each point by sheer force of dedication and knowledge. In the manner of all good teachers he found that the impulse to communicate was itself a wonderful stimulant to original thought. In his case the need for excellence was pitched above that of his normal high standards by the obligation to overcome the scepticism of highly critical students – the pick of the *Reichswehr* – to what amounted, in some minds, to outlandish concepts. Present these well-informed officers with a weak argument and they would rend the lecturer. Convince them and he had recruited disciples.

At the centre of his programme was a theme – that of *Stosskraft* – dynamic punch – and its bearing upon the weapons of the past and the present. Of the disastrous Prussian campaign against Napoleon in 1806 he would ask, apropos the present, 'Do we make the same mistake as they did "to proudly meet the enemy without firing a shot since to take aim with a volley might upset the battalions' upright bearing": in other words do we fail to take cover from enemy fire?' He would jeer at the bayonet: 'One is still regarded as a heretic if one dares impune that sacred symbol of infantry *Stosskraft*', and called Moltke the Elder to his aid, quoting the Master's dictum, 'Fire must be used against the enemy during an offensive in order to weaken him before a bayonet fight ensues'. Caustically he quoted again: '. . . the day of honour at Hagelberg in 1813 when a celebrated bayonet charge cost the enemy all of 30 to 35 dead'. This was his destructive phase prior to the moment of construction.

For he would then go on to demonstrate how *Stosskraft* was subject to technological change. In 1914 it lay with fire-power, '. . . that is to say in the infantry's machine-gun and with other heavy weapons, but largely with the divisional artillery. If the *Stosskraft* was sufficiently strong then the offensive succeeded as it did in the East, in Rumania, in Serbia and Italy. If it was weak, as on the Western Front, it failed . . . The World War proved that *Stosskraft* does not depend upon fire-power alone . . . Guns must be brought close to the enemy lines . . . so that pin-point targets can be recognised at close range and then annihilated by direct fire'. The cavalry sword he would dismiss with a flourish similar to that with which he disposed of the bayonet: 'Even the celebrated attacks by the Bayreuth Dragoons at Hohenfriedberg and by Seydlitz's cavalry at Rossbach were made against infantry who were already shattered. Attacks against fresh infantry were not decisive, as the Battle of Zorndorf confirms.'

From this starting point he could begin his examination of means of 'bringing fire on to the enemy lines' during fast monoeuvres. 'Here', he said, 'only the restoration of an ancient means could help – armour. Armour has fallen out of favour not because it could not be made thick enough to offer protection against rifle shots, but because neither man nor horse has strength enough to carry or move it'. At this moment he could announce the advent and the case for the tank and declaim: 'What then is *Stosskraft*? It is the force which enables the soldier in combat to bring his weapons close enough to the enemy lines in order to destroy him. Only troops with this integral capacity have *Stosskraft* and with it the capacity to attack. We are not unreasonable when we maintain, as the result of our war experiences, that of all land forces the tank possesses most *Stosskraft*.' And at this point, as time went by and his convictions hardened, the teaching of history gave way to the dissemination of tank propaganda at which he became expert.

These were halcyon days in that there was ample time for calm and thorough consideration of problems which, in the foreseeable future, could have no immediate effect upon an army which thought deeply but, in outward form, hardly changed at all. Guderian kept himself thoroughly informed of the latest moves by the Inspectorate of Transport Troops as it took an increasingly active part in the co-operation with Russia and placed the first orders in 1926 for the *Leichter Traktor*, mentioned above. It was ironic, in fact, that as these small but significant movements took place in the direction of an eventual rearmament, Western Europe entered the zone of a tranquillity such as had been unknown for more than two decades. In 1925 the Locarno Treaty was signed and introduced a brief epoch of mutual security between nations and the gradual rehabilitation of Germany: the admittance of Germany into the League of Nations in 1926 and the withdrawal in 1927 of the Control Commission led to the final removal of Allied troops in 1930. On the other hand, when strong moves towards a Disarmament Conference were in train, it was the British who first assembled an experimental armoured force in 1927. And so, by default, when politicians steered hard for peace, a simultaneous tack was taken in the direction of war by military demonstrations aimed at showing how a short, decisive campaign could be implemented. In Russia they were assimilating fast and furiously everything that the Germans, and anybody else, could teach them; it is probable that they benefited far more from Rapallo than did the Germans.

In January 1927 Guderian was at last promoted *Major* in a small Army where circumstances naturally retarded ambition, and in October 1927 his academic work was curtailed by a posting which sent him to the *Truppenamt* and therefore, for all practical purposes (despite the Versailles Treaty), back to the General Staff. There he was assigned to the Transport Section, which belonged to the Operations Department, where his task was, ostensibly, the further development of troop transportation by lorry. It was another shrewd and logical selection for a man who been converted into what is to-day called a Technical Staff officer, inviting him to perform a task which involved both technological and operational subjects. It did not matter that he was not an engineer or particularly mechanically trained. His technical awareness was what counted and produced an individual who was of the greatest rarity in almost every army of the day. Change was in the air: his arrival in the *Truppenamt* practically coincided with that of its new head, *Generaloberst* Werner von Blomberg, whose destiny would soon be linked with German revolution of another kind.

For Guderian a terrific challenge awaited. The *Truppenamt*, prompted originally by Seeckt with his insistence upon cavalry and infantry aided by motor transport, tended to look upon road transport services as an extension, albeit a more flexible one, of the railway. They seemed to postulate that what already went by rail in future should also go by road to satisfy existing organisations and methods. They rather overlooked the obvious defect that Europe's railways were much more highly developed than her highways and were quite unprepared to admit that the composition of fighting formations would greatly alter in the future. Hence they demanded that lorried transport must be capable of carrying the same loads in the same manner as railways, and those loads would consist of everything a cavalry or an infantry division possessed – equipment, men and horses. In so many words they were trying to use lorries as taxis in order to preserve the *status quo* without admitting, as Guderian insisted they must, that past concepts were out of date and demanding of total reconstruction. He says that there were many heated discussions and more sceptics than believers in the possibility of finding a workable solution. The days of tranquillity were past, in fact. In stating his opposition to the unworkable and to concepts which were the antithesis of what he reasoned as essential, he nailed his colours to the mast and embarked upon the course which was to change history.

At about the same time as liaison with Russia commenced, the training of a new staff was demanded. The Transport Department set up its own small school to instruct officers, civilian employees and non-commissioned officers in automotive mechanics. In 1928 it was decided to add a tactical wing to study and teach the employment of tanks and their co-operation with other arms – and who better to found that wing than Guderian. But in the autumn of 1928, when the suggestion was approved, he had to admit that as yet he had not even seen the inside of a tank. This was soon rectified. In 1929 he went with Gretel to Sweden via Denmark, an occasion which prompted him, in *Panzer Leader*, to give a rare insight into his abiding delight in beautiful things – the countryside and the Scandinavian cities – the sort of pleasure which used to pass soldiers like Schlieffen and Erwin Rommel by. As the guest of a Swedish tank battalion equipped with the M 21 tank of German origination, he drove the machine, assessed its performance (judging its limitations and vulnerabilities) and witnessed small exercises in which the tanks co-operated with other arms and made attacks under cover of smoke screens. The M 21 was a poor machine but the experience it gave Guderian marked another turning point in his career. Perhaps he rather over-dramatises his conclusions when he says that it was in 1929 he became convinced 'that tanks working on their own or in conjunction with infantry could never achieve decisive importance', for his early lectures and studies at no time give the impression of a belief that tanks in isolation could prosper. But that year he devised and consolidated a scenario for all future conflict – presenting it both in the councils of the

General Staff and on the training grounds. In the summer of 1929, he ran a divisional-sized field exercise that incorporated a battlegroup of all arms such as an armoured division could deploy – a copy, in fact, of the earlier British experiment such as the Americans and Russians were trying at the same time.

The concept of the armoured division, a formation comprising a balanced force of tanks, armoured cars, motorised infantry, artillery and engineers, was by no means a German invention. The idea had long ago been suggested by British and French protagonists of the tank who saw it as the dominant weapon. It had been discussed in public and was often mentioned in the quite large number of books about tanks then beginning to appear. Indeed, so profuse were the writings on tank warfare that the problem facing the Motor Transport Inspectorate was one of selection before making any recommendations. The Russians were tending towards independent tank formations which could be used in the traditional strategic role of cavalry. The French saw the tank as a strictly infantry support weapon, moving at the speed of marching men, and looked on armoured cars as the seekers of information in the old cavalry role. The British quite noticeably tended towards balanced armoured forces, as their experiments in 1927 had plainly shown, but also were attracted by armoured cars for reconnaissance and heavily armoured tanks for infantry support. Economically the Germans could afford to adopt only one system. Though Seeckt had been succeeded as Commander-in-Chief in 1926 by *Generaloberst* Wilhelm Heye (a milder disciple of Seeckt), Seeckt's authority still held sway: 'The smaller the army, the easier it will be to equip it with modern weapons'. And although Seeckt wrote in 1930 that he could not imagine '. . . armoured engines and the horseman entirely superseded by the motor soldier' the drift of his thoughts ran mighty close to those of Guderian when he added, 'No longer, like Frederick at the end of the day, will we hurl our jingling squadrons upon the tottering foe. The modern Seydlitz will lead his well-nursed troops with their mobile artillery behind the flank and rear of the enemy in order to join with the advancing infantry and other units in securing the final decision.' This, though it excluded the provocative work 'tank', was the essence distilled of Fuller and Guderian.

Fuller's concepts rode the Germans hard. In 1936 Guderian could sincerely acknowledge in public that it was decided to rely mainly on English observations as contained in Part (Vol) 2 of the 'Provisional Instructions for Tank and Armoured Car Training', published in 1927. This document bore the imprint of Fuller and included the conclusions drawn from experience in the First World War plus that gathered in three years' experiments with the latest tanks. It was obtainable, price 9d, from His Majesty's Stationery Office. In due course would appear 'Mechanized and Armoured Formations, 1929' and 'Modern Formations, 1931' which were Security-graded documents, 'not to be communicated either directly or indirectly to the Press or to any person not holding an official position in His Majesty's Service'. Nevertheless they each found their way into unauthorised hands, including those of the Germans. The 1927 book, according to Guderian, contained '. . . the essential basic rules . . . clearly expressed . . . so that trials could be started, but at the same time it gave the necessary flexibility for further development. This was not the case with the well-known contemporary French manual which seemed to hinder all development by the inflexible binding of tanks to infantry. The recommendation to use the English manual was approved by *Reichswehr* Headquarters. It remained the basis for the indoctrination of the officers of the motorised troops destined for the future tank arm until 1933.'

The 'tank' exercises of 1929, deficient in realism though they were because of the absence of real tanks, taught false lessons but heightened the faith of the enthusiasts. Small motor cars, decked out with canvas and sheet iron to look like tanks, made a poor enough impression. Their inability to cross anything other than the smoothest of hard going and their propensity to look silly when the infantry poked their bayonets throught the canvas and made derogatory remarks to the humiliated crews, placed demands upon the pioneers. Coherent lessons were difficult to assimilate but fortunately Guderian had the optimism, determination and imagination to satisfy all demands and to carry his colleagues with him. 'In spite of these shortcomings', he wrote, 'the idea gained ground that it was essential to have a Panzer Command. Those engaged in the tests obtained a clear knowledge of its future employment and organisation. The tests eventually resulted in demands for the development of the weapon'. That year secret orders went out for the building of *Grosstraktor*, the heavier tank with its bigger gun.

Lutz, who became Inspector of Motor Transport in 1931, was carried along by Guderian. Brilliant organiser and clear thinker though he was, he was only a partner – in terms of achievement the junior partner – in a team. *Major* Chales de Beaulieu, who was on Guderian's staff between 1931 and 1933 and again between 1935 and 1937, says: 'Guderian was the brains behind it all and thought about everything in advance which could be important or necessary – in personnel, equipment and in leadership . . . he was an ideal leader'. Lutz provided the authority and tact to help push through Guderian's schemes in the higher councils. He also placed Guderian in the right appointments at the right time. In January 1930 he sent him to command 3rd (Prussian) Motor Transport Battalion (no doubt at Guderian's suggestion) and obtained as its equipment all the elements of a future armoured division less field artillery. There was a company of dummy tanks and an anti-tank company with wooden guns – in fact only the armoured cars of the Reconnaissance Company

49

and the motor-cycles in No. 4 Company were real. There was also another vital piece of equipment missing – the modern communication sets which alone would make the panzer division, as envisaged by Guderian, a viable proposition.

When Colonel Ernest Swinton wrote the first tactical directive for British tanks in 1916 he tackled the communication problem by suggesting that 'One tank in ten should be equipped with small wireless sets, others to lay telephone cable as they advanced, while the rest make do with visual signals and smoke rockets to indicate progress'. At that time, of course, there were no suitable small wireless sets while cable-laying was both frail and an inflexible method related only to short advances. Anybody who has attempted visual signalling from the top of a tank will testify what a thoroughly unsatisfactory system it can be, while the few who have tried it in action, and survived when every weapon in sight is throwing missiles, are most unlikely to repeat the experience. A few tanks were equipped with radio and used it in action before the end of the First World War, but they became specialised vehicles because they could not send or receive messages satisfactorily on the move. They were usually employed as reporting centres only.

Progress in the improvement of radio communications during the 1920s was rapid and the Germans were well up with everybody else, particularly since, in this corner of the military field, the Versailles Treaty did not impose severe restrictions and was far easier to circumvent. In any case enormous strides had already been made in radio transmission and reception during the First World War, and these were further exploited for police and commercial use afterwards. Speech over the air was becoming as common a means of communication as morse, and far less liable to interference when inventors shifted their investigations into the higher frequency ranges. Sets gradually became more robust, smaller and easier to tune, especially when the airmen placed a premium on such things in the interests of reductions in weight. The power of transmitters was steadily increased along with range of operation; the discovery of crystal-controlled master oscillators in the early 1920s opened a new era of accuracy in establishing radio networks.

In 1931 the first demonstration ever of a tank formation being controlled on the move from a single master control tank was made in England. The sets in use were crystal-controlled. If the Germans were further behind at that time they were, however, more seriously committed to the acquisition of comprehensive tank radio networks – largely because of Guderian's insistence. His experience in 1914 left him in no doubt that if highly fluid long-range operations were to be conducted with co-ordinated zeal, radio communication had to be accurate, concise and widespread from the pinnacles of command down to the lowest possible level. Just how low would depend upon the kind of sets which could be built and on the amount of money made available for their purchase. At first Guderian and his collaborators asked that radio communication should reach as far as the headquarters of tank companies, though they knew that the British had gone lower still to troop headquarters and, in some cases, to individual tanks. Walther Nehring, who was one of Guderian's principal staff officers for many years, told the author that from the outset it was realised that, without a comprehensive communication network, the concept of high mobility and deep penetration by panzer divisions was unthinkable. De Beaulieu adds that 'the early use of the wireless for command in battle to the single tank was due to Guderian's insistence . . . He had an eye for the essential and at the same time . . . he was also able to judge when to press for his goal – which is a vital characteristic. Few people know how to recognise the moment.'

Comparatively speaking, as much effort was put into the development of communications as into the fighting vehicles themselves and the signallers took up the challenge with fervour. In fact the Germans had taken a lead in communications during the First World War and had recognised the problems, though they also had the sense to realise, in 1926, that their latest sets were totally inadequate, notably those developed for civilian purposes. Work began on designing a new range of sets which were small, 'undamped' and thoroughly reliable in vehicles on the move. But the dangers of enemy intercept overhearing radio messages and breaking the codes – even those manufactured by machines – also concentrated attention upon the evolution of field telephone and teleprinter networks which could be laid down at such high speed that a pace of 100 miles a day could be kept with an advancing formation. Those units which were compelled by circumstances to use radio alone were warned that their security was almost sure to be penetrated, regardless of codes and disguised speech, and that, therefore, only plans which were to be implemented within a short time, could be mentioned over the air. In parallel extensive monitoring services were created to 'listen in' to the enemy, and so acquire information at all levels of his deployment; for these Guderian was to find another use in moments of desperation.

Within these circumscriptions, intensive trials were launched by the German enthusiasts of fast operations. The all-important trials unit was 3rd (Prussian) Motor Transport Battalion with its 'latest', if dubious, equipment. Every phase of warlike operation was practised – attack, defence, withdrawal, flank attack, direct attack with infantry and cavalry, co-operation with artillery and aircraft. As Heinz-Werner Frank (a *Leutnant* at that time in the battalion), puts it: 'We almost became fanatics in advertising motorisation and building the *Panzerwaffe*, enthusiastic followers of Guderian with his passionate powers of persuasion'. But followers they were fully intended to be by the *Oberst*, as he made clear to them one day after ski training. The young officers had over-enthusiastically overtaken their commander, though nothing was said until that evening. Then, with a twinkle over drinks, Guderian casually remarked: 'In the tank force the commander leads from the front – not from behind!' From the exercises grew, in 1931, the list of essential requirements for the sort of independent Panzer Command which Lutz and Guderian deemed necessary. But resistance to their progress was now appearing since these requirements impinged upon the traditional roles of the cavalry and infantry while financial and manpower restrictions at a time of international economic crisis dictated that, in exchange for something new, something old had to be discarded.

The cavalry was the first to suffer inroads from the new and, to their mind, upstart supply troops who were trying to steal a slice of the operational cake – but at a disadvantage since both memory and the *Reichsarchiv* history told against them, while Guderian's proposals were difficult to refute. In 1932, faced with the question of how they envisaged their future employment, the cavalry opted for the solitary role which seemed viable in the light of recent history – that of a 'heavy' force to apply the *coup de grâce* after the other arms had made the opportunity. Unwillingly, and in an atmosphere of mounting jealousy, they surrendered to the Motorised Troops the role of reconnaissance at which they had invariably failed in the past.

Concessions by the cavalry were, of course, of minor importance when set alongside the much greater shift that was taking place in world and German political and economic evolution. Events conspired to bring about a crisis. An influx of foreign money, which had previously poured into Germany, dried up as a world trade recession turned into the Economic Blizzard. As unemployment rose to almost unprecedented levels the opportunity seemed ripe for the extremist elements in German political life to make their bid for power. Communists vied with Nazis in a succession of elections. The Government reeled and was perpetually in danger of collapse while assassins raised the score of their victims with every month that passed. By 1932, when the Army was contentedly maintaining its separation from politics and was bent upon increasing its size and strength, the followers of Adolf Hitler, the NSDAP, were on the verge of taking over the Government by the nearest thing to constitutional means that violence could countenance.

From these things Guderian tried to stay apart. There was frequent irritation of the scar on his memory from the events of 1919: many of the Nazis and members of the *Sturm Abteilung* had been of the *Freikorps*, and he had several friends in the Nazi Party. Unlike so many of his colleagues he was not divorced from contact with the outside world, but watched and waited in the hope that the *Reichswehr's* part would be decisive in obtaining the 'right solution' for Germany as once it had done under Seeckt. While Hindenburg was *Reichspresident* Guderian was content.

He made no complaint when, in 1927, Heye, the new C-in-C, refused to allow Nazis into the army or, in 1930, when *Generaloberst* Freiherr Kurt von Hammerstein (Heye's successor) began to express strong anti-Nazi sentiments. As a junior officer he was not only remote from the thoughts of the C-in-C, but saw little reason at that moment to imagine that the Nazis might come to power or that Hitler could be the strong man – desirable or otherwise – of the future. But in 1930 a fresh influence began to make itself positively felt through the activities of the head of the *Truppenamt, General* Werner von Blomberg. Blomberg had visited Russia in 1928 in connection with the various collaboration projects and became impressed by the priority received by her army compared with the status of Germany's: he later remarked, 'I was not far short of coming home a complete Bolshevist!' But in 1930 he fell under the spell of Hitler – one of Communism's staunchest enemies – because he seemed a likely candidate as the man to strengthen the *Reichswehr*.

Already Hitler was demonstrating his magnetic persuasive ability to be all things to all men in his search for personal power; as yet hardly anybody recognised him as an evil force because only those in the very closest contact had the remotest chance of doing so. But he knew that the generals were resolved to re-establish the Army not only as a force which could defend Germany's frontiers – notably those in the east – but also as a stabilising factor in the country. So he announced his support for the Army and its aspirations. And as for Blomberg? He felt, as the economic crisis deepened and unemployment increased, that a unification of all the political parties alone would save the nation. He was prepared to utilise nationalist elements in support of that aim and, if that failed, the strongest party. Nevertheless it has to be said that many generals criticised him for his choice of agency if not his selection of aim.

Guderian, rather like Blomberg, was enigmatic in his political association with the Nazis and Hitler – though he does seem to have kept the party and its leaders separate in consideration. A Royalist at heart, he treasured past associations with the House of Hohenzollern: had he not served the Crown Prince in 1916 as a Staff Officer? But he realised that there was no point in a return of the Monarchy and was at one with the people in their disenchantment with the governments which succeeded each other at all too frequent intervals. These, in his own words, '. . . were unable to win over the officers or arouse any enthusiasm for the Republic's ideals.' Vehemently he abhorred the Communists and consistently he hoped for the emergence of a Bismarckian figure. But not so all the officers, for as Guderian wrote in 1947: 'When National Socialism entered the scene with its new national slogans, the young officers especially were quickly roused to enthusiasm by the patriotic ideas which the National Socialist German Labour Party (NSDAP) propaganda held out to them. For years the entirely inadequate armament of the Reich had weighed on the officer corps like a nightmare. No wonder that the initiation of a rearmament programme won them over to the man who promised to put new life into the *Wehrmacht* after fifteen years of stagnation.'

Nobody at that time had the faintest idea of what was in store. The Nazis were but part of a scene of rising disorder and fear. At first Guderian argued against the claims of the Nazis with those of his junior officers who took their part. Like so many of his generation he venerated Hindenburg, writing upon the President's death in 1934, 'He possessed the trust of the world'. And like so many officers in 1932, he too was angry with the tone of Hitler's campaign. He and they would have been appalled had they known that, in December, Hitler considered impeaching Hindenburg, and further disturbed if they had understood Hitler's pathological inferiority complex when dealing with the General Staff. After all, at that moment Hitler was going out of his way to placate the General Staff by giving public praise to the Army!

Six million unemployed and a rising threat by Communists at the polls could not be set lightly aside, however. A desperate situation demanded draconian measures or a scapegoat. Men like Guderian thought that somebody like Hitler could provide the necessary rule of iron and still be kept under control of the Army. The last soldier Chancellor, the arch-intriguer Kurt von Schleicher, over-played his hand and Hitler became Chancellor in his place on 30th January 1933. A few hours later Hindenburg selected von Blomberg as Minister of Defence and Blomberg in his turn picked one of the most able generals to lead the *Ministeramt* (the office with the task of co-ordinating all defence matters – land, sea and air and which, in due course, became the *Wehrmachtamt*), *Generalleutnant* Walter von Reichenau. The elevation of these men, each a Nazi sympathiser, met with Guderian's approval. Of Blomberg he thought well and Reichenau he regarded as 'a modern soldier', though one who was 'very political'. Two things they had in common: that the *Reichswehr* should co-operate with the most patriotic elements and that the tank arm benefit from encouragement, especially from Reichenau who constantly sought outlets for new ideas.

The political stance adopted by Guderian at this moment of political fermentation was of ambivalence, contrived to satisfy what he considered best for Germany and the Army. He retained a tacit belief in Seeckt's principle of non-political involvement, gave approval to generals such as Seeckt, Schleicher, Blomberg and Reichenau (who were knee deep in politics) because they seemed to have the Army's best interests at heart by striving might and main for expansion; kept contact (as did many Army officers) with old *Freikorps* friends such as Adolf Hühnlein who was a member of the *Sturm Abteilung* High Command, and, as time went by, managed, in his mind, to segregate Hitler from the other members of the Nazi Party. He seems not to have reacted one way or the other when Schleicher put an ineffectual ban on the SA in 1932. In 1933, however, Guderian was a mere *Oberstleutnant* who, like the vast majority of army officers, had not the slightest personal contact with Hitler. How could they know the secrets of this man when even the closest of his party colleagues were denied his innermost thoughts? And they were certainly not privy to the councils of the Army hierarchy.

Yet the development of Guderian's feelings towards Hitler are important and brought to light by his wife's letters, which also reflect Goerne sentiments. The Goernes (Gretel's family) were not in the least pro-Nazi, as snatches from their letters show, and yet Gretel leaves no doubt about their convictions concerning Hitler. On 23rd March 1933, after Hitler had been granted dictatorial powers, she described to her mother her exaltation '. . . after all the hideous mess of the past years we get at last a feeling of awe and greatness'. Also she extolled his '. . . beautiful way of speaking, his iron will, his energy and good words for the Army'. It could hardly have been said better by an enthusiast for Bismarck. And next day her father wrote to say how fine it was that the new government had tidied things up: 'All will be achieved without wounds'. A year later, on 3rd June 1934, Gretel still sang songs of high pitched praise to her mother in tune with the majority of the people: 'I am so glad that Heinz has written to you enthusiastically about Hitler. Everybody who gets to know him is very impressed by his personality. Above all his eyes and look send a special message to the heart . . . I do not think we will find a more courageous and better leader'.

Of course by then Guderian was aware that Hitler would help him in the task of building a Panzer Command and so his enthusiasm may have been conditioned by ambition and hope. In 1945 he was to write: '. . . policy was not shaped by soldiers but by politicians and the Army had to accept the political and military situation as it existed' – adding rather typically but nevertheless in confirmation of his distaste for all party men: 'This was unfortunate because politicians rarely expose themselves to the hazards of war, usually remaining safely at home.' But Germany then lay in ruins.

It is easy to criticise the Germans in hindsight and to forget that Fascist parties throughout the world at that time of desperation contained a proportion of highly respected and distinguished people – nearly all of whom were fooled by Hitler. With the economic crisis at its height Germany happened to acquire as her saviour an unscrupulous dictator. The French remained in disarray, the British formed a so-called National Government and the Americans accorded President Roosevelt unprecedented powers to dictate. In the final analysis it was a rearmament programme which raised each Western nation out of the economic depths. Not long after France had been broken in 1940, Britain was hanging on by a thread under the dictatorship of Churchill, and the Americans were on the way back to prosperity in war having used their Constitution to good effect to curb, but not destroy, the power of Roosevelt.

Guderian spoke for others as well as himself when he wrote of this period: 'Literary output did not reach pre-World War I quality because of the Army's rapid expansion which occupied the General Staff to such an extent as to leave no time for unofficial writing'. Absorbed by ambition and the feeling of urgent need in strengthening the *Reichswehr* for defence, in particular, of the eastern frontiers, the senior members of the German Army became fascinated by its task and allowed evil men to take over before they appreciated the implications. With the Army on his side and neutralised as a political force, Hitler had nothing to fear from the intellectuals and industrialists while the people gave thanks as more jobs were created.

5 The Creation of the Panzertruppe

When stupendous events in the clash of revolutionary causes overshadow the diplomatic and political scene and attract the full glare of publicity it is often symptomatic, if not endemic, that trivial changes of great importance also take place – though often unnoticed. Alongside the vivid display of Hitler's initial struggle for supremacy in Germany, with its heavy overtones of racial prejudice, the withdrawal of Germany from the League of Nations and the Disarmament Conference in October 1933; the slaughter of dissident elements such as von Schleicher and a few recalcitrant *Sturm Abteilung* leaders on June 30th 1934; the murder by Nazis of the Austrian Chancellor in July 1934, and the disclosure of the existence of the *Luftwaffe* in March 1935 (only a few days before the announcement of conscription and the reconstitution of the General Staff), significant though less discernible shifts in power and actuation were also taking place. For example the diminution of *Sturm Abteilung* power left room for Heinrich Himmler's *Schutz Staffeln* (SS) to become the strong arm of Nazi power, and the SS was already engaged upon creating its own military wing – the *Waffen* SS – with enormous import for the future. Simultaneously the power of the Army was being reduced by Blomberg and Reichenau in their endeavours to create a central defence organisation – what was to become the *Wehrmacht* – of which the Army, Navy and Air Force were intended to be subordinate parts, answerable to a new central staff. Hitler was giving covert signs of hostility to the Army but so also were some Army officers from within the organisation. Thus the movement by Lutz, a mere *Generalleutnant*, and his Chief of Staff, Guderian (promoted *Oberst* on 1st April 1930), to form a new Command (an army within the Army, as some suggested it might be since it incorporated elements of each existing arm) was only a minor movement within one great revolution, though possibly more likely to prosper since so much attention which might have been hostile was deflected elsewhere. While their main opponents in the High Command were preoccupied, Lutz and Guderian could initially debate in relative obscurity and gain advantages by rational arguments in committee.

But hope and temporary advantages were not enough for Guderian. He needed immediate and positive support from the highest level. Blomberg, as Minister for War, was sympathetic but too remote within the military structure. It was significant that Guderian felt that Hitler was more accessible, or so he implied when, in *Panzer Leader*, he wrote: 'I was convinced that the head of the government would approve my proposals for the organisation of an up-to-date *Wehrmacht* if only I could manage to lay my views before him.' The remark was prompted by Hitler's first inspection of new equipment at Kummersdorf early in 1934 at which Guderian, for half an hour, had been allowed to demonstrate the basic elements of a panzer division – a motor-cycle platoon, an anti-tank platoon, a platoon of the first experimental light tanks (Pz I founded on a Vickers' design and disguised under the name of 'Agricultural Tractor') and some reconnaissance cars; it revealed Guderian's widesweeping concept of a totally restructured defence force in which a unified Panzer Command was the dominant equal of the Infantry and the Artillery. At the same time the oft-quoted remark of the time by Hitler, 'That's what I need! That's what I want to have', may have been misleading in that he did not necessarily say 'why' or in what quantity he wanted a panzer force. Standing beside him that day was Hermann Göring who was vested with enormous powers as a Minister and was in the course of setting up the *Luftwaffe* upon which first priority of expenditure and effort was to be conferred. Although at Kummersdorf Hitler saw something recognisably modern, fast and sensational such as would generate prestige, he said nothing to suggest that he received a vision of revolutionary land warfare. More likely he visualised a force which would add drama to the threats supporting his display of power politics. As a result the panzer force was not accorded any special priority and Guderian was left to fight as hard as ever for recognition.*

Overriding every major consideration in connection with Army expansion – a target of 36 divisions was set by Hitler early in 1934 and revealed to the world in 1935 – was the desire to build a force which was capable of defending Germany's frontiers. The occupation of the Ruhr by the French in 1923 – unopposed because the means of opposition were virtually non-existent – posed a persistent fear of invasion from the west which was second only to the fear of a threat by the newly created states of Poland and Czechoslovakia which, since their inception in 1918, had repeatedly preyed upon their neighbours – Poland more than Czechoslovakia. There is no evidence to show that the General Staff contem-

*In a statement to the Allies in 1945, *General der Infanterie* Georg Thomas, the highly efficient head of the Economic and Armament Branch of *Oberkommando der Wehrmacht* (OKW which was created in 1934), gave it as his opinion that 'up to 1937 Hitler never had any intention of starting a war but that he believed he could, through putting over a bluff of rapid re-armament, reach his goal by peaceable means . . . Hitler attached much importance to the possession of much heavy artillery, many mechanical weapons and anti-tank weapons. The great importance of the tanks was not recognised until the success in the Polish campaign.' Thomas was in a good position to know.

plated offensive operations either before or during the opening stages of rearmament – for practical reasons if no other: they simply could not be ready with a properly constituted force until 1943 because neither financial nor industrial capacity were equal to the task. These constrictions, allied to the dread of another financial inflation if progress went ahead too quickly, overrode the launching of each project in a costly process. Economy had to be the watchword in erecting defences. Offensive weapons were last on the list. In 1936 in the pages of *Achtung! Panzer!* Guderian gave what undoubtedly were his true beliefs, to the effect that Germany could only afford to wage a short war in the hope that it would be brought to a tolerable conclusion before she was crippled. These were not the beliefs of a man who was hungry for war.

Guderian's initial concept for the panzer division, as stated in *Achtung! Panzer!*, was primarily as a weapon of defence; an attack on the French he considered to be hopeless. He feared the threat from the east far more and therefore strove for a highly mobile force which could knock out the Poles and Czechs, should the need arise, while delaying the French in the west. It was with defensively orientated offensive operations that he experimented throughout 1933 in exercises which, as he said, '. . . did much to clarify the relationship between various weapons and served to strengthen me in my convictions that tanks would be able to play their full part within the framework of a modern army when they were treated as that army's principal weapon and were supplied with fully motorised supporting arms'. These supporting arms, he insisted, 'were to be permanently attached'.

The task of the proposed panzer divisions which, to the mind of Guderian, ought to become the pivot around which the rest of the Army revolved, was defined in a news-sheet disseminated at the end of 1933: '. . . the widespread attack against enemy flank and rear – separated from other slower units; but it can also achieve considerable success in a breakthrough on the front. When used in pursuit it can throw a fleeing enemy into confusion. On the other hand it is less well equipped to hold captured territory; for this purpose it is usually necessary to employ motorised infantry and artillery. The manner of its engagement is not in prolonged battles but short, well-timed operations launched by brief orders. The principle is to use the battle tanks at the core of the operations, to concentrate the main fighting force at the decisive point of action . . . on the principle of surprise in order to avoid or avert enemy defensive action.'

Never was the course of progress steady or mellowed by sweet accord, and frequently Guderian was compelled to draw heavily upon his inherent optimism. Alas! His tolerance was not always equal to the task and a tendency to irascibility when under stress became more pronounced. Those among his contemporaries who said he was a 'bull' overlooked the frustrations placed in his way and had ceased themselves to pursue the old Prussian tradition of 'absolute frankness, even towards the King'. There are many who recall, with pleasure, his willingness to hear their case with patience and understanding.

As he became absorbed by the pilgrimage of innovation, the time left for introspection got scarcer, yet something in him sounded a warning note on 2nd August 1934 on the eve of taking the oath of allegiance to Hitler instead of to the Constitution. To Gretel he wrote: 'Pray God that both sides may abide by it equally for the welfare of Germany. The Army is accustomed to keeping its oaths. May the Army, in honour, be able to do so this time'. Gretel took up the theme on the 19th to her mother: 'Over the radio I have just heard the ovation for Hitler . . . We need unity more than ever, it is our only strength abroad . . . Hitler's faith in his mission for Germany and the faith of the people in him are practically miracles. But sometimes one can become a little afraid about excessive elevation.' These were the first signs of trepidation that events were shaping a dangerous course, but they hardly ruffled the surface of satisfaction with a Führer whose guidance was unchallenged. Guderian looked to the Führer for salvation. As a reasonably pious member of the United Lutheran Church he did not often attend its services, for in religion too, according to his son, he was constantly seeking new ideas. Indeed, as the pressures grew heavier at work he seems to have cultivated a grimly intensive self-sufficiency in his assault upon obstacles thrown in his way.

Frustrations there were in plenty. In 1933 acute national financial stringency led to the curtailment, for the last time under Hitler, as it happened, of the major Army manoeuvres. Also Hitler cancelled the arrangements for mutual training and development with the Russians, with the result that fruitful courses had to be ended before the new training establishments at Wünsdorf and Putlos in Germany were working fully. Moreover Lutz had to undertake some delicate negotiations with the Russians in recovering equipment left stranded at the Kama River site.

On the other hand Hammerstein-Equord was replaced as C-in-C by Fritsch, Guderian's old superior officer at Bartenstein. This was a blow to the few who already were trying to resist Hitler, for it has been suggested that Hammerstein, lazy though he was, had the ability, integrity and powers of decision which at any time might have been turned to ejecting the Führer before he became too well entrenched. Be that as it may, Guderian welcomed Fritsch's appointment, rating him a thoroughly sound soldier, who had '. . . devoted a period of detached service to the study of the panzer division'. Between them was a close affinity, although it must be realised that neither were part of a circle of close friends – except for the life-long friendships made in the earliest days with their regiments.

In years to come the Nazi hierarchy would make use of Guderian but it must not be forgotten that, in seeking support for his schemes, Guderian also made use of them. Allies being short within the Army he gathered help wherever it could be found and the head of the National Socialist Motor Corps (the NSKK) a paramilitary organisation under Adolf Hühnlein of the SA, was of fruitful importance. In *Panzer Leader* Guderian merely credits Hühnlein (whom he called 'a decent upright man with whom it was easy to work') with taking him to a Nazi Party meeting in 1933. But Hühnlein's main contribution to Guderian's ambitions was the training of truck and tank drivers in 24 NSKK-*Reichsmotorsportschulen*, about 187,000 being provided between 1933 and 1939 to solve largely the basic preparation of crews for highly motorised forces, all as part of the role of co-operation that evolved with the SA after the purge of its leaders in June 1934.

Obstructors there would always be and notably from three sources. First, from the new Chief of the recreated General Staff, *Generaloberst* Ludwig Beck, an artilleryman like Fritsch but slow and hesitant in decision, who was the opposite of Fritsch in philosophical outlook. Though most German generals, in Sir John Wheeler-Bennett's words, '. . . .did not regard war as the primary role of the soldier, but believed that Germany's rearmament should be of such a degree that they would lessen rather than increase the danger of war by making it impossible for Germany to be attacked or gainsaid with impunity', Beck interpreted this in its military aspects as a sufficiently strong argument for retaining the 'delaying defensive' or, as Fritsch called it, 'organised flight'. Fritsch had the last word and the traditional Prussian doctrine of attack was reinstated – to Guderian's undisguised pleasure.

Suggestions have been made that Beck hampered the creation of panzer divisions because, as a man who became dedicated to the resistance against Hitler, he recognised the immense potency of this new instrument of war and its propensity to strengthen Hitler's powers. There is no evidence in support of this supposition. Hardly anybody on the General Staff is on record for appreciating the potential value of armoured forces in 1934. The following conversations between Guderian and Beck, when proposals were being made, are fairly typical of the general level of understanding in those days:

Beck: How many of these divisions do you want?
Guderian: Two to begin with, later 20.
Beck: And how will you lead these divisions?
Guderian: From the front – by wireless.
Beck: Nonsense! A divisional commander sits back with maps and a telephone. Anything else is Utopian!

The second source of obstruction was generated by the Cavalry who persisted in their efforts to retain a full share of the manpower allocation and of resources. They saw Guderian as a threat to their existence, but in their opposition merely delayed the inevitable since those above them were already determined that progress should be maintained. People who say that the German military hierarchy was against the creation of a panzer force are wrong; but, sound professionals that they were, they rightly demanded convincing evidence before committing themselves to something that was huge, costly and irrevocable at a time of tight budgeting. Guderian had to provide the evidence-in-chief but already many cavalry officers, notably among the younger generation (and not only in the German Army by any means) welcomed the prospects offered by mechanisation. They had long ago lost faith in the operational role of their arm. They, and the rankers, saw practical advantages in learning about mechanical vehicles in the age of the internal combustion engine. Guderian's antipathy to the Cavalry was probably taken a little too far – but his patience was provoked by intransigence. In adopting the line that they might be poor substitutes for the indoctrinated men of the Motor Transport Service, he argued against incorporating horse-thinking soldiers into the *Panzertruppe* which he hoped to form, though he was remarkably successful in encouraging many cavalry officers to transfer independently. Eventually 40 per cent of the *Panzertruppe's* officers were those who had been charmed away from the Cavalry. Reichenau, of course, was fully aware of Guderian's objections to cavalry participation and may well have heaved a sigh of relief when an opportunity to avoid a confrontation was presented by the simultaneous absence of Lutz and Guderian from Berlin in April 1934 at a moment when forward planning for expansion was at a critical point. Calling for Walther Nehring, the senior member of Lutz's staff present, Reichenau made the quite original and unexpected suggestion that the *Panzertruppe* should be built up by attaching the 3rd Cavalry Division as a whole to it. Nehring instantly accepted and, although the scheme was never fully implemented, it did, at least, break the ice.

The third obstruction was later raised by the Artillery, not so much because their status or strength was in peril but because their methods were in question. The demands of infantry for artillery support were much as they had been in 1918 and welcomed by the gunners because they called for more and heavier fire support – and therefore an increased number of appointments for them. But the Panzer Command wanted something different due to the need, as enunciated by Guderian '. . . to follow up a panzer attack which normally opened up very quickly. This led to a demand for self-propelled mounts as early as 1934: but the artillerymen did not believe in such fast-moving combat. Accustomed for five hundred years to draw their guns with the muzzle pointing backwards and to unlimber for action, they successfully opposed this proposal until the bitter experience of war taught them to follow the suggestions of the Inspector General [himself] . . .' The source of artillery resistance was widespread but fiercely concentrated in the highest places. Fewer gunners in proportion to infantrymen and cavalrymen had been killed in the First World War and this preservation, allied to the intellectual quality of the type they recruited, meant that more gunners in proportion to any other type of officer were available for high appointments in the 1930s. All three generals who were to hold the top posts in OKW after 1938 and throughout the Second World War were gunners – that is Wilhelm Keitel, Alfred Jodl and Walter Warlimont. In the Army High Command (OKH) Fritsch and Beck were gunners, as was Franz Halder who succeeded Beck as Chief of Staff in 1938. As a matter of interest it will also be noticed that, from 1938, not one of the most senior generals in Hitler's Army was titled, while Franz Halder, a highly intellectual, rather schoolmasterly Bavarian, was the first non-Prussian to become Chief of the General Staff. These men formed the final court of appeal with direct access to Hitler whenever gunner interests were threatened by Guderian and his kind. They were not in a position to prevent the formation of the *Panzertruppe* in 1934, however. In the implementation of that memorable innovation neither Blomberg nor Reichenau and Fritsch were to be denied.

The creation of the *Panzertruppe* in the summer of 1934, with Lutz at its head and Guderian as Chief of Staff, merely opened a gap in the defences of the opposition. Guderian could never convince Beck of the need for the panzer instruction manual which had been written by him and his staff. The Chief of Staff may have seen the need without approving the contents, but by 1939 the greater part of the necessary regulations had still not been issued to the troops. Of course, Beck saw no need for the *Panzertruppe* at all since tanks, in his opinion, were only of use as ancilliary weapons incorporated with the infantry – in the manner of the French. It was true that the sight of the first light tanks – the Pz Is which were intended only for training purposes and which were formed into their first battalion in 1934 under the command of *Major* Harpe – did little to inspire confidence. They bore not the remotest resemblance to dominant weapons, being hardly more than machine-gun carriers of limited cross-country performance. Yet in August 1935 this battalion and another, plus the bits and pieces – real and pseudo – assembled by Lutz and Guderian into makeshift units over the past five years, took the field in special manoeuvres and, in four weeks' intensive experiment, proved the viability of the comprehensive system they represented and the immense faith of all their men in a new way of warfare that lay so close to hand. The major failures occurred mainly in highly mobile situations when the limited communication facilities were quite inadequate. Clearly far more elaborate radio nets were needed. But the creation of the Panzer

Command was then but a formality and obtained formal recognition in October, with Lutz, promoted to the first *General der Panzertruppen*, in command. Three panzer divisions were formed – without tanks since equipment was still in short supply and enough officers and men had yet to be trained. Even then the project was robbed of its full entitlement, for Beck refused the new Command equal status with the Infantry and Artillery, and the promotion of Guderian to command the 2nd Panzer Division removed him from the hub of progress and policy-making where he was most effective. With him out of the way, Beck at once, and almost unopposed, formed a Panzer Brigade the task of which was to co-operate closely with the ordinary, slow horse and foot divisions – a task which Lutz and Guderian had admitted in their 1935 report as being one of a number of uses it could have. This was the first, but by no means the last, time Guderian was to be sidetracked by a Chief of Staff.

Let it not be thought, however, that Beck was alone in resisting the Panzer Command or that the Panzer Command was the only modern scheme which he opposed. He merely represented the focal point of wholesale resistance by those influential members of the General Staff who remained unconvinced of the viability of the new weapons and systems – be they tanks, aircraft or the new *Wehrmacht* Central Staff with its challenge to the old supremacy of the General Staff. Guderian was not being unfair when he remarked, after 1945, that this type of general '. . . dominated the Army General Staff and pursued a personal policy which insured that the leading General Staff positions in the Central Branch were always occupied by men of their way of thinking'. This, after all, is a familiar story in most armies, but it was provocative to eager men like Guderian – and Hitler – who also pursued personal policies. Each protagonist was full of good intentions to himself.

Nevertheless, even without Guderian close to its helm, the strong organisation he had formulated gradually grew. The officers who had been trained in Russia, the staff he had imbued with his ideas at the Panzer Command and the blueprints laid down had merely to be implemented as funds and new equipment became available and the original instructors and men in the lower echelons caught the enthusiasm of their leaders. The tank industry, too, was directing its energies on lines which had the approval of Lutz and Guderian, though it was expending so much time on research and development that production tanks of the required type were a long way from being built in worthwhile numbers. But, of course, industry was treading fresh ground and this slowed initial production: for example, there were all sorts of problems involved with the working and mounting of armoured plate.

With the other types of supporting cross-country vehicles there were problems, too, due to the inadequate specifications put forward by the General Staff. Guderian is remembered for his temerity, at a disastrous demonstration of these soft-skinned vehicles in 1937, marching up to the Commander-in-Chief of the time, Fritsch, and roundly condemning the two-wheeled drive vehicles that had been shown, concluding with, 'Had my advice been followed we would now have had a real armoured force'. The remark is significant in its meaning rather than in its smack of insubordination, for it showed that, by demanding not only the very high establishment of 561 tanks in the original armoured divisions but also armoured infantry-carrying vehicles, he was a true disciple of Fuller who has invariably (and wrongly) been criticised for over-stating his demands for the tank. Both Fuller and Guderian thought in terms of a truly armoured force even though, perhaps, Fuller used the word 'tank' rather loosely when referring to supporting armoured vehicles. And one day, in the march on Russia, lack of four-wheel drive transport was to prove fatal to the German Army.

A prolonged debate, concerning the type of tank needed, retarded industry. The final specifications did not meet all of Guderian's requirements either for, although he attached far more importance to fast-moving machines, he also stated the desirability in 1936 for a heavy tank '. . . to assault permanent fortifications or fortified field positions', tanks which must have '. . . a good destruction, gap-crossing and wading capability besides strong armour and armament of up to a calibre of 150mm' – and these machines, he thought, would come out at 70 to 100 tons and might be too expensive. They would, he said, be used independently in small numbers but 'They are extremely dangerous opponents and should not be underestimated'. With trepidation he appreciated that the heavy French 2 C was barely vulnerable to a 75mm gun.

But because of the restrictions imposed by expense and his demand for high numbers, Guderian had to settle for the smaller solution represented by lighter, faster and cheaper machines: in any case an upper weight limit of 24 tons had to be imposed because of the weight restrictions on existing field engineers' bridges. Two types of tank were fixed upon in 1934: as a stop gap, a light tank for reconnaissance with a top speed of about 35 mph and as main armament a 20mm gun, called Pz II; and a medium battle tank (to be called Pz IV) with an initial weight of 18 tons, a top speed of 25 mph and a short rather inaccurate 75mm gun as main armament, whose primary purpose was direct support, not for tank-versus-tank combat. Neither of these tanks in their initial production form had armour in excess of 30mm, and therefore they were only proof against small arms fire and shell splinters, not against direct hits from field artillery and special anti-tank guns such as were already in service. Moreover neither the 20mm nor the short 75mm gun had a good performance at battle ranges against the existing type of heavy French tank. However, bearing in mind that although much reliance was to be placed upon mechanised infantry anti-tank guns (deployed in depth) for dealing with enemy tanks, tank-versus-tank combat was rated a certainty in 1935 and so a third type of battle tank was proposed. This was to be Pz III, a slightly smaller version of Pz IV, whose prime purpose was as a tank killer since neither the 50mm gun, suggested by Guderian, nor the 37mm gun finally installed by the Chief of the Ordnance Office in consultation with the Inspector of Artillery, would fire a satisfactory high explosive round such as that fired by the 75mm gun on Pz IV. Hence the initial equipment for the panzer divisions was to consist of three complementary types of tank, not one of which was the equal of the heavily armed and well-armoured tanks being laid down by the French. Moreover the standard infantry anti-tank gun was inadequate before it came into service, though the overall design of the Pz III and IV was good. Both, however, had ample capacity for expansion in armament, armour and power plant if the need arose – as Guderian knew, from the study of history and the application of plain common sense, that it must. The arrangement of crew seating was also good and so were the optical instruments provided for turret gunners: hence fighting efficiency was high, while crew morale was well taken care of by the provision of excellent escape hatches.

But though the proposed tanks themselves were suspect, while possessed of immense potential, there was one vital field in which the Germans were moving far ahead of their prospective opponents – that of superlative command and control procedures allied to a revolutionary and unique philosophy which had advanced beyond the most extreme ideas of other armies after 1934. The extent to which German thinking had overtaken all others was defined in an article, written by Guderian in 1935 with a view to refuting criticisms of mechanisation which were being made in military and non-military journals, the Berlin Stock Exchange Journal for one. In this article Guderian reflected upon von Schlieffen's call in 1909 for methods that made possible the existence of 'a modern Alexander'. He developed the proposition that 'Only leaders who drive in front of the troops will influence the outcome of the battle – the best aviators did so and so did the British General Elles at Cambrai'. He was opening a campaign to raise the scale of wireless sets so that radio communication could be extended below company level (as it stood until 1936) to give each tank a set of its own. 'The modern Alexander must bend modern technology to his will and instil it into his soldiers . . . If he forges his sword with a firm, clear mind to protect the honour and freedom of his people, that is a task set him by Fate.' The paper was endorsed by *Oberst* Fritz Fellgiebel, the Inspector of the Signal Corps, who declared that modern signal systems were the only way to make the panzer weapon work. But midway through the paper a poignant sentence tells us something additional about Guderian: the comment 'Alexander was a king – not a mere divisional commander', has a wealth of expression along with its insight into the uphill struggle in which he was engaged.

For Beck, as usual, took the opposite view: to him human beings and not machines were the real instruments of war, as he said in a speech before Hitler in October 1935.

The radio network which Fellgiebel was engineering for the *Panzertruppe* had a performance pitched to meet the specifications of the sort of long-range operations Guderian anticipated. The two worked closely together. Diagrammatically the sets were to appear as under, though with variations, of course.

Formation level	Set Type	Frequency Range Kcs	Normal max range in miles	
			Voice	Key
Corps to Pz Div	1000 W S b	1090–6700	300	700
Pz Div to Pz Bde also to some armoured cars	Fu 12 80 W S a	1120–3000	25	80
Pz Bde/Regt to Pz Bn	Fu 8 30 W S c	1120–3000	15	50
Pz Bn to Pz Coys or tanks	Fu 8 as above *or* Fu 5 10 W S c *or* Fu 6 20 W S c	2720–3330 2720–3330	4 8	6 10

These sets were simple to operate and reliable. They were constructed in units which could be easily secured to panels or connected to each other, thus permitting quick assembly or dismantling: their design so good that exceptional performance was possible with tuning to close limits even in a vehicle such as a tank with its enormous vibrations. A point was to arrive when, as Albert Praun, who worked closely with Guderian and was, in due course, to become Chief of *Wehrmacht* Signals, said: '. . . it was possible to maintain uninterrupted strategic and tactical control of armoured units while they were engaged in any form of movement; indeed, this control became simpler, more flexible and more reliable than the control of the non-mechanised units.' Paradoxically it was the main stumbling block to many officers believing in Guderian: the scope of his vision and experience extended far beyond their limited imagination.

Paradoxically, too, the Infantry, despite the half-heartedness of their main sponsors, also desired mechanisation, as exemplified by the motorisation of their anti-tank company, against the advice of Guderian who feared for the squandering of limited resources: these guns should be horse-drawn, he maintained, because they travelled in company with foot soldiers. (For the same objection against diversification of industrial effort he opposed, in 1938, the provision of assault guns for the Infantry.) But these digressions were as nothing compared with the dilutions which took place once Guderian had been despatched to command a division, and the cold and more pliable *Oberst* Friedrich Paulus took his place as Chief of Staff to Lutz. Lutz without Guderian was unable to prevent the erosion of the *Panzertruppe* by sectional interests. Whereas Guderian might have just been able to maintain the unity of the entire armoured force as he desired, his successors permitted the fragmentation of the force so that, for example, the reconnaissance units were handed over to the Cavalry, and the motorised rifle units to the Infantry along with the creation of motorised Infantry Divisions. As a further diversification, Light Divisions, with only a low tank content, were formed and put under the Cavalry, though with the proviso that when more tanks became available they would be raised to full Panzer Division status. The *Panzertruppe* was reduced to responsibility only for the actual tank units, although XVI Corps staff was formed to control all three Panzer Divisions and placed under a special Group Command 4 along with the two other Corps which commanded the Motorised Infantry and the Light Divisions. This Group was placed under *Generaloberst* von Brauchitsch, who had conducted the early experiments of 1923, and given the mission of studying the operational employment of mechanised formations.

None of this was as serious as Guderian made out, providing there remained ample time for experiment. But in 1936 Hitler began to push Germany along the pathway of aggression, a route which dangerously resembled a tight-rope. In March, when barely a trickle of modern arms had begun to flow from the factories and the panzer divisions were little more than inscriptions on paper, he chanced his arm and remilitarised the Rhineland. By the end of that year the better informed generals in OKH began to realise that Hitler was embarked upon war. He coined for propaganda effect the word *Blitzkrieg* – the lightning stroke by air and land forces aimed at the country concerned. Campaigns, if necessary, were to be short in duration since Hitler, according to *General* Thomas, '. . . always rejected all measures of preparation for a long war (economic mobilisation) in favour of the creation of new divisions' – presumably also for propaganda effect. Thomas opposed *Blitzkrieg* in the press, in military periodicals and in public lectures '. . . because I felt sure that a new war in Europe would mean a new world war for which the German economic resources would be inadequate unless she had strong allies'. But Hitler hoped to conquer without war.

Guderian was among those who held the opposite opinion to Thomas over *Blitzkrieg*: he believed in it. As 1936 moved into 1937 his efforts were geared to preserving the *Panzertruppe* as part of a defence force – though gradually its predatory value was being noticed and exploited. In the autumn of 1936 Lutz suggested that public support might be generated in a book setting out the reasons for and the role of the panzer divisions. That winter, in great haste and in addition to his other duties, Guderian wrote *Achtung! Panzer!* – a collection of his lectures, integrated with the best of the articles and arguments he had deployed in the past decade. As a result the book's style was somewhat uneven. But the impact was considerable. It became a military best-seller and the Guderians bought their first car on the proceeds. It was closely studied by the General Staff Intelligence branches of the world and from 1937 to 1939 was essential reading, along with Fuller's books (but not Liddell Hart's), for the *Kriegsakademie* of the Austrian Army, whose leading tank expert, Ludwig von Eimannsberger, was also strongly advocating panzer divisions, based upon Fuller's doctrine.

Achtung! Panzer! disclosed no secrets – the Pz IIIs and IVs were not mentioned – and the latest thoughts about the ambitious role of panzer divisions for deep penetration were muted. But support for Hitlerian opinion was evident in those sections where it led towards Guderian's objectives. He quoted from Hitler's speech at the 1937 Motor Show: ' "It is cosiness, not to say indolence, which protests loudly at all the revolutionary innovations which demand new efforts of mind, body and soul" ' and ' "This much is certain: the replacement of animal power by the motor leads to the most tremendous technical and consequently economical change the world has ever experienced." ' The Four Year Plan, which operated under Hermann Göring, was invoked to show how, very soon, Germany's dependence upon imports of petrol and rubber would be eliminated, thus minimising a fundamental objection to mechanised forces to the effect that Germany could not support them in time of war. Guderian's peroration went far beyond the call for a defence force, however: 'One thing is certain, only strong nations will continue to exist and the will for self-determination can become reality only if supported by the necessary power. It is the duty of politics, science, the economy and the armed forces to strive towards the establishment of German political power. Only by providing the Army with the most modern and effective armaments, equipment and intelligent leadership can peace be safeguarded . . . But it is an indisputable fact that, as a rule, new weapons require new techniques in tactics and organisation. One should not pour new wine into old bottles. Deeds are more important than words. The goddess of battle will crown only the most daring with laurels.' The 1930s were days of the propagandists led by Dr Josef Goebbels: Guderian learnt well from him.

The book flattered Hitler and all that he stood for, as probably it was calculated to do. Walther Nehring points out that Guderian did not have many contacts with Hitler prior to 1939 – indeed it would have been surprising for so junior an officer; he only became *Generalmajor* in August 1936. Nevertheless he did far better than the Chief of the General Staff. Guderian's opponent, Beck, seems to have had only one private meeting with Hitler throughout his term of office from 1935 to 1938 and this must have hurt Beck.

Conflicting emotions were tearing at the German generals as Germany approached Armageddon. In November 1937 Hitler had told Blomberg and Fritsch that he intended to expand to the east, if necessary by means of war in 1943 – and they had surprised him by their horror. These men Hitler now removed by means of charges (trumped up in the case of Fritsch) that denigrated the moral standing of both officers. The resignation of Blomberg and the defamation of Fritsch on 4th February 1938 deeply disturbed Guderian. But the consequential assumption of C-in-C the *Wehrmacht* by Hitler, the appointment of Wilhelm Keitel as Chief of the OKW, of Brauchitsch as Army C-in-C and Reichenau as Commander of Group Command 4 (and thus virtually in charge of mechanised development) can hardly have displeased him. Keitel may have been advantageous to his prospects for, in addition to the family connection, Wilhelm's brother, Bodewin, who was of his regiment and his wife's relative and now too a general, was also Chief of the Army Personnel Office – a position of great power and influence in arranging postings and appointments. It mattered less that Wilhelm Keitel was a mere sycophant of Hitler (picked by the Führer with the cry 'That's exactly the man I'm looking for', after Blomberg, who was Keitel's father-in-law, had reported that Wilhelm was, 'nothing but the man who runs my office'): he might be used as one more channel direct to the Führer, particularly now that the Führer was set upon employing the OKW Staff as his personal instrument to the gradual exclusion of the Army Staff. Reichenau he welcomed as 'a progressively minded intelligent soldier for whom I felt a comradely friendship'. His own elevation to *Generalleutnant* and to command XVI Corps, with Paulus as Chief of Staff, was not unwelcome either, even though it meant supplanting Lutz, who was made to retire. And yet a letter written to Gretel on 7th February transmits foreboding while making it obvious that, not for one moment, did he suspect Hitler's complicity in what had taken place:

'However pleasant and honourable the new appointment, I do not go with an easy mind because, apparently, serious and real tasks are before us and, indeed, differences of opinion which will require strength and nerve. I will have to provide myself with a thick hide. The report to Hitler [in connection with Blomberg and Fritsch] has provided me with insight into things which would better not have happened. The Führer has acted, as usual, with the finest human decency. It is to be hoped that he will be approved by his colleagues [the Nazi leaders].'

This letter must be contrasted with Guderian's comments in *Panzer*

Leader where he refers to 4th February as 'the second blackest day of the Army High Command' and goes on to defend Fritsch and criticise Brauchitsch for not waiting for the promulgation of a Court of Inquiry upon his predecessor before taking serious steps. At the same time he points out that 'For the majority [of German generals] the true state of affairs remained obscure'. There is also evidence in the letter that Guderian saw Hitler as somebody apart from the Party.

Now came the 'serious and real task', an order to command the leading troops in the surprise occupation of Austria on 12th March 1938. The thrill at this honour and the opportunity it gave to demonstrate the panzer forces and their potential in a long march was paramount. It also allowed a *Waffen* SS formation to make a showing and it was a suggestion from Guderian, passed to Hitler by Sepp Dietrich, the commander of the SS *Leibstandarte*, which led to the vehicles being decked with flags and greenery as 'a sign of friendly feelings'. Guderian had friendly feelings for Dietrich, too, the *ex-Landskneckht* who provided yet another direct link to Hitler and to whom Hitler referred as 'simultaneously cunning, energetic and brutal' – a fitting description for most of the world's best fighting men.

Standing proudly beside Hitler on the balcony in Linz when the Führer addressed the people, Guderian was deeply moved by this reunification of German nationals. So, too, was Gretel whose emotions overflowed in a letter to her mother:

'One can as yet hardly believe that Austria has become German. One Reich, one people, one Führer. He who does not understand that Hitler is a very great man and leader cannot be helped. I am deeply moved and cried for sheer joy . . . I felt tremendously proud that my husband was permitted to experience this historic event in close proximity to the Führer. The Führer on several occasions affectionately pressed his hand and was very pleased with the surprisingly quick march through Austria. The achievement of the *Panzertruppe* was specially praised.' And then she got ready to lead the wives of the garrison to welcome Austrian troops with flowers when they arrived for training in the German method.

Nevertheless, shortcomings in the reliability of his vehicles (with a 30 per cent official breakdown rate among the tanks, that was probably higher, plus supply difficulties) were failings which he would tackle with customary vigour when the celebrations were concluded. He was working at fever pitch to perfect the three panzer divisions under his command in XVI Corps as fresh political clouds blew up over Czechoslovakia and the German minorities in the Sudetenland. The exercises of autumn 1937, in which he acted as umpire, had exposed the logistic failings of the Corps and had been disagreeably confirmed during the march into Austria. Since war in the autumn of 1938 was now possible (in May Hitler had told Keitel to prepare for an invasion of Czechoslovakia) there was no time to

71

be lost – but as yet there were only a handful of Pz IIIs and IVs in service, and the issue of radio sets to all tanks was minimal.

As usual the theory of panzer operation reached far ahead of practical implementation. A paper written in 1937 (as rebuttal to criticisms in a General Staff publication, *The Review of Military Science*) had postulated startlingly original reasons in support of the concept of independent action by fast tank groups. Guderian propounded the theme: '. . . until our critics can produce some new and better method of making a successful land attack other than self-massacre, we shall continue to maintain our belief in tanks – properly employed . . .' His faith was based upon strategic speed: '. . . to be able to move faster than hitherto: to keep moving despite the enemy's defensive fire and thus to make it harder for him to build up fresh defensive positions'. This was essentially different from the reason commonly espoused by others – of speed as a means of tactical protection against enemy fire: to this Guderian never gave much weight, accepting that '. . . in unusually unfavourable conditions the hostile artillery can have serious effects on the movement of tanks'. As usual he could not restrain his sardonic wit: 'It is said "The motor is not a new weapon: it is simply a new method of carrying old weapons forward." It is fairly well known that combustion engines do not fire bullets . . .' This sort of jibe in conference or on paper did not endear him to opponents among the Army hierarchy who lacked his sense of humour.

Reports from the world's tank battlefields in 1937 were not beneficial to Guderian's case. Italian light tanks had made a poor showing against badly armed tribesmen in Abyssinia in 1935; the Japanese had tried only a limited use of inferior machines in the Far East; and in Spain, where some of the ineffectual Pz Is had been committed to action under the advice of *Major* Ritter von Thoma, as part of the *Kondor Legion*, the results had been anything but encouraging. German and Italian tanks fighting on the Fascist side, and Russian tanks with the Republicans, had been used in relatively small numbers. They were poorly supported and therefore did not achieve worthwhile gains. Thoma, a Bavarian and a bachelor of uncertain swings in mood and opinion, intensely annoyed Guderian with reports which suggested that tanks were a failure and that there was no need for each to have a radio set. These reports arrived at a critical moment during the negotiations for funds to buy fresh equipment and hampered his efforts to expand the panzer force. Staunchly Guderian pointed out the inadequacy of the tanks and the techniques that were being employed on unsuitable ground. In *Achtung! Panzer!* he declared that 'neither the war in Abyssinia nor the Civil War in Spain can be regarded, in our opinion, as a sort of "Dress Rehearsal" with regard to the effectiveness of the armoured fighting vehicle', but he was really only stonewalling. The fact remained that operations by the tank's sister weapon, bombing aircraft, were regarded in precisely that light – as the demonstration of a match-winner. Blood-curdling accounts of destruction from the air dominated the world's newspapers to strengthen the proponents of air warfare, who claimed it as a prime means to a decision when aimed at the civil populace. Tanks could lay no such claim and therefore were held much lower in esteem and in the order of priority for resources.

Believing with the utmost sincerity in the essential nature of his demands and fearful that his opponents would rob Germany of the fruits of his labours (undoubtedly he cast himself in the role of a military apostle), he began to react more out of character as the strain upon him increased. For example, during the training exercises of 1938 when Hitler was present and witnessed an awful muddle due to inept orders from the commander and staff of Panzer Regiment I, he saw red. In the concluding discussions Brauchitsch and *General* J. von Blaskowitz let the miscreants off quite lightly – they may even have relished a debacle in one of Guderian's units. But Guderian took them all to one side and told them in no uncertain terms what he thought of them. His elder son, then a young officer, was present and remarks that it was a pulverising performance – one upon which his brother junior officers commented favourably afterwards because they thought the 'rocket' overdue. Most unusually, however, Guderian followed up his reprimand by posting a number of senior officers, the sort of action he rarely took. He was more accustomed to making the best use of the available material – men, land and equipment.

The stresses and strains being imposed upon his superiors now began to recoil directly upon him. Beck, a tragic figure who found it hard to convert conviction into action and was among the very few senior officers with the insight to understand the threat that Hitler posed, was urgent in his attempts to persuade Brauchitsch to make a stand over the treatment of Fritsch who, in February 1938, was falsely accused of scandalous behaviour. Brauchitsch declined. Convinced of the folly of attacking Czechoslovakia, Beck next endeavoured to resist Hitler's intentions on the grounds that Germany was unprepared for war. But Brauchitsch again would not challenge the elected representative of the people, – and sold the pass. From this moment nothing the generals could do, other than by outright rebellion, could halt Hitler or prevent their degradation. Beck resigned and the hunt was on for a more compliant Chief of Staff. *General* Warlimont, whose impressions of Guderian between 1933 and 1939 are chiefly of '. . . a passionate panzer man – nothing more', seems to recall that Guderian was considered as a possible successor to Beck. It seems unlikely that this was a serious proposition though its mere suggestion in high places was bound to arouse antagonism among the alarmed generals. While Guderian lacked the requisite seniority and prestige for such an august post, he was also the representative of a minority military faction and clearly a favourite of Hitler. Franz Halder eventually took over from Beck and also continued the scheme of resistance to Hitler – though with muted zeal.

The dialogue between Hitler and Guderian had become closely personal. Invitations to dine and to accompany him to the opera led to discussions upon tank problems. The habit of giving Guderian a leading part in military operations became almost a formality. Thus XVI Corps received the role of occupying the Sudetenland after the Munich Agreement had postponed war. To Gretel on 5th October he wrote describing the 'suffering and repression' which the Germans of the Sudetenland had suffered under Czech rule – they had 'lost all hope' – and in *Panzer Leader* he tells of enthusiastic crowds greeting the Führer and his troops. When Hitler entered Guderian's car 'he shook hands with me in a very friendly way . . . A very great man!' he wrote. 'To achieve such a victory without a stroke of the sword is perhaps unprecedented in history. It was of course only possible because of the new, sharp sword in our hand and with the will to use it had peaceable means not been possible. Both these determinations were evident from this courageous man.'

He went on to tell of the occupation: '. . . the enemy fortifications not nearly as strong as thought, yet better taken this way'; the 'lively satisfaction of everyone, including the Foreign Minister, von Ribbentrop, that war had been avoided'; his happy accord with Reichenau, 'we were in full agreement. His staff not so helpful. Pity!' There can have been few in Germany at that moment who disagreed with his assessment of Hitler. The injustice of Versailles was being wiped out at no cost in lives. But the long-term effects were more ominous and Guderian seems to have given little consideration to them at this moment, so uncritical was he of the Führer.

Resources were in short supply as the rearmament programme got into gear. The spectre of inflation loomed large as Austria was digested, as Hitler reached out for the Sudetenland and Czechoslovakia, and as the financial manipulations of the Minister of Economies, Dr Schacht, came close to collapse: the taking of Austria and of the Sudetenland merely added to rather than subtracted from Germany's debt. In 1937 Schacht had fixed both a limit of time and amount on the money available for rearmament and in January 1939, as President of the *Reichsbank*, told the Economics Minister to declare the Reich bankrupt by refusing to make a routine monthly advance. According to Göring, the head of the Four Year Plan, Schacht was at once dismissed on the grounds of his impossible attitude. But world opinion was turning against Germany and Guderian, who visited Britain about that time, must have known it.

When Czechoslovakia was seized in March 1939, and the pressure was next put upon Poland, there could no longer be doubt in the minds of the generals where they were headed. The Army General Staff, conjoint with the civil populace, adopted what amounted roughly to three different opinions. Subject to the usual reservations about generalisation and allowing for all shades of variation in opinion, there were those like Guderian who welcomed the Hitler regime as a means of restoring Germany's prestige and authority, whose pride was in the army they were rebuilding, and whose fascination was with the new weapon systems they were creating – sharpened, undoubtedly and rather understandably, by an inquisitive ambition to see if their ideas would work. This group was probably most fearful of the Poles and abhorrent of the Communists: the Western Powers to them (as to the other groups too) poised a counter-weight to their most acquisitive ambitions since they were apparently too strong to attack. Then there were the disgruntled soldiers and civilians who had been removed or snubbed by Hitler – Hammerstein-Equord and Schacht, for example, and Beck who favoured peace chiefly because he thought Germany was not ready for a major war: with them Guderian also concurred since he knew too well the imperfections of the panzer force and the rest of the Army. Finally there was the vast majority, those in harness who agreed with the second group but either would not resign, were not sacked or who soldiered on without caring to think too deeply about the issues that were involved. Beck and his kind would gradually form an active resistance movement against Hitler. Halder would debate and temporise with the conspirators in their tentative schemes to assassinate Hitler at an appropriate moment but, when it came to the crunch, he would withdraw, pleading the compulsion of the Oath sworn to Hitler on 3rd August 1934, or his sense of duty to the Army in the hope that, while remaining at duty instead of resigning, it might yet be possible to achieve something good. Argue though Halder would against those of Hitler's schemes with which he disagreed, he nevertheless complied with his orders and prosecuted the preparations for war.

Likewise the Commander-in-Chief, von Brauchitsch, whose second wife had strong Nazi inclinations, did little to halt the General Staff's slide into decline except by attempting to stop any rot he saw within the Army hierarchy. He had watched Guderian's personal triumphs with Hitler in Austria and the Sudetenland and seems, first in conjunction with Beck and then with Halder, to have decided to put Guderian out of harm's way – whether from fear of the threat Guderian seemed to pose as a Nazi sympathiser and rival for power, or whether from jealousy, there is no way of determining. But from this moment it becomes increasingly apparent that the opposition to Guderian was no longer so much aimed against his ideas as strongly and directly against his person.

There was another factor which neither soldier nor civilian could ignore, although at times it was overestimated. It was the prevailing adulation of Hitler by a large proportion of the people, because he had lifted Germany from the depths of depression, reduced unemployment, and made a real start in restoring her pride. Goebbels underlined that claim. There were quite as many Germans in the lower orders who were as devoted to their country's honour as there were among the upper strata. It was indicative of an abiding political sense, for which the General Staff is rarely credited, that their dissident factions believed in the necessity for popular support in any attempt to curb Hitler. None had forgotten the sight of revolutionary soldiers and crowds in 1918 and Hitler was the most potent crowd-raiser of his day, who expertly cloaked his activities in the guise of popular legality.

Even so, those senior German officers who had experienced *Freikorps* methods at close hand and who knew (as all must) that a hard core of the Nazi Party was composed of old *Freikorps* fighters who were unable to readjust to normal life, should not have harboured delusions about the deeds these men were capable of perpetrating. For one thing they cannot have been unaware of the persecution of the Jews. Reichenau, for example, is on record for his approval of that policy. Guderian evaded the subject, though there is no record of his involvement in any form of racial atrocity – which is hardly surprising since, although he loathed the Communists and resented the Polish resurgence, he was innocent of bias as regards race or religion. There is nothing in his papers to suggest it – quite the reverse. It has to be faced that many German officers were blind if, by 1938, they could not recognise an impending holocaust of war, but they were in no position to visualise the Final Solution and its awful implications because at that time it was an unimaginable nightmare.

For Guderian there was a point beyond which Hitler and his followers could not go without sacrificing his esteem. The treatment of Fritsch was a case in point. His indignation at the manner of the late C-in-C's thoroughly unjust disgrace, and a half-hearted exoneration by Brauchitsch, after Fritsch's innocence was proved, was not simply reserved for the pages of *Panzer Leader*. His forthright expression of delight in public during the parade at Gross-Born in August 1938, when Fritsch was paid honour, left nobody in any doubt where his heart lay. Despite the Oath of Allegiance to Hitler he stood staunchly by the old Prussian codes. In due course he withheld approval for Hitler's plunder of Czechoslovakia in March 1939, yet, as usual, when controversial politics became too embarrassing, his conditioned safety mechanism came into action. There is no comment in *Panzer Leader*, merely a discourse on his attention to military duties, and a description of his work in collecting useful war material from the Czech arsenals. Guderian, though he withheld from protest, was too honest later to make out a false case in justification of evil inflicted on a non-German people. On the other hand he could be gullible. His elder son recalls that 'We were sceptical because Germany had deviated from the legal way of uniting all Germans in one

State', and remembers asking his father a question which drew '. . . an argument that, I think, came from Hitler, that it would be necessary to eliminate the aircraft carrier in the midst of Germany considering the attitude of the Western Powers'. All too readily he believed, in 1939, what Hitler so glibly pronounced.

Gretel, however, had taken an opposite and more passive view at the height of the crisis in September 1938. Some of the euphoria had evaporated when she wrote on the 29th: 'The most beautiful present would be the maintenance of peace from the meeting at Munich to-day. If this is a failure we shall need all our courage and faith. I will do my best to be a brave soldier's wife and mother'. But though Guderian leant heavily upon her when his personal affairs were in difficulty, there is little reason to suppose that he adhered to her political opinions. And at that time he was about to become, once more, an instrument of political manoeuvre, partly as one of Hitler's several unwitting tools in denigrating the military hierarchy. Playing his part of being all things to all men, Hitler appeared to push wedges between the factions within the General Staff – whether intentionally divisive or not cannot be ascertained. It could be that, recognising Guderian and the Panzer Command were a source of disruption within the Army, he used them to widen an existing rift. In October 1938 he had intervened, ostensibly to strengthen the Panzer Command, in collaboration with Brauchitsch (probably at the latter's suggestion) to create a Chief of Mobile Troops controlling all the motorised troops – panzers, infantry and cavalry. Guderian, without being told that Hitler approved the change, turned the job down since it lacked sufficient authority to overcome the resistance of the traditionalists in the High Command. This he eventually explained at length to Hitler (after Bodewin Keitel had intervened), who quietly overruled him with the promise that, if he was obstructed, he was to report in person. His promotion to *General der Panzertruppen* was some mollification but: 'Naturally,' he writes, 'there was never any question of my writing a direct report, despite the difficulties that immediately arose'.

That is the gist of the Guderian version in *Panzer Leader*. But his old friend, Hermann Balck, at that time a staff officer in Department *In 6* working with *Oberst* von Schell on motorisation, says that it was Schell who created the post of Chief of Mobile Troops in response to a conspiracy hatched by Brauchitsch and Beck (continued by Halder when he took over) designed to deny Guderian an influential role. Schell, who was later made an Under-Secretary of State, made impossible Balck's attempts to co-ordinate panzer and motorisation policy and so Balck attempted to arrange a meeting at which they would resolve their differences. 'With a laugh', according to Balck, Guderian agreed to try, but Schell refused point blank – a refusal which was inevitable if conspiracy there was and he was the agent of the C-in-C. It is impossible to verify this story. Guderian seems unaware of this particular plot though, as time went by, he felt no doubt that officers in high places were working dangerously against him. It is interesting, however, that he bore Schell no grudge and, indeed, later aided him in misfortune. But this was the second attempt to side-track Guderian, coming swiftly upon the suggestion that he might become Chief of Staff.

Rightly Guderian felt that, as *Generalleutnant* and commander of XVI Corps, he would have had more effect: not unexpectedly all his efforts to bring cavalry establishments into line with the panzer formations met with initially unyielding resistance. Inevitably he became a political catalyst instead of a military coagulant. At the same time he began to win recognition even among his enemies as one with the ear of the Führer who might – in a pinch – act as a middleman to help span a widening gap in communication and persuasion between them and the Head of State. For the time being they tried to keep him under their thumbs, engaged upon any sort of sterile task so long as it isolated him from the heart of policy-making. They allowed him free rein to waste his energy and that of his small and dedicated staff in a futile attempt to weld together the squabbling *Panzertruppe* and Cavalry. Incapable as he was of ready compromise in his approach to this problem, he attempted an integration by leading the Cavalry towards new objectives as part of a modern role which would enable them to function effectively in the sort of war he envisaged. But the instruction manuals which he had brought up to date and tried to persuade the General Staff to adopt, were rejected, and the Cavalry successfully evaded each suggestion to change shape because they did not want to lose their horses – and in the sure knowledge that the C-in-C and Chief of Staff were in sympathy.

As a further irritant it was announced that his appointment in time of war, if mobilisation was decreed, would be that of a Reserve Infantry Corps Commander, dooming him to a walking-on part and total divorce from the armoured forces with which he was expert. It was either a calculated insult, which suited the conspiracy, or it was stupidity. Guderian writes that 'it took considerable trouble to get it changed'. We may be sure it did. Maybe the Keitel connection was valuable upon this occasion; there is no way of telling how his fortunes were restored since he is silent on the matter. It is small wonder, however, that at this, a nadir in his career, his contemporary writings exhibit pessimistic tendencies that were most uncharacteristic. Probably he felt that the forces of tradition were too strong.

The summer of 1939 passed in a whirl of intense preparation for a war that could only be decided in Germany's favour by a miracle. The parades in Berlin, with Guderian's tanks rolling in phalanx down the chaussées to the cheers of the crowds and the respect of foreign observers, while Göring's *Luftwaffe* roared overhead, merely represented a facade shielding little of substance. But they invoked the sort of impression Hitler sought as part of his grand bluff – even though Guderian curtly dismissed them (without much perception of political motives) as 'more exhausting than impressive'. Like so many of the new breed of mechanised soldiers he had meagre time for ceremonial, though he was shrewd enough to appreciate the attraction to soldiers of a striking uniform. His panzer soldiers were dressed in dramatic black overalls and wore a black beret, somewhat similar to that already adopted by the British Royal Tank Corps.

As the crisis approached, Guderian seethed at each manifestation of wasted time and effort. Ambition spurred him on while his opponents coolly held him back even from his nearest goals. Yet while he expended practically every atom of energy in his pursuit of the heights of military achievement, he had a remarkable facility for relaxation. Spending 95 per cent of his time with military matters he was able to set the job aside when the opportunity arrived. Unlike Schlieffen, he could never dismiss the view of a beautiful valley 'as of no significance as a military obstacle': nor, like Rommel, sit through an opera and fill the time in contemplation of how to deploy an extra battalion in some forthcoming offensive. The creator of the *Panzertruppe* had much in common with his British counterpart, Percy Hobart, who was also a man of immense verve and frustrated zeal, and who, too, was being side-tracked. Each, when under the direst stress, was capable of writing sensitive and perceptive letters to their wives and able to cast off the cares of their task once they crossed the threshold of their homes.

But in August 1939 home was to look a little more remote. The ultimately exhausting event was about to engulf them all.

6 Vindication in Poland

Throughout a summer in which tension with Poland was stimulated by German agencies, Guderian and his staff were preoccupied with plans for major exercises in which the mechanised divisions were to be tested as never before, manoeuvres which demanded the initial stages of mobilisation. Crew training, however, was far from complete in every unit and while they had over 3,000 tanks with which to play, only 98 of them were Pz IIIs and 211 Pz IVs, and therefore most were the light Pz Is and IIs. But the latest communication systems had arrived almost to scale and improvements had been made to the supply services. Then came a change that can hardly have been unexpected. On 22nd August Guderian was ordered to take command of the newly formed XIX Corps (with Nehring as Chief of Staff) at Gross-Born and, under the cover title of 'Fortification Staff Pomerania', build field fortifications along the frontier with Poland. Next day Hitler announced the signing of a non-aggression pact with Soviet Russia and ordered the Army to attack Poland on the 26th. Preparations would be incomplete and mobilisation only in the preparatory stages, but the mechanised units were ready: some had been fully mobilised since July.

Poland's ability to defend herself depended mainly upon a fiery determination to preserve her newly won independence. Of modern weapons she had few – a mere 225 tanks, not all of them modern, and only 360 aircraft to set against Germany's 1,250. For combat technique she relied upon the sort of linear defence and positional warfare by horse and foot armies which had been the fashion in 1920, and which still largely dictated the methods of her allies in the West – the French and the British. From them she could not expect speedy help since they would take weeks to mobilise the massed-style armies of a previous epoch; nor was she likely to assemble her own full strength of 45 divisions and 12 brigades in the short time permitted by the Germans. It was about to be revealed to an astonished world that, for special reasons, Poland never had a chance; that six Panzer Divisions and four Light Divisions aided by massive air intervention could achieve in a few days what the remaining 45 German cavalry and infantry formations might never have accomplished in weeks. As Professor Michael Howard has said, 'The Germans were almost unique in 1939–40 in that they appreciated with the minimum of practical experience . . . the full implications which the new technological developments held for military science and embodied them in their equipment and their doctrine. I find it difficult, off hand, to think of a comparable example. Usually everybody starts even and everybody starts wrong.' If Howard had substituted 'Guderian and his adherents' for 'the Germans' he would have been precisely accurate.

Ironically, though symbolically, Guderian was to be denied a part in the main initial armoured drive which was directed by *Generaloberst* Gerd von Rundstedt's Army Group South (Chief of Staff, von Manstein) with two Panzer and three Light Divisions from Silesia towards Warsaw. In so-called good tank country Guderian's old XVI Corps, commanded by *General der Kavallerie* Erich Hoepner, was told to lead the assault and was to make striking progress from the moment it was launched on 1st September – the alteration from 26th August being enforced by diplomatic circumstances. Guderian's XIX Corps, with its single panzer division – the 3rd – and its 2nd and 20th Motorised Divisions (which had no tanks) was to be sent as the spearhead of Army Group North (*Generaloberst* Fedor von Bock) and Fourth Army (*General der Artillerie* Günther von Kluge) against far tougher opposition on a potentially less lucrative mission into the strongly defended Polish Corridor where fortifications made good use of the delaying effect of two river obstacles – the Brahe and the Vistula. Yet it was the magnitude of an awkward task which gave Guderian, from the outset, the opportunity to demonstrate, with a minimum of time for preparation, the versatility of his creation.

On the 24th – the eve of battle as he erroneously took it to be – he wrote a bracing letter to Gretel: 'We have to keep our ears stiff and be prepared for strenuous work. I hope all will turn out well and also quickly . . . As regards the Western Powers it is not clear what they will do, though surprises are not out of the question, but now we can bear that with fortitude. The whole situation has improved considerably and we can go to work full of confidence . . .' – an approving reference to the Soviet Pact which he welcomed as a re-establishment of the bridge with Russia. He realised how her mother's heart would be worried for their two sons, both of whom were in the Army and soon to receive their baptism of fire along with the *Panzertruppe*. But 'Please be a brave soldier's wife and, as so often before, an example to other people. We have drawn the lot to live in a warlike way and now have to put up with it'.

Nowhere does Guderian show remorse for the Poles. It would have been surprising had he done so. Poland was an excrescence to many Prussians, a nation which had come into being at the expense of the tribal homeland. Since 1918 they had posed a constant threat to Germany's eastern frontier: Frontier Defence Force East had been as much concerned with checking depradations by the Poles as by the Bolsheviks. And Guderian was particularly pleased to play a part in recapturing the old family property. His letter to Gretel indicates how '. . . the old family estates, Gross-Klonia, Kulm now take on a special significance . . . Is it not strange that I especially have been commissioned to play this role'. But he cannot have had detailed knowledge of the briefing of the Commanders-in-Chief by Hitler on 22nd August, although no doubt he was aware that Brauchitsch had promised the Führer 'a quick war'. So, likely though it is that he was informed through the usual flow of news circulating in higher military circles that the British and French might be intransigent, it is unlikely he heard then that Hitler had also pronounced on the 22nd: 'I have ordered to the East my "Death Head Units" with the order to kill without pity or mercy all men, women and children of Polish race or language'. And even if he had known there was nothing much he, in his position, could have done about it, for the slide into degradation by the political and military forces under the Nazis had already been permitted to pass the point of no return. All the military could do now, apart from an act of outright revolution for which they were neither adjusted nor organised, was mitigate the worst ramifications of evil perpetrated by the monster they had permitted and, at times, welcomed into their midst. Those who have never suffered a situation similar to that in Germany in 1939 are entitled to maintain that the generals should have behaved differently, but they should also view the situation from the generals' point of view – and ask themselves, too, how many Allied generals, faced with circumstances they did not approve – such as the Bomber Offensive against civilians – made a worthwhile protest?

Predictably Guderian decided that XIX Corps' main effort should be made by 3rd Panzer Division along his right flank where a deep penetration would benefit from the protection provided by two streams running parallel with the division's boundaries. That way, too, he would have the satisfaction of quickly capturing the family home of Gross-Klonia. The two motorised divisions were told to enter less promising territory: one rather feels that Guderian attached little importance to their role.

He travelled with the leading tanks of 3rd Panzer Division in one of the latest armoured command vehicles, equipped with radio that enabled speech to his main headquarters in the rear and such other formations as he needed. His account of the first day's action in *Panzer Leader* embodies the full fury of the prejudices he had acquired through frustration in the past decade: his anger with the artillery when they fired into the morning mist against orders, bracketing his vehicle and frightening the driver into a ditch: his disgust when he arrived at the Brahe to find stalemate, a complete loss of impetus without a single senior commander in sight to re-inject momentum. In sight of the family home he was enraged to discover that the commander of 6th Panzer Regiment had halted because

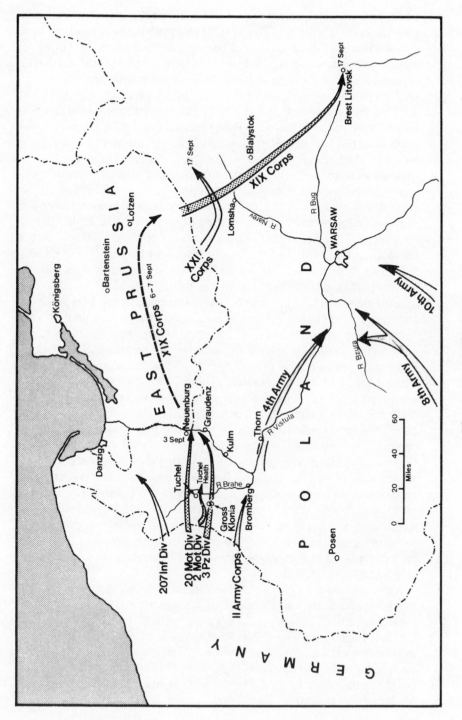

The Campaign in Poland

he thought the river too strongly defended, and that the divisional commander, *Generalleutnant* Geyr von Schweppenburg, was nowhere to be found. Geyr, by his account, had been called back to Army Group for consultation – a barely credible state of affairs when one realises that his division was entirely fresh to battle and demanding of personal leadership. It took the example set by a young tank commander, who had found a bridge that was undemolished, and by his own intervention in conjunction with the commander of 3rd Rifle Brigade, to get things moving again. Soon infantry, supported by tanks, were across the river at hardly any cost. The main casualty was Schweppenburg's injured pride: his petulant protests were loudly to be heard, both then and in after years when he complained about Guderian's interference. Schweppenburg, of course, was a disappointed man and jealous of Guderian, who had overtaken him in the race for promotion. Yet he had little cause for complaint at his treatment on 1st September if he was absent at the crucial moment of decision and had failed to implement his Corps commander's orders.

Fear of Polish horsed cavalry on the part of his staff and by infantry officers bothered Guderian as he toured the battlefield in his endeavours to overcome the inhibiting fears of troops who were largely inexperienced and under fire for the first time. His disgust at a commander who felt compelled to withdraw at news of the presence of Polish cavalry makes entertaining reading: 'When I regained the use of my voice I asked the divisional commander if he had ever heard of Pomeranian grenadiers being broken by hostile cavalry.'. There came an assurance that the positions would be held. And in due course it was his personal leadership in the van of the attack which sent the motorised infantry division into an attack towards Tuchel. This, the first twenty-four hours' experience of combat, was vital to the future self-confidence of the panzer force. Guderian, by his untiring efforts in supervising the establishment of both a technique of command at the front and also his own reputation for fearlessness and undeniable authority, where the fighting was heaviest, made success a certainty. Even if a few senior officers were bruised and disgruntled, the rest of his officers and men were deeply appreciative. All were impressed. It is after 1st September that one begins to detect that look of frank adulation on the faces of soldiers when they were photographed talking to Guderian.

Resistance by the Poles was, in fact, disjointed but usually fierce. The charge by the Pomorska Cavalry Brigade against 3rd Panzer Division's tanks was but one of many gallant but quite fruitless attempts to redeem disaster. Polish deployment had been wrecked by air attacks upon communication centres. German tanks were exploiting that disruption by almost unchecked advances, blazing away at those enemy columns they caught on the roads, helping infantry and engineers in their assaults upon fortifications, moving cross-country in sweeping, outflanking attacks whenever the natural line of advance was blocked. Always they were on the move and thoroughly self-sufficient within the organisation of the all-arms panzer division; only rarely were they very much assisted by bombing attacks because, primarily, the *Luftwaffe* was engaged against targets deep in the Polish rear and, secondly, the means of close liaison between ground and air forces was as yet in its infancy. This was not surprising: the *Luftwaffe* was only luke warm to direct support of the Army. The Air Field Manual No. 16 laid down that 'The mission of the *Luftwaffe* is to serve this purpose [the defeat of the enemy military forces as part of a process of breaking the will of the enemy] by conducting air warfare as part of the overall pattern for the conduct of the war'. And *Generalleutnant* Wolfram von Richthofen, who had experimented with close air support of armies in Spain, and who, in due course, was to make his reputation as the commander of an air force which carried out the most effective and devastating operations by bombers in close support of Guderian's panzer divisions, was an opponent of the dive-bomber. Such difficulties as 3rd Panzer Division suffered were much more the outcome of failures in equipment and organisation than the result of the enemy's retaliation. The little Pz I tanks and also the Pz IIs were far too thinly armoured to withstand even the light Polish field artillery and anti-tank gun fire. It was only the handful of Pz III and IV tanks, most of them manned for the sake of experience by the Panzer Demonstration training units, which produced a rare advantage. Supply problems were hampering too. On 2nd September Polish counter-attacks, which cut 3rd Panzer in two on the eastern bank of the Brahe, might have been more quickly contained had the tanks not been stalled for lack of fuel – the supply columns being deprived of adequate orders to send them forward in time to replenish the tanks after the first day of battle. Each inadequacy and breakdown was noted and, whenever possible within existing resources, put right on the spot by Nehring and his staff at Corps HQ or by the divisional and lower staffs when there came a lull in the fighting after the collapse of Polish resistance in the Corridor on 5th September. The bearer of victory was Guderian's Corps which had sealed off the major Polish formations and made it impossible for them to break the cordon. Thus armoured troops had done all that Guderian claimed for them – broken through in a direct assault, carried out a pursuit and held vital ground under enemy pressure – and they had done these things at that lightning pace which he insisted was essential.

Recounting the first day's fighting in a letter to Gretel on 4th September he cheered at his successes, mourned the dead and gave credit to the foe. 'Series losses occurred at Gross-Klonia where a tank company lost one officer, one officer cadet and eight men due to the sudden lifting of the morning mist [despite bombing, the Polish artillery often fought to the end]. At the decisive point I exerted myself personally with success in order to overcome a slight set-back. The 3rd Panzer Division was the first to reach its objective in the night. The others were unable to push back the hard-fighting Poles quite so quickly . . . though fighting in woodland area with, here and there, heavy losses. With the deployment of a further infantry division and after some crises in heavy fighting, we succeeded in encircling completely the opposing enemy in the woods north of Schwetz to the west. On the 4th the encirclement was tightened. Several thousand prisoners, light and heavy batteries and much material was captured . . . Lively small skirmishes will continue for a while in the large woods as many scattered troops are still roaming about. The troops fought brilliantly and are in an excellent frame of mind.' Then followed the names of officers who had fallen and a mention of his delight at meeting their younger son, Kurt, at a point 'from where one can see the towers of Kulm', his own birthplace.

Already Gretel had caught the excitement of his mood and on the 5th she had written: 'I know that my men are the best soldiers. May God send them back to me with Victory – that Germany may live and at last find peace . . . I am burning to know where and how your troops are victorious . . . I followed your hard work and strife: now may God give you undisputed success.'

A momentous occasion for Guderian was his opportunity on 5th September to conduct Hitler, Himmler and their entourage round the battlefield – the party shepherded along by an officer who had once commanded the 10th *Jägers* – Erwin Rommel, in his capacity as Commander of Hitler's headquarters in the field. For the first time the Führer was given a partial insight into the essentials of modern war. Some of his illusions were shattered, but the educational process was superficial – as time would show. Yet there is vast significance in his question to Guderian concerning the sight of shattered Polish artillery: 'Our divebombers did that?' and Guderian's emphatic and proud reply, 'No! Our panzers!' At that moment it was faintly born upon Hitler, along with Guderian's announcement of a mere 150 dead in his entire Corps, that the truly dominant weapon on land might be the tank force. Up to then he had been enslaved by Göring's claim for the omnipotence of air power. Now he was shown that tanks were an ubiquitous, life-saving weapon and that airpower had its limitations. And the rapid advance of the other armoured formations to the gates of Warsaw and through the mountains in the south told the same story, leaving nobody of balanced judgement in any doubt that, even in unfavourable territory, panzer divisions could make a decisive impression.

But the campaign, though won, was far from over. Next day XIX Corps was sent across the Vistula and transported through East Prussia, close to Bartenstein, to concentrate on the left wing of the German Army as it prepared to drive south towards Brest Litovsk. This provided an opportunity for the Corps Commander to relax while his staff did the donkey work, and it was part of Guderian's make-up that he could do so – in style. On the night of the 6th he slept in the bed which once had been used by Napoleon in Finkenstein Castle: with amused vanity he relished the privilege. The following night, while his troops drove up for action, he went deer shooting and bagged a large twelve-pointer. Fortunate the staff which has such a trusting commander. Within a few hours he was planning again, receiving his orders from Bock and negotiating for alterations so that his Corps, now strengthened by the substitution of 10th Panzer Division for 2nd Motorised Division, should be left free to make full use of its immense striking power. The initial scheme put forward by OKH to von Bock's Army Group North on the 4/5th September was anything but productive of wide-ranging, fast panzer attacks. XIX Corps was to be kept in close attendance of Third Army and held back at infantry speed. Moreover the fear of strong intervention by the French in the West (the fact that it had not yet taken place after the Anglo-French declaration of war on 3rd September was the cause of some amazement) deterred OKH from committing major forces too far east when it appreciated that, already, the Poles were broken. Incursions east of a line Ostrow Mazowiecka – Warsaw were forbidden. Bock, whose concept of mobile operations was acute, protested without avail long before Guderian was told of the restrictions and had the chance to add his own vehement objections to Bock on 8th September. But on the 8th it suddenly transpired that Army Group South had not, after all, captured Warsaw: nor had it crossed the Vistula as it had claimed. In fact, 4th Panzer Division had taken a hammering, with the loss of 57 out of 120 tanks, as it tried to break into the city, and there were signs of a major Polish counter-offensive opening along the River Bzura to the west. In these changed circumstances Bock now obtained permission to use XIX Corps to wider and better effect, bringing it under direct command on the left of Third Army and aiming it against Brest Litovsk, far to the east and rear of Warsaw. While Rundstedt and Manstein were preparing for a tactical envelopment on the Bzura, Guderian was given the opportunity he yearned for – a strategic envelopment from north to south with massed panzers.

Already XXI Corps had begun to push across the River Narew against the sternly resisting Polish Narew Group and was aided initially by the presence of 10th Panzer Division. But the moment that division was withdrawn from command and switched to the left flank where XIX Corps was being pushed through by Guderian, the impetus of XXI Corps' operations was lost. Here, as elsewhere, infantry unsupported by armour had a rough ride against a determined enemy – and this applied equally to 10th Panzer's infantry regiment. Last-minute changes of plan also caused confusion in XIX Corps whose inexperienced troops as yet lacked a common method of operation. Moreover unsubstantiated reports by the leading troops, which claimed advances that had not yet taken place, gave a false impression and caused the operation to be launched in a haphazard manner. It was the same in 10th Panzer as it had been with 3rd Panzer on the first day: local commanders were too far to the rear to enable them to both understand and have control over the situation: operations ground to a halt for lack of leadership. While the tanks remained on the home bank of the river, awaiting ferries or the construction of a bridge, the infantry were held up, and not until 1800 hrs on the 9th were a sufficient number of tanks across to join the infantry in an attack which was immediately successful. Guderian was on the spot, urging on the attack and ordering the building of bridges that would carry the tanks next day.

Again there was confusion after he had left the front and returned to his main headquarters for the routine evening exchange of views and orders with Nehring. During the night the commander of 20th Motorised Division, which was under orders to cross the river on the right of 10th Panzer, demanded and received the bridges which Guderian intended for use by the tanks. Progress was made only slowly against extremely stiff resistance from the 18th Polish Infantry Division which had already given XXI Corps a rough handling and now was withdrawing southward. It was 20th Motorised Division's turn to grapple with 18th Division while the two panzer divisions began their drive towards the River Bug. Immediately the dangers to unarmoured troops in maintaining a deep penetration were exposed. 20th Motorised Division called for help almost at once, and 10th Panzer had to be diverted to their assistance. Meanwhile 3rd Panzer Division, moving into the lead on the left flank, felt itself in danger from the remains of the Narew Group and the Podlaska Cavalry Brigade which lurked on the left flank and rear from the vicinity of Grodno and Bialystok. Guderian ignores this threat in *Panzer Leader*, but the War Diary (KTB) of XIX Corps does not make light of it. Nehring realised the threat and, moreover, on the night of the 10th/11th was prevented with Main Headquarters from joining Guderian because Polish troops had cut the road. Rightly Guderian admits to moving the headquarters prematurely over the Narew: there was no need since the radio sets were well within range of each other and a headquarter's effectiveness is reduced each time it makes a move. Furthermore the perils of a roving commander in the forefront of the battle were enunciated at this moment of maximum Polish reaction. That day Guderian himself was cut off and had to be rescued by motor-cyclists, and on the 12th the commander of 2nd Motorised Division, travelling ahead of his formation on reversion to Guderian's Command, was cut off for several hours by Polish troops. These were the penalties of over-confidence allied to a failure to realise that, within the confines of a grapple when the enemy was present in strength, the major portion of panzer divisions was every bit as vulnerable as other troops and that the comparative safety inherent in vast movement was nullified until conditions of untrammelled mobility had been created.

These conditions were fully satisfied on 13th September when 18th Polish Division surrendered. OKH now took advantage of XIX Corps' location deep among the enemy in the east to make use of it as a flank guard to the rest of the forces to the westward, and began to reinforce it by XXI Corps against the threat of flank attack from the forests to the east. Complex traffic control problems immediately arose, not only those caused by XIX Corps' immense train of motor vehicles pouring from north to south along the inadequate road system towards Brest Litovsk, but also in passing XXI Corps' slower moving, horse drawn transport from west to east across the XIX Corps' axis. It said much for the system of traffic control which had been devised before the war, and the understanding among the staff, that this operation was actuated with a minimum of confusion. XIX Corps ran free and arrived at Brest Litovsk on the 14th, with its two panzer divisions leading and the motorised divisions echeloned back as flank protection on either wing. Speed was the essence of victory: at Zabinka the sudden arrival of 3rd Panzer Division caught Polish tanks in the act of detraining and destroyed them.

The Polish garrison of Brest would not surrender and was well entrenched among the ancient fortifications. This provided yet another opportunity for Guderian to demonstrate his corps' versatility with a full-scale direct assault that lacked none of the power associated with heavily supported infantry forces in the past. Tanks, artillery and infantry from 10th Panzer and 20th Motorised Divisions were thrown into a deliberate attack on the 16th while 3rd Panzer and 2nd Motorised Divisions continued their advance to the south in pursuit of the Corps' mission. But if there was nothing to prevent a drive to the south, overcoming the defences of Brest was another matter. Resistance was fierce and accidentally stiffened when German artillery fire fell short among its own infantry. At this the infantry faltered and failed to follow close upon the heels of that part of a creeping barrage which was accurate. Next day the matter was settled, by mutual consent, the final German assault coinciding with a despairing Polish attempt to break out. This, as Guderian wrote, marked the end of the campaign. Isolated garrisons throughout the country would prolong the fight for the sake of honour, but the entry of Russian troops in eastern Poland eradicated any Polish hope there might have been of establishing a coherent defence in that region.

In the closing phases was heard the mutter of yet another storm to come. On 15th September Bock decided to split XIX Corps in two, sending half north-eastward towards Slonin and the rest south-eastward – a task which he estimated would take an infantry corps eight days to complete but which motorised troops could accomplish in a fraction of that time. To co-ordinate this operation with XXI Corps he introduced Kluge's Fourth Army. Hotly Guderian protested to Kluge at the splitting of his corps. It offended the principle of concentration which was sacred to his philosophy of armoured warfare and it would also, as he forcefully pointed out, make command and control almost impossible. Events precluded the movements, but at this moment was born a mistrust of Kluge that was to distinguish his dealing with that officer (and Bock) over the next five years. Yet it was these two who recommended him for the award of the Knight's Cross of the Iron Cross – an honour he deeply appreciated since '. . . it seemed to me to be primarily a vindication of my long struggle for the creation of the new armoured force'. It is equally likely that Bock and Kluge were motivated by immediate considerations and the reflected glory they would gather from Guderian's accomplishment. For he – and they – could claim a 200-mile advance in ten days against tough opposition for losses which were lower, in proportion, than those of the other groups. Since September 1st XIX Corps had suffered only 650 killed and 1,586 wounded and missing – a mere 4 per cent of its strength. Tank losses for the entire Army were 217 and the number of dead 8,000, of whom the vast majority were in the infantry and only 1,500 in Army Group North.

There were matters which gave less cause for rejoicing in the aftermath. Guderian shared the soldiers' disappointment that Hitler's promise of an automatic withdrawal of opposition by the Western Powers once Poland was conquered, was not fulfilled, though he was hardly surprised. In his letter to Gretel on 4th September he had told her: 'In the meantime the political situation has developed in so far as a new world war is in the making. The whole affair will therefore last a long time and we must stiffen our necks'. Now they had to face an offensive campaign in the West at which they boggled and for which there was no plan. The redeployment of an army which had suffered heavy wear and tear in battle had to be swiftly implemented, initially as a defence measure against an expected French offensive which never came. At least half the tanks needed major workshop overhaul. In the haste of withdrawal from the sectors which were to be turned over to the Russians, some equipment had to be abandoned, but the bulk of the Army (Guderian included) was spared the horror of watching the SS units at their deadly work of extermination in that part of Poland which Germany retained. Heinz-Günther Guderian remained for two months, however, and records the 'deplorable impression' made by the Jewish ghettos in Warsaw and Lublin.

The campaign's lessons should have been patently obvious, but although the Germans were avid in correcting relatively minor sins and omissions in their equipment, their methods and organisation, it was plain that the full meaning of their achievement in Poland eluded even their own commanders. At the heart of misunderstanding was a universal belief that the Poles never had a chance, that the might of Germany was certain to prevail against an inferior opponent – as well it might in course of time. Such a belief suited the adjusted arguments put forward by opposing factions. The panzer men claimed everything for themselves, as did some airmen. But whereas history tells us that the latter played an important role within the broadest concept of air power as an instrument of force, it also reminds us that only land forces seize ground. That was what the panzer troops did with such speed and effectiveness that Polish resistance never had a chance of adjusting itself to changed circumstances. It was upon the infantry that the higher German leadership, for a variety of reasons, heaped recrimination. It was said that they had failed to fight with the fervour of their forefathers and it could be inferred that, if the Army had gone to war with the horse and foot organisation Beck had preferred, execution of the campaign might have been so slow as to preclude a decision in time to pre-empt an irresistible offensive in the West. Hence it could be argued that, if Guderian had not engineered the panzer idea against the opposition of the majority, the war would not have been practicable. Few so argued, but Hitler had drawn his own conclusions.

As it was, Bock severely critised the performance of the infantry divisions (as part of an effort to restore their sense of purpose) coupled with a complaint that the artillery was immobile and far too slow in deploying its fire. Henceforward he demanded that the artillery must not delay the infantry and, moreover, should be capable of giving direct support from the front line. This was merely a reiteration of Guderian's early arguments in favour of the tank. Manstein went further: tracked, motorised assault guns were required, he said. So it was that, as the inadequate Pz I tanks were gradually withdrawn from front-line service, they were rebuilt and fitted with larger guns of Czech origin, mounted, for limited traverse only, behind armour.

With none of these things could Guderian seriously quarrel, even though he resisted digressions from the turretted tank because they were, in his opinion, retrograde steps. He felt the tanks had stood up well against the Polish tanks – many of which were better armed than his own – and so he sought increases in the fire-power and armament of German tanks and expressed dissatisfaction with the standard of command at the lower levels. The Light Divisions, with their low tank content, had failed – as he expected they would – but with tank production reaching 125 per month and good Czech equipment becoming available it was now possible to up-grade these divisions to full panzer specifications.

At the same time it was quite easy to resist a bizarre bid by the Cavalry to increase their establishment, even though horsed formations had amply demonstrated their terrible vulnerability in the late campaign. Yet the 'Great Manoeuvres' in Poland had not seriously altered the fundamental objections to all that Guderian stood for.

All Guderian could do was recommend. He was without direct power since the post of 'Chief of Mobile Troops' had been dissolved – unmourned – upon the outbreak of war when the representation of panzer interests had been transferred to the Commander of the Replacement Army – a somewhat anti-panzer officer called *Generaloberst* Fritz Fromm. In Guderian's opinion the personalities who were made responsible for panzer matters were 'not always in concert with the importance which the Panzer Command enjoys in modern war'. Nevertheless, if educated German military specialists were unwilling to come to terms with the changes which had been wrought upon the art of war as the result of Hitler's 'little war' in Poland – and there is ample evidence in support of Guderian's contention – an incredulous and ill-informed world was even less likely to do so. Though the major military powers, particularly Germany's neighbours, realised that tanks and air-craft had played a vital role in the Polish debacle, they tended to minimise their effects on the grounds that this had been an unfair test against an impotent victim. Nothing such as had happened in Poland could possibly take place against France, it was argued. They would not long be left in doubt, if Hitler had his way, for Hitler was uplifted by success and this reinforcement of his self-confidence. He had seen the magic of his new weapons work: they were better than a bluff. No sooner had the dust from Poland settled than the Führer was giving the order, on 27th September, to prepare for an early invasion of Western Europe, a project which so alarmed some German officers, who rejected its feasibility let alone the attendant risk of really starting a Second World War, that they reactivated the project to assassinate Hitler. Among these dissidents were Hammerstein, Beck and a few civilians.

Guderian was not among the plotters – he might well have been the last they thought to invite – but he was far from content with the condition of Army affairs in addition to his worries about the state of the armoured forces. In October, at table, he had sensed what he took to be the Führer's mood after the presentation of his Knight's Cross. Seated upon Hitler's right hand he gave a soldier's reply to Hitler's request for Guderian's reactions when the Soviet Pact was announced in August; he said that it had given him a sense of security since it reduced the likelihood of a two-front war such as proved Germany's undoing in the First World War. In *Panzer Leader* he expressed surprise that Hitler should look at him in amazement and displeasure, and says that only later did he come to understand Hitler's intense hatred of Soviet Russia. It is possible that

Guderian's reply actually pleased the Führer, who had come to believe that most of his generals were whole-heartedly against the war and therefore against the Pact: it may have encouraged him to find one among the few who recognised the wisdom of his diplomacy and who did not flinch from fighting. But Guderian, unlike so many of his fellow professionals, had come to believe in Germany's power to win battles and, in conversation, transmitted that conviction on the eve of the next round. For November 12th was the date chosen for the invasion of the West and the dissident generals had worked upon Brauchitsch and Halder to stand firm against what seemed, to them, a fatal step.

On November 5th Brauchitsch presented the case against invasion to Hitler, quoting the weather as a prime reason for postponement – an argument with which Guderian would have concurred because the mud produced by so much heavy rain would stop, or at least slow, the tanks. But Brauchitsch also threw doubt upon the fighting qualities of the infantry and this drove Hitler to fury. The Army Commander-in-Chief became a target for a vitriolic attack both upon his own integrity and that of the entire General Staff. At the height of his tirade, according to Goerlitz, he told Brauchitsch that he knew the generals were planning 'something more than the offensive he had ordered', an accidental shot in the dark which shook Brauchitsch to the roots. A thoroughly demoralised C-in-C went back to his Chief of Staff and tendered his resignation to Hitler. This, as Supreme Commander of the *Wehrmacht*, Hitler refused to accept. In much the same way, too, he brushed aside Keitel's offer to resign when he detected the flight of his Führer's confidence. Discipline was reasserted. The plot had to be called-off by the dissidents, of course. Not only did it seem possible that they were discovered, but neither Brauchitsch nor Halder were prepared to resist further, and without them there could be no progress. The postponement, on the 7th, of the offensive was almost incidental – the first of many deferments which were to recur at regular intervals throughout the winter.

On 23rd November Hitler felt provoked into reading his commanders a sharp lecture and left them in no doubt, as Guderian (who was there) put it, that, 'The *Luftwaffe* generals, under the purposeful leadership of party comrade Göring, are entirely reliable; the admirals can be trusted to follow the Hitlerite line; but the Party cannot place unconditional trust in the good faith of the Army generals'. At this time Guderian and his XIX Corps were concentrated near Koblenz and under command of von Rundstedt's Army Group A in readiness for the invasion. It was to Rundstedt's Chief of Staff, his old friend Manstein, to whom Guderian first turned for consultation upon this matter which touched them all so deeply. Manstein agreed that something should be done but Rundstedt would not move in a positive manner – he kept to the letter of his oath. The same attitude he found among the other generals he consulted in his efforts to organise a protest. Finally he visited Reichenau who suggested that Guderian himself should speak to Hitler, and it was he who arranged an audience.

The record of that meeting is Guderian's alone* and is in the character of a man who cherished the Army's honour above all else, besides being the possessor of a quite unquenchable spirit of aggression when posed with a problem which struck at the heart of his beliefs. Guderian's correspondence leaves no doubt that the meeting took place and, if his account is true, contradicts Wheeler-Bennett's claim that 'Not a voice was raised in criticism or even in comment', although it must be remembered, as Wheeler-Bennett remarks, that the main body of the Führer's lecture gave rise to a wave of enthusiasm. Guderian says he was closeted with Hitler for an hour in which time he put the case for the generals and the plea that somebody had to speak out after the Führer told the Army generals that he did not trust them. In return Hitler blamed it all on the C-in-C, to which Guderian responded: 'If you feel you cannot trust the present C-in-C of the Army then you must get rid of him . . .' But after Hitler had asked him to name a suitable successor and Guderian had failed to suggest a single acceptable candidate from the top men, the soldier fell silent.

Now occurred the first of those increasingly recurrent scenes in which Hitler deemed it profitable to spend thirty minutes or more trying to convince a general whom he regarded as different and, perhaps, more sympathetic than the rest. There poured out a long diatribe in castigation of the generals and their resistance to Hitler's wishes over the preceding years but, in the end, nothing constructive to settle the problem in the way that Guderian would have wished. The broken and pliable Brauchitsch remained as C-in-C and the schism widened between Hitler and OKW on the one hand and with the General Staff and OKH on the other. It is significant that Hitler should have felt the need to convince Guderian. Perhaps he felt that Guderian, because of his 'modern' outlook and personal struggle against the Army hierarchy, had a closer affinity with Nazi ideology than most Prussian military leaders (in a way he could have been right even though Guderian was no Nazi). Maybe he hoped to recruit another sycophant who one day, like Keitel, would supplant the recalcitrant members of OKH: if that is so he was hopelessly misled, for Guderian was incapable of sycophancy. Possibly he simply hoped to foster Guderian's goodwill as that of key leader of the Army's most potent striking force on the eve of the most testing campaign – but, in practice, he was to show that he had still not fully comprehended the meaning of the panzer divisions. It is more likely that a combination of all three motivations, plus several more of typically devious Hitlerian ingenuity, persuaded Hitler in an attempt to win the support of Ger-

*He recounted it immediately afterwards to General Engel who gives corroboration.

many's most controversial operational commander. Perhaps he wished to evaluate Guderian as a potential Commander-in-Chief.

Guderian had demonstrated, as had several of his comrades, the absurdity of Seeckt's demand that the Army should stay out of politics. He actually played an important part in thrusting it deeper – if unwittingly and against its will – into the political field. If he believed, as sometimes it is said he did, in political detachment, it is merely another example of his blindness to reality. This isolated him from those with whom he was destined to collaborate and created the divergences of view which were fundamental to his effectiveness as a leader. For Guderian was a target for the German generals' distaste when they had the opportunity. Angrily he wrote to Gretel on 21st January 1940:

'The recent evening with Herr v R [Rundstedt] began quite pleasantly and ended with a debate started by him and Busch [*Generaloberst* Ernst Busch the commander of Sixteenth Army] about the *Panzertruppe*. It was a debate which I thought impossible in its lack of understanding and, in part, even hatefulness after the Polish campaign. I went home deeply disappointed. These people will never see me again. It is completely fruitless ever to expect anything from this well-known group of "comrades". To these people can be traced back the reason for our irreplaceable equipment standing immobile out of doors for months on end to perish in the extreme cold. The damage arising from this is inconceivable.

'Apart from this great annoyance I have that evening contracted a nasty infection and am suffering from catarrh and a cold of the most evil kind. And we continue to wait . . .

'I have a lot to do for the next fortnight with regard to training courses. But everything suffers on account of the bad training facilities. Had they only left us at our depots! But that cannot be put right now.

'It freezes, it is snowing. The big brook carries floating ice. It is mostly cloudy and dull. The months pass and what remains is a big question mark.'

Gretel probably smiled compassionately when she received that letter, knowing that a sick and despondent husband would recover and eventually forgive his tormentors. Forgiveness came easily to him on this occasion, as it happened, for on 11th February he could happily report to Gretel after a meeting at which the future campaign was discussed as a 'war game': 'Apparently von R himself has the feeling that I was right to defend myself recently. At the meeting he was kindness itself . . .' It mattered less that, in the same letter, he could complain: 'I suffer from loneliness because I constantly meet strangers to whom I cannot speak freely – and so one talks banalities and what is closest to the heart remains unsaid.' But this was the end of the period of isolation. Rundstedt's change of mood marked a change in the fortunes of the creator of the *Panzertruppe*, for the plans they had discussed were the ones that

Hitler favoured and which Guderian recognised as the revelation of a dream.

Nevertheless the fluctuation of sympathy towards Guderian among the German generals acted as a barometer which pointed to the climate of opinion of the Germans – not only towards the controversial subject of tank warfare but also with regard to Hitler's grasp upon a war situation. As a politician Hitler had secured his position but his pretensions as a 'military genius' were as yet hardly suspected. Guderian held out a key that might unlock the door to a military revolution by destroying the orthodox armies of a previous decade. At the same time he could help prove the prowess of the amateur Supreme Commander as the equal of professional soldiers. Much more than the issue of one campaign hinged upon the plan to invade Western Europe.

7 The Green Light through France

Without a plan and lacking much time to make one, since Hitler demanded its execution on 12th November, the German General Staff went to work on 28th September preparing an invasion of the West. But since, from the outset, Brauchitsch and Halder had little faith in the feasibility of their task, it is hardly surprising that the product of their deliberations lacked inspiration. It was essential, they reasoned, to outflank the Maginot Line which guarded the French frontier between the Swiss frontier to Longwy, south of Arlon, where the man-made defences merged with the allegedly strong natural defensive terrain of the Ardennes. Indisputably, they decided, the main effort should be made north of the Ardennes, in the general direction of Namur while, concurrently, Holland was subdued on the extreme right flank. Left flank protection could be obtained by pushing a relatively strong force through the Ardennes to reach the River Meuse between Givet and Sedan. This was the basis of the plan which was to suffer persistent postponement until, on 10th January 1940, it appeared to be compromised when a German staff officer's aeroplane carrying its details made a false landing in Belgium. (In fact, the papers were burnt before capture and little was disclosed.)

Long before January the plan had come under piercing criticism. Manstein complained that it was unlikely to achieve complete victory since it could not bring about the total destruction of the enemy's northern wing and failed to create a favourable strategic situation from which to launch subsidiary thrusts: in essence it lacked penetration and versatility. He realised that an invasion must achieve all – quickly – since failure to do so would condemn Germany to a protracted war she could not sustain. He desired an annihilating encirclement such as the elder Moltke used to demand, that the younger Moltke had sought and missed, and which he and Rundstedt had recently achieved in Poland. Hitler also was dissatisfied with the plan, though his strategic insight was that of a tyro compared with Manstein's. On 25th October – before Manstein had seen the OKH plan – he had suggested that the drive through the Ardennes might be enlarged by aiming the main attack across the southern Meuse and then extending it towards Amiens to the Channel coast with the intention of cutting off a large portion of the enemy. On the 31st, quite independently of Hitler, Rundstedt sent OKH a reasoned project which looked remarkably similar to the one Hitler had conjured out of a dream.

This brought Guderian into the debate as the acknowledged expert whose qualifications in the tank sphere were far superior to those of Brauchitsch, Halder and the rest. For, despite the sniping which still went on among underlings against the *Panzertruppe*, nobody in supreme command doubted that the coming invasion would depend upon aircraft and tanks. Indeed, the principal reasons for the postponements were fear that aircraft could not fly in bad weather and that the tanks would bog down in the winter mud. After Hitler mentioned his idea to Jodl on 9th November, Jodl discussed it with Wilhelm Keitel, and Keitel called Guderian into consultation on the feasibility of passing strong tank forces through the Ardennes. Guderian omits mention of this in *Panzer Leader* and only writes of a similar discussion with Manstein in the latter half of November – by which time he had had the time to calculate the demands in terms of forces needed for the project. No doubt recalling his close experience of the Ardennes during the hectic days of 1914 and his sojourn at Sedan during the staff course in 1918, he had confidently informed Keitel that panzer divisions could be sent through the Ardennes. But on 11th November, when told that his own XIX Corps might be the leading formation in a drive for Sedan, he insisted that the two panzer and single motorised divisions proposed were quite insufficient for the task. Later still, when faced with a searching examination by Manstein, as the latter developed his more ambitious scheme, he expanded still further his own requirements: now he bid for seven mobile divisions in the van.

As the winter advanced Manstein became ever more urgent in his memorandums and personal pleas to OKH until at last they rid themselves of this insistent Staff Officer by appointing him to command of an infantry corps. Nevertheless OKH opinion was veering. The January war games conducted by Rundstedt demonstrated the potentiality of a blow against Sedan at the joint between the strong northern flank and its weaker extension along the Meuse, though Guderian's insistence that the panzer divisions should lead the attack into the Ardennes, execute the river crossing and also spearhead the advance deep into France, was treated with outright scepticism if not scorn. (The bitter *Herrenabend* had reflected the nadir of his part in the argument; it was from that moment that he began to stamp his personality on the victory to come.) Halder insisted that the infantry divisions must catch up at the Meuse since they alone would have the power to perform a major obstacle crossing operation against prepared positions. He said that Guderian's intentions were 'senseless' and he was supported by Rundstedt. Guderian stood firm and contradicted them both, reasoning in favour of a surprise stroke in mass, '. . . to drive a wedge so deep and wide that we need not worry about our flanks . . .' Support appeared from some of the other generals. Halder began to waver. Then Manstein, during a routine interview with Hitler on 17th February, took the opportunity to describe his plan in person. At once Hitler was re-enthused and next day told Brauchitsch and Halder – as if it was his own idea – that this was what he wanted.

There was no further delay. A new plan appeared in which the full weight of the assault was to be thrown into the Ardennes leaving only a single panzer division (9th in XXXIX Corps) committed to Holland, and two more (3rd and 4th in XVI Corps) temporarily leading the initial thrust against Belgium to the north of Namur. Moving across the northern face of the Ardennes, XV Corps, with 5th and 7th Panzer Divisions, was to tackle the Meuse near Dinant, thus covering the northern flank of *General der Panzertruppe* Georg-Hans Reinhardt's XXXXI Corps. The offensive's *Schwerpunkt* was to consist of a special Panzer Group under *General der Kavalerie* Ewald von Kleist, comprising XXXXI Corps, Guderian's XIX Corps and Wietersheim's XIV Corps, placed within *Generaloberst* Siegmund List's Twelfth Army which in turn came under Rundstedt's Army Group 'A'. Reinhardt was given 6th and 8th Panzer Divisions only, but Guderian, upon whom all hopes were pinned, had 1st, 2nd and 10th Panzer Divisions plus the crack motorised Infantry Regiment *Grossdeutschland*. The armoured strength of Kleist's Group would thus amount to about 1,260 tanks (with a larger share of Pz IIIs and IVs plus the first *Schützenpanzers*) out of a total German tank availability, on the day of assault (10th May), of about 2,800. But, in addition, priority of air support was promised during the advance to the Meuse, along with a massed bombing attack during the actual river crossing operation. This obviated the need to push heavy artillery and the attendant road-cluttering ammunition columns along tortuous routes which were to be filled by the fully motorised mobile corps.

As the hard winter gave way to a cheering spring and the *Wehrmacht* opened the campaigning season with the swift subjugation of Denmark and Norway, Guderian and the rest became absorbed by training and planning. Map exercises predominated since, although tank crews spent a few nights practising driving along difficult country lanes, shortage of fuel precluded intensive rehearsal. Due to shortage of ammunition some tank crews never once fired their guns, though the artillery, including the long 88mm anti-aircraft guns, were given considerable practice in direct fire at small targets, such as pill-box slits, in addition to their orthodox role. Over and again infantry and engineers rehearsed the techniques of an assault river crossing in rubber boats, and then the tank ferrying and bridging operations that must follow once the infantry had secured a foothold on the enemy bank. The training on the River Moselle was notably realistic since its approaches were so like those of the Meuse. Tirelessly Guderian travelled from one exercise to another, goading his men to more intensive activity, analysing faults in their methods, synthesizing each lesson and feeding fresh ideas through Nehring and his staff for dissemination throughout XIX Corps and, indirectly, to the other panzer formations whose prospects were constantly in his thoughts. For though Guderian gave most attention to his own corps, he never forgot the welfare of the entire armoured force. All ranks came to recognise and value the bustling general with the eager look bearing down upon them with purposeful questions, terse comments and shrewd assessments of their performance. *Der Schnelle Heinz* enfolded them all with the stern but fair fatherly spirit which he lavished upon his own family. Those who survive have affectionate and enduring memories of him and his catch phrases that the privileged among them loved to throw back at him – *Klotzen, nicht Kleckern* (which can be translated in all sorts of ways but means 'Don't feel with the fingers but hit with the fist') and 'Joy riding in canoes on the Meuse is forbidden' are but two. It amounted to a feeling of absolute mutual confidence, the essence of outstanding leadership.

How much confidence did Guderian himself repose in the prospects of the oncoming adventure – an enterprise which, at one time, had been as unthinkable to him as it still was to many of his contemporaries? He says in *Panzer Leader* that French reticence to take advantage of German preoccupation in Poland suggested over-caution on their part – but this was insufficient in rating them inept. Far more important was the knowledge that French strategic and tactical doctrine had dictated, certainly until September 1939, a mode of positional warfare waged at the pace of 1918. Though the French were thought to be superior in number of tanks (they and the British between them could actually assemble about 4,200) it could be assumed that these machines would neither be used at speed nor in mass, and that their scale of radios was low and under-implemented. Therefore they would be spread along the front and must be slow to react in a fast-moving situation. This, Guderian felt sure, would prove fatal. He was aware, however, that many of the latest French tanks, the Somua S 35 and the heavy Char B, carried twice the armour of his Pz IVs and, in their 47mm gun, had a superior anti-armour weapon to any mounted in his own tanks. Thus, in a tank-versus-tank contest, his machines would be at a disadvantage and so too would the infantry whose only anti-tank gun was the same 37mm as carried by the Pz III. The use of field artillery along with 88mm guns in the forefront of the battle, alone, would compensate for this deficiency – that and the ability to outfight the enemy by manoeuvring for his flanks and rear and defeating his armour by directing accurate fire at the smallest exposed weak-spots – a testing exercise for nervous gunlayers in the heat of battle.

German knowledge of the enemy positions in the Ardennes and along the Meuse was quite comprehensive – and generally encouraging to them. They realised, from extensive reconnaissance by every possible means, that the defences were shallow and, in places, incomplete. Taken on balance there was good reason for Guderian to have confidence that superior, surprise handling of his armour could surmount shocked opposition in the good defensive country of the Ardennes and bounce a way across the Meuse before the enemy could recover from initial setbacks. His only recorded doubts before the action became related to fear for inadequate support from his superiors, though, to be fair to them, it has to be said that only a man of Guderian's conviction could have been happy with the prospects. Hitler was out of his depth in the realms of educated military thinking. Though his 'intuition' put him on the course that was to prove right, his frequently expressed doubts often undermined his composure. Brauchitsch and Halder had vacillated so much at first, and become converts so late to the new scheme, that it was impossible to place solid trust in their consistency if a crisis arose. List wanted infantry divisions to lead across the Meuse. Rundstedt had wavered and demonstrated a lack of tank appreciation by declining to consider deep penetration beyond a Meuse bridgehead. Kleist had no experience of armour though his cavalryman's instinct for movement and his recognition of opportunities were by no means dim. Busch did not think Guderian would manage to cross the Meuse at all, while Bock, whose Army Group in the north had been deprived of the original dominant role prescribed in the first plan, spoke for a majority with reasoned objections (by conventional standards) when he told Halder:

'You will be creeping along, ten miles from the Maginot Line flank on your breakthrough, and hoping that the French will watch inertly! You are cramming the mass of tanks together into the narrow roads of the Ardennes as if there were no such thing as air power. And you then hope to lead an operation as far as the coast with an open southern flank 200 miles long where stands the mass of the French Army!'

There Bock went wrong, for sufficient intelligence of Allied intentions in the event of an invasion of Holland and Belgium had been gathered throughout the winter months to make it almost certain that the mass of Allied armies would move forward into Belgium and thus create a vacuum in the open space Panzer Group Kleist was to enter. Yet it is interesting that Guderian once called the advance via Amiens to Abbeville a raid. Perhaps it was the careless use of a word: maybe it reflected uncertainty of the final outcome and he was prepared to back-pedal if necessary – mentally he was as flexibly attuned to retrograde panzer movements as to progressive ones, as the Supreme Command would one day learn.

In a mood which reflects repose, and certainly not bombast or over-confidence, he sent his feelings to Gretel as his headquarters got ready to advance:

'Your guess was right. I now say farewell to you. We have strenuous days ahead of us and I don't know when I will have a chance to write again. I would like to have said farewell in person. Now it has to be done by means of an insipid piece of paper and all my tenderness remains unspoken and undone. The last beautiful leave is still fresh in my mind and even a short repetition would have been a blessing, but it was not to be. Great activity is developing in the beautiful spring countryside, but it is not in harmony with the splendour of the blossom and so, despite all the confidence, one is filled with a gentle sadness. Your thoughts will now speed increasingly to our boys and I wish and hope with you that you may hold them safe and sound again in your arms after the victorious campaign. We must now direct our thoughts towards our task. Everything else, therefore, must take second place . . . I have left my comfortable quarters and will move forward tonight . . . If a big success materialises none of the discomfort will be of account.'

Stretching back a hundred miles from head to tail XV, XXXXI and XIX Corps began to wend their way from woodland hiding places down the roads leading across the frontier. Ahead the opposition, such as it was, fell to pieces under the impact of surprise: in places the defenders, quite literally, were caught napping by infiltrators dressed in civilian clothes who had previously entered the zone on the pretext of being 'tourists' and who neutralised as many demolition devices as possible and saved bridges and defiles from destruction. Working alongside the tank and infantry combat teams were the assault engineers whose job it was, expeditiously, to remove and demolish those road blocks which stood. Everywhere the advance flowed smoothly and to schedule. Halder called it a 'very good marching achievement'. Indeed the preliminary movements were largely a struggle by engineers and logisticians to remove barriers and overcome the choking traffic jams which inevitably, at random moments, impeded Guderian's advance. The appearance of a screening French cavalry division (half in lorries and half in tanks), at the approaches to the River Semois caused only the slightest pause since it was soon swept away, artillery and all, in a brief skirmish. German tanks infiltrated much as they pleased and the terror they inspired was exaggerated by rumour into a dreadful spasm which passed from the mouths of stragglers and refugees of battle to the ears of uncommitted formations in flank and rear. Yet, on the German side, Kleist, the cavalryman, logically and loyally credited French horsemen with a prowess he contended ought to be theirs, and deflected 10th Panzer, squeezing it along Guderian's left flank, southward from its planned axis to counter a nebulous cavalry threat at Longwy. Guderian protested vigorously against this 'detachment of one third of my force to meet a hypothetical threat' but compromised and shifted the division's axis in order to staunch Kleist's fears. But in this effort to placate a superior Guderian erred, for the diversion of 10th Panzer impinged upon its neighbour, 1st Panzer, which at that moment was XIX

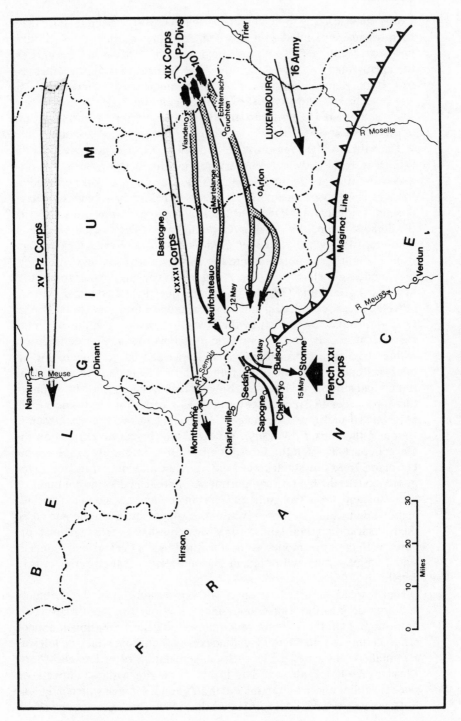

The Attack through the Ardennes

Corps' main striking force and preparing to cross the Semois. 1st Panzer then became entangled with 2nd Panzer further north and they in turn encroached into XXXXI Corps' sector, stalling 6th Panzer. Fortunately the enemy made no air attacks upon the snarled up columns, otherwise irreparable damage besides further chaos might have been caused. This was but the first and smallest of many vacillations to come from every level of command. These were the perfectly natural reactions to a quite unprecedented operation of war – classical examples of 'friction'.

The battle for the Semois was settled before XIX Corps arrived, for the French were already in voluntary retirement to the Meuse. Infantry waded the river on the night of 11th/12th May and the tanks crossed by fords at dawn. Nehring and Guderian established their headquarters in the comfortable Hotel Panorama with 'a splendid view over the valley of the Semois' and paid for their over-indulgence under an accurate enemy bombing attack which showered Guderian with glass and a lucky escape from a falling boar's head mounted on the wall above his desk. After that they tended to behave a little less ostentatiously and Guderian became surprisingly cautious. The old, undecided question of how and when to cross the Meuse cropped up and now demanded a firm answer. 1st Panzer Division, flanked on the left by the 10th, though a little in the air on the right because 2nd, due to its traffic problems, was falling behind, was within striking distance of the river. Kleist had by now overcome his doubts. Reports from the other fronts made it clear that the main allied armies had moved into Belgium. News of tank-versus-tank skirmishing in the approaches to Hannut, between XVI Corps and the French Light Mechanised divisions (the nearest equivalent in the French Order of Battle to the panzer divisions), indicated a technical superiority on the German part. Though the French tanks were comfortably proof against German 37mm shot, their return fire was slow and inaccurate due to the poor layout of the fighting compartment. In French tanks the commander also laid and fired the gun: in German models the commander just commanded while another crew member aimed and fired the gun. Also the French spread their tanks over a wide and shallow frontage in accordance with their out-moded tactical methods while the Germans concentrated on attacking vital points in turn and defeated their opponents in detail.

Kleist opted 'to attack at once, without wasting time'. Immediately and according to the War Game plan, OKW put two Air Corps at his disposal. But Guderian demurred because 2nd Panzer Division might not arrive in time to join the unified attack on a broad front which he felt was essential. In any case, time for the dissemination of orders was short. Kleist overruled Guderian. The incident was not without importance since it implies uncertainties in Guderian's mind, some of which might, as has been suggested by Alistair Horne, have been implanted by the shock of the narrow escape from bombing. This is unlikely though it matches neatly with Fuller's ideas in 1918 that to bomb enemy headquarters might 'neutralise clear thinking'. It certainly indicates that, for all Guderian's criticism, Kleist possessed a clean grasp of panzer time and space potential. More shocks were to follow. On the return flight after the interview with Kleist, Guderian's pilot lost direction and nearly came down in the French lines. It was Guderian's quick recognition of their actual location – a throw back to the skills of 1915 when he flew on reconnaissance – which saved them.

Planning the assault over the Meuse was a classic example of mixed improvisation and General Staff foresight. Kleist's Group was to attack at 1600 hours on the 13th and to be preceded by an intensive artillery and air bombardment instead of helped by simultaneous air support as the troops began to cross the water. There was insufficient time for both the army and air force staffs to write and disseminate the necessary complex written orders for a formal river crossing, but Nehring recognised that the situation coincided so closely with that envisaged in a recent War Game that it was only necessary to reproduce the War Game's orders with times amended to a start at 1600 hours instead of, as originally, 1000. They went out from Corps at 0815 hours on the 13th, and those by 1st Panzer were issued at 1200 hours. The Air Force, faced with a similar communication problem, simply ignored Kleist's orders and proceeded with the predetermined plan that had been made with Guderian. But the Air Force was snug and intact at its bases whereas XIX Corps could not be sure that 2nd Panzer would arrive at the start line in time, while XXXXI Corps also was short of the river at daybreak. In other words, an intended simultaneous assault by five divisions could easily be reduced to a piecemeal incursion by two. Both corps were committed, in the event, to an opposed assault crossing of a major water obstacle on the run – the sort of operation which few commanders had welcomed in the past and at which many were to boggle in the future. Guderian did not have to be bombed in order to acquire a few reservations about the outcome of the next twenty-four hours!

Though the battle for Sedan opened with 1st Panzer Division leading, it was, in actuality, to be an artillery and air engagement in which tanks took little part and infantry captured ground only after a duel with high explosives had been settled. The Germans were to find that not only were they prevented from crossing the river while French guns were in action, but that their own guns were at a disadvantage in the approaches to the river. For while Guderian allowed the conventional field units to employ the usual indirect fire, he demanded that Anti-Aircraft Regiment 102 should support the crossing 'for which purpose it is to commit its guns very far forward'. In effect he was asking the powerful 88mm anti-aircraft guns (of a type which one day would arm his heaviest tanks) to execute the direct fire role he envisaged for tanks, the reason being that this highly accurate gun of large calibre had a far deadlier effect against pin point targets than the smaller, less accurate tank guns of the day. This was the moment when a heavy tank or an armoured assault gun would have been useful, but only 55 of the latter were as yet in service (and mostly with Guderian) and they were equipped only with the same inaccurate 75mm guns as in Panzer IV.

Here and there French fire hindered the German deployment, but mostly it was restricted in order to conserve ammunition and in the conventional belief that it might be four to six days before the attack would come. At 1600 hours the first waves of bombers arrived – the heavies to carpet selected areas, the dive-bombers to swoop on individual gun-pits. In Poland this method had achieved only marginally good results because the Poles were difficult to intimidate. Near Sedan, second-rate French divisions were unequal to the shock. Mostly the men went to ground, ran or were withdrawn upon receipt of supine orders from above. For five hours the bombing continued: with every minute that passed the French return fire slackened. Unsupported by artillery, front-line French infantry wavered while those who shot at the gathering German infantry, as they dragged their assault craft to the water's edge, were struck by 88mm fire that came straight through the pill-box embrasures. As evening encroached the German infantry gained a first foothold and began to work their way inland. Throughout the night the work of constructing tank ferries and bridges would go on but the first tank would not be across until dawn. In the meantime Guderian boated across himself to be met by his old comrade, the exultant commander of 1st Rifle Regiment, *Oberstleutnant* Hermann Balck, with a ribald reproof for 'joy riding in canoes on the Meuse', and the news that a bridgehead was secure. Balck needed no reminding that Guderian wished them to go on advancing all night: each German was well rehearsed. By daybreak 1st Rifle Regiment and the *Grossdeutschland* Regiment on his left had formed a bridgehead that was three miles wide and six deep as reproof to Guderian for a previous, galling remark that infantry '. . . slept instead of advancing at night'.

Yet on this terrain where, in a German historian's words, 'the noise of fighting had almost stopped' the tank had won a victory where no German tank set track. The tank terror which had undermined German morale in 1917 and 1918 was turned upon its originators. French infantry fled from key and unthreatened positions at the mere hint of a tank's engine, though the engines they heard and reported in fear were those of French tanks, moving to the rescue for a dawn counter-attack. This French attack, if it had been pressed, might have thrown the battle back to the river, but the two light tank battalions which caused such alarm halted in case they multiplied a panic they had already raised in the night among

106

the shattered defenders. In consequence they were far from the start line at dawn, and when next they moved it was to find themselves firmly opposed by German tanks and guns whose intentions were deadly and purposeful in the spirit of von Seeckt, the general who had once demanded of the good commander that 'He will always fix his goal somewhat beyond the point he feels to be really attainable. He will leave a margin for luck, but wise restraint and an artistic sense are necessary to prevent him fixing the goal too far outside a reasonable sphere of action'.

That was advice Guderian had now to heed as information began to accumulate of the existence of that breach in the French defences he had hoped to open. His mind was always fixed upon the raid to Amiens. But first there had to be what one of the major-generals on the British side, Bernard Montgomery, was one day to entitle 'the dog-fight'. And since the dog-fight mainly concerned the opposing armoured formations, to recall their fate is to understand the confrontation. To match the Germans, the French fielded three *Divisions Légères Mécaniques* (DLM) each of which had 194 tanks including the good S 35s and four *Divisions Cuirassées Rapides* (DCR) each of 156 tanks including the heavy Char Bs. There were, in addition, 25 independent battalions of light tanks for infantry support. The DLMs were sent into Belgium, and badly chewed by XVI Corps: besides many machines, they lost the will to fight and for the remainder of the campaign were jumpy at the very mention of German tanks. Guderian saw nothing of them. Nor did he meet the 1st DCR which, like its fellows, had only recently been formed and lacked the organisation, the communications, the philosophy or the techniques of panzer divisions. They were short of infantry and supporting arms, still wedded to the concept of close infantry support in linear positions as well as slow and untutored in their deployment and battle drills. 1st DCR had also gone to Belgium and on 14th May was sent towards Dinant to oppose a sudden breakthrough by Hoth's XV Corps. In three days' combat it was virtually wiped out during a series of scattered engagements. Invariably it was short of fuel (because of logistic ineptitude): never was it co-ordinated due to weak command procedures and chaotic traffic control.

Two of the remaining three DCRs tried conclusions with panzer divisions and the result of their labour resolved itself into a study of contrasts between prowess and trepidation, professionalism and amateurism. 3rd DCR began to arrive south of Sedan at Chémery on the 14th as part of XXI Corps, whose task it was to push Guderian back into the Meuse. Once more the dissemination of orders by the French was dilatory (the converse of Guderian's) and refuelling disorganised and slow. As with 1st DCR a second chance for recovery was denied, first by 1st Panzer moving against Chémery and later by *Grossdeutschland* Regiment and 10th Panzer pushing resolutely on to the high ground of Bois Mont Dieu and denying 3rd DCR its assembly area. Third DCR complied with enemy pressure, reverted to the defensive, and thus was dispersed. But in dispersal it also became engaged in a hard and bitter struggle for the village of Stonne, and this prompted a manoeuvre which was to exemplify the foundation of Guderian's concept of armoured warfare – and incidentally induce another clash with Kleist.

As his troops moved into the Bois Mont Dieu, Guderian appreciated that the twelve-mile gap which had opened between this piece of high ground and the Meuse was wide enough to allow his entire corps to turn right and move westward towards the Channel. The one inhibiting factor was an air report of French tanks concentrating against the exposed flank. In fairness he felt it right to ask the commander of 1st Panzer Division if he was prepared to take his whole division or whether a flank guard should be left behind. From the division's Ian *Major* Wenck, came the answer: '*Klotzen, nicht Kleckern*'. In any case a strong flank guard was provided on both 1st Panzer's flanks. On the right, XXXXI Corps was at last beginning to make progress westward after crossing the Meuse near Monthermé, and 2nd Panzer was moving its tanks close alongside – furious Allied air attacks on the bridges having failed in their mission. On the left, *Grossdeutschland* and 10th Panzer were absorbing the intervention of French XXI Corps, particularly in the vicinity of the key village of Stonne. Here, throughout the latter part of the 14th and most of the 15th, 3rd DCR and *Grossdeutschland* strove for ascendancy. 3rd DCR began to lose tanks when they tried to take up their advanced defensive positions and fell back; once more the sheer pace of the panzer attack had pre-empted them. Early on the 15th *Grossdeutschland* took possession of Stonne. At that moment 3rd DCR came under orders, once more, to make a phased attack towards Sedan. But the division, once it had been dispersed, was incapable of concentrating again in so short a space of time. Instead it indulged in a piecemeal counter-attack against Stonne and at once met emplaced German infantry anti-tank guns. A desperate battle ensued, tank versus gun and gun versus tank in the manner envisaged in *Achtung! Panzer!*. The casualties mounted on both sides and the ordinary riflemen cowered in impotence. For a moment the heavy French Char Bs dominated since their armour proved impenetrable to the German 37mm guns. Eventually only one German gun remained in action – but this proved sufficient. At 100 metres range the layer detected a small ventilation grill in the tank's side and through this posted his shots. Then, in quick succession, he destroyed three Char Bs. Even so, at 1800 hours, Stonne was once more in French hands, for *Grossdeutschland* was exhausted.

Guderian watched this struggle on the 15th, anxious that his risky decision of the previous night should not rebound in its rashness, conscious too that he was acting against the wishes of Kleist who had resisted the early westward shift of XIX Corps for fear of the sort of threat which was now developing. There had been strong words: Guderian had railed at Kleist's desire to halt and consolidate as 'a plan which throws away the victory'. Kleist had given way, but there was justification for his anxiety. Guderian could be accused of taking an awful risk, of despising an enemy who was yet to be categorised as effete. News from 10th Panzer was disturbing. They were receiving a heavy tank attack on their extreme left and could barely spare their reserve infantry to reinforce *Grossdeutschland* at Stonne. Everything hung in the balance. One concerted push by the French, even if their offensive went in with only attenuated strength, could have swung the issue their way. It might not have crippled XIX Corps (for XIV Motorised Corps was arriving close to Sedan and, in a dire emergency, 1st and 2nd Panzer Divisions could have been brought back) but the mere suggestion of a brake upon Guderian would have reasserted the dominance of Kleist and permanently inhibited Guderian's future attempts to maintain the Seecktian doctrine of an ambitious goal. As it was the French halted their attack when it was on the verge of making progress and the crisis for Guderian passed. On the following day a fresh German infantry division arrived to stabilise the front.

In five days half the main French armoured formations had been eliminated.

Next it was the fatal turn of 2nd DCR which was in the dangerous process of sending its tanks in small packets by rail to Hirson and St Quentin and its supply lorries by road from Châlons to Guise and thence eastward to Signy L'Abbaye on the 15th. Nobody warned them they were heading into the path of Kleist's Group since nobody on the French side was sure how far Kleist had advanced. While the battle at Stonne raged on the 15th, Reinhardt's XXXXI Corps on Guderian's right, was accelerating in its westward drive and already, with impunity, was overrunning French formations. Its 6th Panzer Division (leaving its companion, the 8th, on the east bank of the Meuse) had driven through the French defended areas and entered the exposed communication zone to begin playing havoc with supply columns, communication centres and dumps. Among the lorries they caught were those belonging to 2nd DCR, the survivors racing southward to escape but thus becoming divorced from the tanks they were meant to supply. Those tanks were at that moment beginning to off-load from trains between St Quentin and Hirson and from the outset would be marooned, presented, fuelless, for mopping up by Reinhardt.

Reinhardt was at Liart at midnight when the leading elements of XIX Corps still lay far behind at Poix-Terron, though 2nd Panzer had at last broken clear of opposition. XIX Corps had suffered from the worst of the dog-fight by being compelled to dissipate part of its strength in holding the hinge of the southern flank and having also collided with a few well-led French infantry units which stood and fought strenuously. There was furious fighting for the village of Bouvellemont in which Balck's

109

exhausted 1st Rifle Regiment, supported by tanks, at last overcame part of 14th Division commanded by a future Marshal of France – Lattre de Tassigny. Here, once more, Guderian managed to arrive at the psychological moment – at dawn on the 16th when the French were beginning to withdraw – when the Germans were longing for a rest and the necessity for fresh impetus had need to be injected into a pursuit.

It was in moments such as this – in triumph or in crisis – that Guderian appeared at his best. Paul Dierichs, who often accompanied Guderian and referred to him as 'a modern Seydlitz', wrote at the time:

'He radiates a sensation of positive and personal calmness. He is never ruffled. But that does not mean that Guderian cannot astonish his officers. For instance, when he arrives at a command post of a subordinate unit and states its next task, many a person might think it a joke that the goal would be placed so far ahead. But in short, clear terms the general explains the feasibility of the operation. At such moments he speaks in a fascinating way to put over his intense desire to advance'.

Vibrant haste was not the only product of his habitual eagerness. As so often before he felt anxious about the shortage of time in which to produce convincing results – the invariable bane of the *Panzertruppe* from the day of its inception, and the spur to its brash ambition. The previous evening he had held a hectic telephone conversation with Kleist who once more was expressing anxiety about the southern flank. Again Kleist had justification for caution. The situation at Stonne was still obscure and there was insufficient evidence to prove that the French no longer had the capacity to mount a decisive counter-stroke. Neither Kleist nor his superiors were to know that French armoured forces were virtually extinct, that only 1½ of these major formations remained intact or that the moral fibre of the French High Command had cracked at realisation of the calamity which had befallen their armies.

German leaders at the tip of the spearhead, where it broke through the final layers of the French linear positions, may not have been so well supplied with statistics and sophisticated politico-military intelligence as their High Command, but they were right in claiming that this was the moment to take risks for they could smell the atmosphere of enemy decay and recognise from instinct and experience the sight of victory. Nothing like this had been seen by Guderian when he rode near the head of the breakthrough at the Marne in 1914, and yet it was a reference to this somewhat dubious historical precedent which he flung at Kleist as Kleist endeavoured to have him stop. Kleist yielded and granted him another twenty-four hours' grace. But Guderian was not to know then (since Kleist was unswervingly loyal to his superior officer), nor does he seem to have known later, that Kleist was simply obeying orders from above – orders, moreover, which neither reflected the current mood of OKH nor OKW.

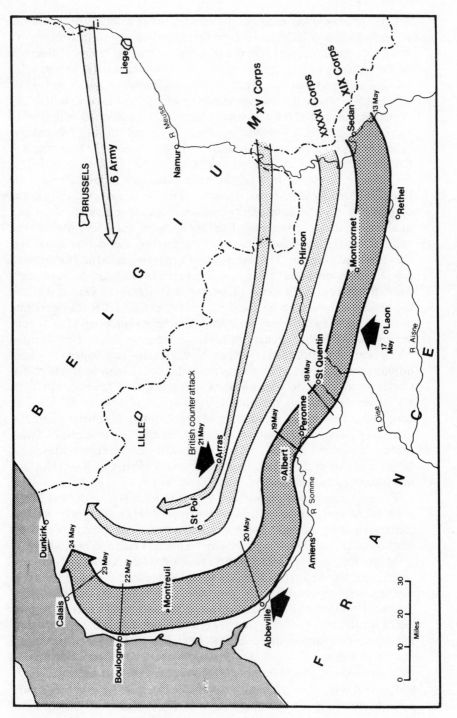

The Drive to the English Channel

On 14th May OKW and OKH had concurred in withdrawing XVI from Army Group B in Belgium so as to reinforce the success of Rundstedt's Army Group A in France. On the 16th Halder was expressing delight at a breakthrough which '. . . is developing on almost classical lines', an opinion which found support at OKW. Rundstedt, however, had begun to fuss on the 15th, when the advance from the Meuse had barely started. His War Diary suggested the necessity of halting on the River Oise for fear of the threat from the south and because the enemy must in no circumstances be allowed a success '. . . on the Aisne or later in the Laon region'. On the 16th these fears overflowed.

Guderian thrust forward on the 16th with only 1st and 2nd Panzer Divisions, leaving 10th Panzer Division and *Grossdeutschland* Regiment to the south of Sedan as insurance against interference from the south and in deference to Kleist's anxiety. The French again repeatedly attacked the hinge at Stonne and caused losses to the arriving German infantry. But they made no progress. The rest of XIX Corps shot ahead and by nightfall was 40 miles distant at Dercy on the Serre at the same moment as a battlegroup from XXXXI Corps arrived at Guise on the Oise and began the process of mopping up the stalled tanks of 2nd DCR. Conveniently overlooking Kleist's twenty-four hour time limit, Guderian blandly sent out radio orders that evening to continue the advance next day, orders which were monitored by Kleist's headquarters and which, at once, brought down a peremptory counter-order along with instructions for Guderian to report to Kleist next morning. At 0700 hours on the 17th Kleist stepped from his aircraft at XIX Corps Headquarters and, without ado, roundly accused Guderian of deliberately disobeying orders. Guderian at once tendered his resignation. Neither could be credited with much common sense at that moment, but both were on edge – Kleist to a far greater extent than Guderian could have known. For Kleist was not much more in favour of a halt than Guderian.

The uncertainty was germinated by Rundstedt. Again his War Diary reflected tremors of doubt, for after it recorded, on the 16th, that the commanders of the motorised formations were convinced they could push on over the Oise '. . . especially Generals Guderian and Kleist', it went on: 'But looking at operations as a whole the risk involved does not seem to be justified. The extended flank between La Fère and Rethel is too sensitive, especially in the Laon area . . . If the spearheads of the attack are temporarily halted it will be possible to effect a certain stiffening of the threatened flank within twenty-four hours'. It is apparent that Kleist did not bother to explain Rundstedt's underlying anxieties to Guderian – their relationship was already too far strained. But Rundstedt was shaken when Guderian's report of resignation arrived. Things had gone too far when a favourite of Hitler did that! He sent him a curt order to remain in his post and await a plenipotentiary – no less than the

Twelfth Army Commander, *Generaloberst* List. List arrived in the afternoon, swiftly declined Guderian's resignation and with the authority of the Army Group Commander told him to begin a 'reconnaissance in force', leaving Corps HQ where it was. In effect this gave Guderian a free hand, one which he made all the freer by laying cable to his tactical headquarters so that his orders could no longer be monitored by superior officers. List confirms these events as well as Guderian's request to be peacemaker on his own behalf with Kleist.

Between resignation and reinstatement Guderian sat down to pour out his troubles in a letter to Gretel. It no longer exists but its purport is made plain by her reply on 27th May, in which she wrote, 'It would be lunacy and tragic if at the crowning moment of your life's work you stood aside . . . Despite all your troubles, do not take steps that will harm you and which you will regret for the rest of your life. Darling, I beg of you from the bottom of my heart not to do this. If you have to act I think you should send a direct report to the Führer: anything else would be, as always, to your disadvantage.' She went on to warn him to have care in what he wrote – 'that important letter of yours was opened by the censor' – and added, 'I almost asked Bodewin [Keitel] yesterday for an explanation but could not make up my mind since I was not sure if it would be in your best interests.'

The vigilance of the Army authorities – it is unlikely that this act of censorship was State-inspired – seems to throw a revealing shaft of light upon their mistrust of Guderian. That the mail of a senior general should be censored (even by a rampant bureaucracy) was, to say the least, unusual, while the despatch of a *Major* to instruct his wife to keep silent about the letter's content demonstrated a distinct official uneasiness at what had passed. But the disagreements that had raised the incident were but a storm in a tea-cup compared with what was brewing between the leaders of OKW, OKH and Army Group A.

That day Hitler became scared at success and drove to see Rundstedt (a ready fellow worrier) to tell him it was more important to maintain a flow of safe successes rather than take a risk by reaching for the Channel. The scope of Guderian's advance once more outreached the Führer's limited notion of mobile operations: ripples of the Führer's worries washed through OKW, sometimes in the form of direct instructions to specific Army divisions, and aroused anger in Halder who, that morning, was perfectly satisfied that there was 'no danger whatsoever'. He assessed the situation with the same, accurate insight as the spearhead commanders, and kept his head in the days to come as Hitler and his entourage soared between euphoria and melancholy, over-confidence and funk.

Brauchitsch, however, endorsed Rundstedt's decision to halt at about the same time as List, on Rundstedt's authority, was letting Guderian loose again, though that evening Halder persuaded Hitler, for the time being, that all was well. The brakes were again released but a precedent had been set. From now on Hitler pestered Rundstedt who had revealed himself as the willowly sort who, unless he lost an otherwise even temper, would bend when Hitler blew.

Almost unnoticed, and certainly unreported to Kleist or registered with much emphasis at HQ XIX Corps, an event, exaggeratingly fixed in the history of armoured warfare, had taken place in the period the German commanders were locked in vituperation at the rear. Moving fast and unco-ordinated along the road from Laon, a battalion of French Char Bs and two battalions of light tanks had hit the left flank of 1st Panzer Division. This was the point of 4th DCR, a partially formed, under-trained formation commanded by de Gaulle, who had taken up the appointment less than a week before. Appreciating, like Guderian, that speed was salvation, he had attacked Guderian's flank in the hope of catching the softer administrative tail of the division. As it was, and quite by chance due to the stand-fast imposed by Kleist, he hit muscle – though not without profit. Light German units were brushed aside and at 1600 hours, when Guderian was talking to List only a few miles distant, the French had broken into Montcornet, threatening the supply columns. But at this moment the French attack, for want of infantry and artillery support and from shortage of fuel, turned back when blunted by a defence which was beginning to stiffen. Now the *Luftwaffe* harried the French tanks and, though destroying only one, chased away the rest down the road they had come. After the war pro-de Gaulle propaganda made much of this attack, but in actuality, apart from within 1st Panzer Division, there was hardly a twitter of alarm on the German side.

Why should there have been? Again the French had displayed lack of determination and already 10th Panzer was on its way to rejoin the spearhead approaching Rethel and poised to hit de Gaulle in flank. Moreover the leading German troops, deep in France, were better sup-plied with fuel and ammunition than the French. German stocks were being built up at maintenance areas in rear, at Hirson for example, their system working all the better as practice made perfect: the French arrangements were falling apart. On the evening of 18th May 1st Panzer Division was approaching Peronne, scarcely disturbed by further isolated outbursts of French resistance and taking an interested look at the first British troops to fall into their hands. At the same moment Halder managed at last to persuade Hitler that the way to the Channel was open with the result that OKH overrode Rundstedt and Kleist was allowed to give Guderian his head. Paradoxically this acted as the signal for Guderian to slow down – though not from choice. The tanks were in need of maintenance, 10th Panzer had been held up at Ham, there was a fuel crisis because of a report that the newly created petrol depot at Hirson had been destroyed by fire, and air reconnaissance discovered a big

French tank force – 4th DCR of course – concentrating to the north of Laon and threatening Guderian's flank and rear. Guderian, in *Panzer Leader*, makes no mention of the fuel crisis or the need to slow down (one fancies it might have made him look slightly ridiculous), and he rather glosses over slow progress while paying his respects to de Gaulle: '. . . a few of his tanks succeeded in penetrating to within a mile of my advanced headquarters in Holnon wood . . . and I passed a few uncomfortable hours'. But he was right when he wrote that: 'The danger from this flank was slight' (the air reports exaggerated 150 tanks into several hundred) and 'assumed that the French, conditioned by the doctrine of positional warfare, would not make a major attack until the Germans stood still'. Guderian had no intention of standing still and 4th DCR's attack (the only one with any hope) was beaten off without making a serious indentation in XIX Corps' flank. The French never again enjoyed a better opportunity for, by the evening of the 19th, XIX Corps' ailments had been cured. It also transpired that the fuel dump at Hirson had not been destroyed after all: the signal reporting it had been corrupt and, in fact, as originally drafted, read that it was ready to make distribution.

Next day, the 20th, XIX Corps made its longest and most dramatic advance in a single day – the most in twenty-four hours by any tank formation in that campaign – 56 miles from the Canal du Nord to the sea at Abbeville. XXXXI Corps, on its right, almost kept pace and thus, that evening, Kleist could boast of having three panzer divisions lined up on a 15-mile frontage from Abbeville to Hesdin with virtually nothing to prevent them turning either south towards Dieppe and Le Havre, or north against Boulogne, Calais and Dunkirk. The Allied armies were not only cut in two, they were in imminent danger of being isolated from their bases.

An officer in 1st Panzer Division remarked that 'We had the feeling such as a fine racehorse may have, of having been held back by its rider, coldly and deliberately, then getting its head free to reach out into a swinging gallop and speed to the winning post as winner'. But racehorses, as Fuller once wrote, 'do not pull up at the winning post' and Guderian never willingly held back a galloping mount. Indeed he had felt the need to drive 2nd Panzer quite hard on the 20th when it came up with the well-worn excuse of a petrol shortage in order to take time for a rest. No doubt Guderian recalled Richthofen's horse-shoe problem in 1914 at the time of the breakthrough in the same region: this time an excuse was to no avail and 2nd Panzer somehow 'found' the fuel to carry it to Abbeville. Halder was certainly taken by surprise and delayed until midday on the 21st before deciding to turn north against Boulogne instead of going south. At the same time Hitler's confidence waned again as he surveyed that exposed southern flank on his map and allowed his imagination to dwell on the threat posed by French armies undisclosed.

There was nothing of offensive value to disclose in the French Order of battle. There had been a change of C-in-C (another German achievement) and there was much talk of a counter-offensive to cut the panzer corridor. But the French and British already knew that this was practically beyond their capacity and the Germans were also able to calculate the same, and quite as accurately, on the basis of air reports, radio intercepts and information from undercover sources and prisoners of war – including several very senior French generals who had been swept into the bag.

Halder plumped for a northward movement, but it was evening before Kleist set off again, directing Guderian into the void of the defenceless Allied rear, against Boulogne and Calais. This day the shape of ominous events emerged. The British attacked southward with tanks at Arras and caused Rommel's 7th Panzer Division heavy losses. His difficulties were cleared up by nightfall since weight was lacking behind the British attack: but the repercussions were considerable. Though Halder was not in the least disturbed – he welcomed, as did Guderian, any abortive Allied attack which further helped to destroy their forces against a resilient and economic German defence – Kleist took the orthodox step of withdrawing a division – 10th Panzer – into reserve, thus weakening Guderian still further since elements of the Corps had also to be left behind at Abbeville and a few other key localities guarding the River Somme crossings. Reinhardt, too, felt bound to redeploy a division eastward as a precaution against the Arras threat. Inevitably Rundstedt went on fretting and needless to say Hitler fidgeted: neither could bring himself to believe in total victory, and the pliable Brauchitsch lacked enough strength of will to reassure or silence them. In the upper echelons only Halder demonstrated a real affinity with Guderian and his colleagues.

Meanwhile the Allied armies in the north had been put on half-rations and urgent measures were being taken to evade complete encirclement. Small British groups were being sent from England to garrison Boulogne and Calais and bar the way to Dunkirk from whence an evacuation by sea was in prospect. But it would be the morning of the 22nd before Boulogne received its main garrison and so it follows that, if Guderian or Reinhardt had been sent there immediately on the 21st at the same rate as they had travelled on the 20th, they would have found the port virtually undefended. Likewise they could have had Calais for the asking since that port's garrison was not properly in position until the 22nd. As it was Guderian made no movement on the 21st because, as mentioned above, neither OKH nor OKW had previously made up their minds: he was thus a victim of his own speed. Nevertheless there was still time enough to achieve all the objectives at low cost. He moved off northward at 0800 hours on the 22nd, his original intention being to send 10th Panzer to Dunkirk, 1st to Calais and 2nd to Boulogne. This plan had to be abandoned when 10th Panzer was taken from him by Kleist and so only 2nd Panzer was immediately available to lead the advance to Boulogne – and this Guderian despatched without awaiting Kleist's permission, as the Corps' diary tells. Strong resistance from French units was met on the way and, on the heights above the port, British troops, supported by heavy anti-aircraft guns used in the same way as the comparable German 88mm guns, held firm. Now the Germans had a fight on their hands of a kind they had only occasionally met from first-line French units.

It took some thirty-six hours to clear Boulogne. In the meantime 10th Panzer Division was once more released to him and he was told to invest Calais on the 23rd. Though British troops were known to be arriving, Guderian gave no special priority to taking the port which clearly would fall in due course. His aim, and that of Kleist, was to place a solid barrier between the coast and the Allied armies to the east, thus forcing them to fight their way to safety through an ever-thickening German ring. As his contribution to forging the ring, Guderian sent 1st Panzer Division in the direction of Gravelines and Dunkirk – above all Dunkirk – on the 23rd. XIX Corps' War Diary leaves no doubt about it.

Play is made in the British Official History of the campaign that Guderian gave these orders in ignorance of the difficult country into which he was throwing his troops. This overlooks the fact that Guderian knew the area too well from the First World War (and had flown over it) to be in ignorance of the risks to tanks in this terrain. On 23rd May the difficulties of ground were well outweighed by preponderance of opportunity and strength. At this critical point Kleist's Group (despite 10 per cent losses since 10th May) outnumbered its opponents and easily outclassed them. So obviously complete was German dominance that Guderian was saying, through the Corps' War Diary, that it was 'opportune and possible to carry out its three tasks [Aa Canal, Calais and Boulogne] quickly and decisively' – a revealing abandonment, in terms of confidence, of his normal insistence upon concentrated effort. By the morning of the 24th Boulogne had fallen, the Aa Canal had been crossed by 1st Panzer Division (which had brushed aside British tanks when they made a foray from Calais), and the panzer divisions of Reinhardt and Hoth, reinforced by additional motorised infantry divisions, were roaring up to join them. This was a formidable and versatile force. Moreover the southern flank was being gradually secured by infantry divisions marching as fast as they could towards Abbeville, and the defences of Boulogne were being worked on by Allied prisoners – a breach of the rules of war.

At this moment, with Dunkirk but 15 miles distant and ripe for the taking next day (in British appreciations this was rated a probability), came the celebrated halt order. Without entering into a detailed discussion as to the reasons for the order and the attendant sequence of events, it is sufficient to note that it originally emanated from Rundstedt on the evening of the 23rd. Once more he had lost his nerve and was striving to hold back the advance in order to close up his forces before they became involved in heavy fighting against a desperate foe – a view with which Kluge, the commander of the marching infantry of Fourth Army, concurred. It was purely coincidental that, on the same day, Göring had suggested to Hitler that the *Luftwaffe* be given the honour of finishing the job at Dunkirk which the Army had nearly completed. Hitler, still nursing the anxieties which had beset him since the 15th, was delighted to find a new solution, particularly since it would enable a truly Nazi orientated organisation to seize a larger slice of glory. On the morning of the 24th he once more visited Rundstedt, learnt of the standstill order and happily confirmed it. Guderian says: 'We were utterly speechless. But since we were not informed of the reasons for this order it was difficult to argue against it'. Soon he was to learn that it was a Führer order. Yet another precedent had been set for the future: Hitler had intervened decisively in the conduct of a battle and overriden the Chief of Staff in an operational matter.

There were rumblings. Halder was disgusted, made a strong protest and was overruled. Two SS infantry formations, which arrived to take over from 1st Panzer on the Aa Canal, pushed forward on the 26th to improve their positions and were spurred on by Guderian. Sepp Dietrich, the commander of SS *Leibstandarte* Division, had Hitler's ear. That afternoon, quite unexpectedly or perhaps because the true Nazi SS was now involved, Hitler relaxed his embargo. But now the British and French had come back in strength, the original German momentum had been lost and the going was hard. Slow progress was made on the 27th and 28th, with Guderian up at the front in observation. Fearful that Germany's best troops would be wasted, he returned to his headquarters and sent advice to Kleist in a report which he does not mention in *Panzer Leader* (probably because, after the war, he had no access to the Corps Diary):

(1) After the Belgian capitulation [which had taken place on the 27th] continuation of operations here is not desirable as it is costing unnecessary sacrifices. The panzer divisions have only 50 per cent of their armoured strength left and their equipment is in urgent need of repair if the corps is to be ready again in a short time for other operations.
(2) A tank attack is pointless in the marshy country which has been completely soaked by rain. The troops are in possession of the high ground south of Dunkirk; they hold the important Cassel-Dunkirk road; and they have favourable artillery positions . . . from which they can fire on Dunkirk.
Furthermore 18th Army [part of Bock's Army Group B] is approaching [Kleist] Group from the east. The infantry forces of this army are more suitable than tanks for fighting in this kind of country, and the

task of closing the gap on the coast can therefore be left to them.

This was the view which had been put forward by Hitler and OKW on the 24th when the way was clear. This time Kleist was bound to agree and move XIX Corps into reserve to prepare for its next task which was to be a renewal of the offensive in a southerly direction.

The British Official History implies that if Guderian had known about the state of the ground at Dunkirk on 23rd May he would not have been so keen to enter that area with his tanks, and it has sometimes been suggested that Guderian was not as yet fully aware of the inhibiting effect of difficult ground on tank forces. Neither accusation warrants exhaustive examination. The pages of *Achtung! Panzer!* fully reject the latter suggestion and it is irrelevant to compare the nature of the consolidated defences of Dunkirk on 28th May with those that barely existed on the 23rd. Though Guderian is made to appear in agreement with Hitler this was far from the case.

In the meantime the *Luftwaffe* tried to do by bombardment what the Army had wanted to achieve by occupation. Guderian's men were thus privileged to be spectators of the first major attempt by air power to win a land battle in absolute terms on its own – the first of many signal failures to come.

There could no longer be any doubt that panzer divisions had won their spurs. Not even their most hardy opponents within the German military hierarchy could deny them as a dominant weapon. Those who still harboured sectional reservations wisely maintained silence as, on 28th May, Hitler conferred the command of a Panzer Group upon Guderian. It consisted of XXXIX and XXXXI Corps, each of two panzer divisions and a motorised infantry division, with the addition of certain supporting formations – a composition which made Panzer Group Guderian (prominently identified by a large letter G upon its vehicles) into an army, except in name. This clear distinction was retained to keep the eager tank men in their place. Panzer Groups were denied full army status and kept under command of an army – in Guderian's case he was put under List's Twelfth Army – so that the traditional authority of the old system should not be weakened and denigrated.

Victory was assured for the Germans. Not only could they assess the Allied formations and equipment which had been destroyed by counting the carcasses on the battlefield and the prisoners in their hands, but through wireless intercept they built up a comprehensive picture of the improvised defences opposing them from the Maginot Line to Abbeville. They knew the defences lacked both depth and sufficient mobile armoured troops. Because they were aware of these things their task appeared relatively easy; at last there was harmony in their construction of plans for the southward directed offensive. Guderian had made his peace with Busch and Kleist, and both had been generously sincere (to his delight) in their praise of his achievement. All was peace with Rundstedt under whom Twelfth Army and Panzer Group Guderian now came. Enemy weak spots could be recognised. In a mood of relaxation – almost of over-confidence – liberties could be taken. The offensive was to begin when individual Army Groups had recovered from the exertions of the past weeks and had completed their redeployment. Army Group B, on the right close by the sea, started forward on 5th June whereas Army Group A was held back until the 9th. Moreover the infantry were to be given an opportunity to re-assert their influence, with permission to lead the offensive and punch holes for the panzer divisions.

Penalties had to be paid. The French and a handful of British divisions fought hard and Kleist's Group took a mauling south of Amiens on the 6th and 7th. It was Hoth's Corps on the extreme right, led with characteristic dash by Rommel's 7th Panzer Division, which made the first clear breakout and began a non-stop drive for Rouen, Le Havre and Cherbourg. But things did not go well on the 9th, the date on which Guderian was intended to exploit an initial infantry crossing of the Aisne and Aisne Canal between Chateau Porcien and Attigny. At dawn the infantry made heavy weather of the crossing and established only one small bridgehead at Chateau Porcien: elsewhere they were repelled. It was nightfall before the leading tanks of 1st Panzer Division could begin to enter the bridgehead. Throughout the day Guderian had motored tirelessly from one place to another, seeking information about infantry progress and trying to co-ordinate his future operations with them. In the course of it he trod on a few corns and managed to have a sharp (victorious) tussle with List who falsely assumed that inactivity among the tank crews designated for the assault was a sign of Guderian's disobedience. This was symbolic. Though List was quick to realise his error, many senior commanders held implacable convictions that Guderian would sabotage their plans to prove panzer superiority over infantry: they were ever ready to find examples of his insubordination for which he had a well-founded reputation by this time.

It made no difference that Guderian had become the equivalent of an army commander. Unlike Kleist in the first days of May, he was frequently at the front, urging on everybody from regimental to corps commanders and encouraging the fighting men themselves. This could so easily have been mistaken by his subordinates as interference in their province. It rarely was, partly because they now needed little urging, largely because they realised that Guderian's main purpose was to dovetail their activities at the utmost speed with flanking formations by using his superior communication system to give them the maximum assistance by short-circuiting the time-honoured, statutory links of command.

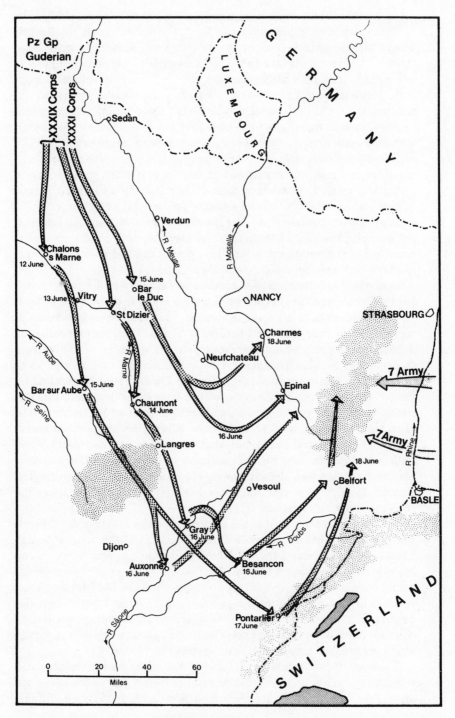

The Drive to Switzerland

Once more the superiority of mobile armour was demonstrated in the battles which developed amid the French defences south of Rethel. Where infantry attacked unsupported they were frequently held: once tanks were injected into the battle, operations got fluid. Where time was lost by the Germans and French tank counterstrokes developed – even those involving just a few of their Char Bs – there came a pause in the advance while the tank battle was resolved. Overcoming the miserable hesitation which had stigmatised their performance at Sedan, the French tank crews this time countered each German penetration promptly. The outcome was finally settled by superiority of German numbers and techniques rather than superiority of German tanks. On the spot, Guderian personally carried out trials against a Char B using a captured French 47mm anti-tank gun (which he knew to be superior to the German 37) and found that, frontally, the Char B was invulnerable. Shots bounced off the French armour and the wrecks of German tanks and guns in the countryside at Juniville confirmed his opinion that German armour was too thin and their guns not powerful enough.

Soon the breakthrough was made and instantly mobile operations began. Try though they might, by throwing in the last remnants of their mobile divisions to restrain the avalanche, the French were doomed – as they had been since the initial reverse at Sedan. Their morale collapsed once more after only a temporary resurgence. There is no need to retrace in detail the account of Panzer Group Guderian's race to the Swiss frontier. Random impressions are sufficient. On 11th June he watched 1st Panzer Division take Béthenville with a copy-book tank and infantry attack supported by artillery fire, and recalled to mind September 1914 when, in the depths of defeat after the Marne, he had arrived there, bereft of his command and all but what he stood in, and had learnt of the birth of his first son. Now he was the victor, surrounded by his triumphant host, and the son was already among the wounded. A letter to Gretel, written on 15th June (the day after Paris fell) neatly summarises the evolving situation as he saw it:

'I wrote to you recently that the front would enter a state of movement. The day after Chalons, Vitry le Francois and St Dizier fell; yesterday Chaumont and to-day Langres. I believe we have broken through and hope to reach Besançon to-day. That would be a great success which would have a retrogressive effect upon the whole of the Maginot Line, and would also have political repercussions. I am very happy that this performance should be achieved despite enormous difficulties due to constant alterations of directions. The battle against one's own superiors sometimes makes more work than against the French.

'The country is in a catastrophic condition. As a result of the enforced evacuation there is an indescribable refugee misery and all the cattle are dying. Everywhere places are plundered by refugees and French soldiers.

Up till now we have come across only scanty civilian populations. The Middle Ages were humane compared with the present.'

This letter, composed in the heat of combat, is unusual from the pen of a combat general in its expression of compassion. By conditioning and circumstances the breed can rarely afford to reflect too deeply upon suffering when actually engaged in battle. Cynics may well categorise these as crocodile's tears from a typical product of the Prussian military machine. This was not in the nature of Guderian: there is a profound sincerity about his letters, in the reflective portions of his book and in his conversations, which reject such aspersions. Of course he prided himself on his accomplishments in manipulating his forces to destructive effect, but that is the clinical pride of the technician. This man was devoid of racial hatred, and registered his distaste for destruction and the by-products of war.

The same letter also warrants comment by its reference to 'alterations of direction'. Vacillating orders originated from the top – from Hitler – though only the very highest in command were aware of it at the time. Halder remained consistent in the conventional requirement that '. . . the object of our operations must be the destruction of the remaining enemy forces'. Hitler, on the other hand, bent Brauchitsch to his will on 6th June with the demand '. . . first . . . to secure the Lorraine iron ore basin so as to deprive France of her armaments industry' – a truly incredible desire in the light of quite obvious indications that France was prostrate and in no position to prevent Germany taking anything she wanted almost at once. Furthermore he ignored the General Staff's logical argument that, until an enemy's forces were destroyed, territorial occupation was worthless. The confrontation was made meaningless in the present context because, within a matter of days, France sued for an armistice. In the longer term, of course, a fundamental principle had been established: in future Hitler would interfere as of routine in detailed Army planning and play one General Staff Officer against another in the realms of strategy and tactics. The Chief of the General Staff was once again reduced in power and influence while the C-in-C became a mere cipher – with vital repercussions for Guderian at a later date.

To Guderian the almost daily switching from essential to prestige objectives was a source of annoyance rather than concern. One day he would be told to divert and take Verdun, the next St Mihiel, with their evocative memories of the past, instead of shaping a steady course towards targets which would lead to destruction of the enemy's forces. Naturally, as enemy resistance vanished, it became easy to overcome these difficulties. Guderian merely kept XXXIX Corps moving in the strategically desirable direction and used XXXXI Corps to mop up extraneous objectives. A flexible response is easier to apply when there is a superfluity of resources. On the 17th (his 52nd birthday) XXXIX Corps reached Pontarlier on the Swiss frontier, but this was a symbolic incidental compared with the important 90-degree turn in a north-easterly direction made by that corps' two panzer divisions the previous day. Using both his corps, Guderian delivered a broad-fronted drive into Alsace to complete the greatest encirclement of the campaign. In conjunction with 7th Army, moving in from the east, over 400,000 French troops, including the garrisons of the Maginot Line, were gathered in. Their contribution to the defence of their land had been worthless.

The manoeuvre, a truly remarkable feat in terms of the military art, goes practically unnoticed by history – perhaps because Guderian and Nehring made complexities of that sort seem so simple, probably because larger events were impending. But when Patton or Montgomery executed similar changes of direction in the years to come, their prowess was acclaimed to the roof-tops. It was to another that tribute should have been paid for designing the methods which made their triumphs possible.

An armistice was signed at Réthondes on 22nd June. Hitler and Germany basked in fame. So, too, did Guderian, for he suddenly found himself renowned throughout the land, a hero whom the propagandists praised for his contribution to the victory. Group Guderian was credited with 250,000 prisoners in 13 days' activity. Josef Goebbels and his agents uplifted Guderian and had him broadcast to the nation. He told Gretel, 'How lovely that you heard my speech. I really enjoyed making it'. There was an enormous fan-mail and gigantic correspondence. 'The other day a former *Gefreiter* [lance corporal] from the First World War sent me a harmonica from his factory. It's fantastic how kind some people are'. As soon as the war was over he told his propaganda officer, Paul Dierichs, to find films of the campaign and show them to the troops. Later this material would be made into a documentary extolling Guderian's command and the *Panzerwaffe*: never once did he forget to publicise his organisation (and thus, be it said, himself) as counter to those who still resented the triumph. But as Dierichs points out, 'Though he realised the meaning of his success, it did not go to his head'.

There were more serious matters to contemplate, among them a genuine hope that the fighting was over in the belief that Britain would give up. That hope would soon die: the British fought on, but in any case neither Guderian nor anybody else on the German side were aware that Hitler was formulating schemes which outlawed peace.

Yet Guderian himself displayed the same conquering restlessness as his Führer when, on 27th June, he shared his views with General Ritter von Epp, who called in during a visit to the front. He explained to Gretel that they discussed 'Colonial questions'. They did indeed, for Epp was an expert on the subject: but the discussion also ranged over the course to take if Britain went on fighting, and the manner of carrying the battle to the remaining enemy. It is reflected on pages 136 and 137 of *Panzer*

Leader and is worth study as an indication of Guderian's contemporary attitude, as well as a demonstration of his accurate reading of the strategic situation and the shifting balance of power – at a time when the vanquished French were turning in anger upon the British and the Italians had already entered the war on Germany's side. He claimed, after the war, that 'in view of the insufficiency of our preparations in the air and on the sea, which were far below what would be needed to invade [England], other means would have to be found of so damaging our enemy that he would accept a negotiated peace'.

He went on: 'It seemed to me, then, that we could ensure peace in the near future by, first of all, advancing at once to the mouth of the Rhône: then, having captured the French Mediterranean bases in conjunction with the Italians, by landing in Africa, while the *Luftwaffe*'s first-class parachute troops seized Malta. Should the French be willing to participate in these operations, so much the better. Should they refuse, then the war must be carried on by the Italians and ourselves on our own, and carried on at once. The weakness of the British in Egypt at that time was known to us. The Italians still had strong forces in Abyssinia. The defences of Malta against air attack were inadequate. Everything seemed to me to be in favour of further operations along those lines, and I could see no disadvantages. The presence of four to six panzer divisions in North Africa would have given us such overwhelming superiority that any British reinforcements would inevitably have arrived too late.'

Epp, of course, was a dyed-in-the-wool Nazi, one of the original *Freikorps*' fighters who had won a reputation as the ruthless exterminator of German Communists and who had helped finance the Nazi Party at the outset. As a member of the *Reichstag* and Chief of the Nazi Party's Department for Colonial Policy, Epp had the Führer's ear, even though he was among those who doubted the wisdom of Germany's involvement in a major war. Guderian claims that Epp put his scheme to Hitler but that Hitler was not interested in exploring the possibilities further. This is not strictly correct. Hitler, inspired not a little by Jodl, explored a multitude of projects after the fall of France, among them collaboration with the Italians in an invasion of Egypt that was firmly rebuffed by Mussolini who wanted to snatch a little glory for himself in his own sphere of influence. He also made overtures to Spain in connection with a drive to Gibraltar and, through the Armistice Commission, to spread his political influence into French North Africa. Admiral Raeder, too, put a strong naval case, linked with the U-boat offensive, for seizing strategic points in Africa, including the West Coast. There are few now (and maybe fewer then who were in the know) who would dispute the soundness of that maritime strategy or its veritable certainty of success.

Hitler, however, was a land-animal who recognised the allurements of the sea but left maritime adventures to sailors, preferring to send his Army

inland, exclusively in its natural environment engaged upon operations
which Hitler felt he understood best. Unknown to anybody else, Hitler
had never forgotten the project he always had in mind and fixed his
predatory gaze upon Soviet Russia.

By 22nd July both Brauchitsch and Halder were aware of their Supreme Commander's intentions and had formulated an outline plan of
campaign. There would be nothing to spare for other projects, worthy
though they might seem. Instead the spectre of the two-front war, which
Guderian and every sane German feared above all, was being resurrected.

8 The Fate of a Hero

At dawn on 22nd June 1941 Heinz Guderian, a darling of the propagandists and commander of the strongest among four German Panzer Groups, watched his corps and divisions roll into action against the Russians. In close attendance an official war artist, stiffly garbed in uniform and steel helmet, tried on sketch block to catch the mood of confidence radiating from one of Goebbel's stars. But of those who marched eastward on the day that 'the world held its breath', how many felt assured by Hitler's promise of victory within eight weeks, and how many were free from a sense of doom?

Guderian was far from at ease though, of habit, he had given everything by the way of duty to make the best of a bad job. The year of rapture that followed the triumph in France had also been one of bewilderment. On the one hand he had frankly revelled in the pleasures of adulation, but on the other recoiled with disgust as the fruits of victory were wasted. On 19th July 1940 he had been promoted *Generaloberst*, sharing the same promotion list with twelve senior generals who were raised to *Generalfeldmarschall* – among them Brauchitsch, Keitel, Rundstedt, Bock, Reichenau, List and Kluge. But on that occasion the notable exclusion from advancement (and subject for puzzled surprise) was Halder who, paradoxically, had come to understand the orthodox role of the *Panzertruppe* almost as well as Guderian. He, to his misfortune, had fallen foul of Hitler. The war for the Army seemed to stand still as the Navy and Air Force, with totally inadequate resources, tried to conquer Britain in the aftermath of Hitler's failure to make peace. Guderian reverted to the old routine of training panzer divisions for a campaign that was, as yet, unrevealed; endeavouring to obtain for them more and improved equipment. The necessity to do so was quite obvious. A world in arms was industriously copying Guderian's methods and Germany's survival would depend upon keeping a jump or two ahead in the armaments race. Hitler – momentarily – was under the spell of the tank – his enthusiasm for technical innovations fluctuating as wildly as it did in politics and strategy. With a campaign against Russia firmly in prospect, he asked for tank production to be increased from the existing level of about 125 to something between 800 and 1,000 per month, his aim being the doubling of the number of panzer divisions. Dr Todt, the Minister for Armaments and War Production, explained that a programme of such magnitude could not be mounted overnight and that, in any case, it would cost 2 billion Marks, require an additional 100,000 workmen and technicians and, inevitably, result in the cancellation or reduction of other projects such as U-boat and aircraft construction. It was ironic that the industrial resources of the conquered nations would provide only limited assistance and that none of thousands of captured armoured vehicles were compatible with German methods of tank warfare. Submissively Hitler ordered a doubling of panzer divisions by halving their tank content (to a strength which varied between 150 and 210) – or, put another way, doubling the infantry component. Guderian complains that his opinions were not sought in these matters, but it would have been surprising had this been so. His views were well known and, in principle, accepted. They had been underlined by the reports he and the other commanders had submitted after the French campaign. Moreover the scheme to invade Russia was a closely guarded secret known only to a few in the autumn.

Practically unanimously the panzer leaders rejected the light tanks – Pz I and II – which had failed in action except when employed on subsidiary tasks. These machines would be phased out. Furthermore they realised that the Pz IIIs and IVs were in need of up-gunning and up-armouring to compete with the improved enemy tanks that must soon appear. The race between weapons and protection was an historical inevitability from which tanks could not escape. But entry into that race would automatically introduce production delays at the very moment when the call for increased numbers was loud and when intelligence reports were silent about those enemy, particularly Russian, tanks which were better than lightly armed and armoured. OKW and the Ordnance Office had finally compromised – as is usually essential in arriving at a weapon's specifications – by increasing the armament of the Pz III with a short L 42 50mm gun of much lower velocity and accuracy than the long L 60 being introduced on field mountings for the infantry. As for the infantry within the panzer divisions, they were given a few additional armoured half-tracks though the actual proportion of units thus mounted was less than one in three as in 1940. The rest continued to travel in awkward, unarmoured, wheeled vehicle of indifferent cross-country performance and zero combat effectiveness.

Nevertheless the combat power of the panzer divisions in 1941 was higher than it had been in 1940, partly as the result of replacing the light tanks with mediums but principally due to increased confidence and experience among the large number of officers and men who, from practice, had gained priceless insight into the potential and techniques of armoured, mobile warfare. In terms of prowess the Germans, with a galaxy of talent, had taken what amounted to a three years' lead over their future enemies.

In November 1940 Guderian heard about the plan to invade Russia – and was flabbergasted.* By his own authoritative estimate, disclosed in *Achtung! Panzer!*, Russia possessed 10,000 tanks in 1937. Now it was reliably reported that she had 17,000. But it was the inherent dread, shared with every educated German officer and many others besides, of the fatal consequences of entering into a war on two fronts (such as had wrecked Germany in the previous conflict) which caused his 'disappointment and disgust'. Though OKW might infer that nothing of the sort would occur, since Russia ought to be eliminated before Britain could make a renewed contribution to the war, the lessons of history were too deeply imprinted on German minds to be erased by a glib excuse. Morbidly the General Staff looked to the precedents by studying Napoleon's 1812 campaign. A translation of Caulaincourt's *Memoirs* had appeared in the bookshops in 1937 and, overnight in 1941, became required and gloomy reading by those involved in planning an advance upon Moscow. Guderian had bought his copy before the war!

In protest Guderian did more than some. He sent his Chief of Staff to complain to OKH, but OKH did not want to hear. Brauchitsch had long since given up effective resistance to Hitler and OKW (preferring personal tranquillity at a time of war), while Halder, realising he would lack support from his C-in-C and feeling that, perhaps, the project was feasible, absorbed himself with means to hasten a military conclusion. But this campaign was not to be the sole project of the year. Digressions supervened. Two panzer divisions had to be sent to Libya in February 1941 to bolster the failing Italians who had been thrashed by a small British armoured force. The invasion of Yugoslavia and Greece had, rather unwillingly, to be undertaken in April to strengthen a southern flank which had become vulnerable due to Italy's abortive attempt to conquer Greece. These major diversions, in addition to commitments in a multitude of minor schemes, sapped the strength of the forces destined for the Russian adventure and made total concentration on the greatest military operation in history impossible. War on two, if not three, fronts was already assured.

Filled with trepidation, Guderian applied himself to a military requirement that characteristically fluctuated as it developed in response to diverse opinions amid long debates and war games. Three Army Groups – North, Centre and South – were to drive respectively towards Leningrad, Moscow and into the Ukraine, but, as in France, disagreements masked the campaign's objects as well as the military objectives. From a nebulous debate appeared a blurred aim, partially directed against territorial and economic targets, partially with the purpose of destroying

*Suggestions to the contrary from some sources are not substantiated by Guderian's private papers, particularly letters to his wife.

Russian forces, although, in fact, the divergent objectives were virtually synonymous with one policy. Moves in the direction of Leningrad, Moscow or Kiev were assured of drawing the Russian forces into battle. It was at the juncture between political and military requirements that confusion arose. Along with an ingrained conviction concerning the indispensability of destroying the opposing army, Guderian was convinced of the historic psychological necessity to seize a political objective. To him the capture of Moscow was an end in itself – a belief he was to hold until the end of the war. But what he and so few of his contemporaries recognised was the need to win a truly psychological political victory in a country whose size precluded total occupation. On the evidence of Wilfried Strik-Strikfeld, who was to liaise with dissident Soviet elements whose desire it was to bring down the Stalin regime and who conversed with Guderian in 1945, Guderian had not the remotest conception, until after the war, that the capture of Moscow need not have been conclusive but that an honest declaration of collaboration with anti-Stalinist activists might have produced the desired result.

Russia was to be subjugated by brute force, her population cowed by the Nazi elements operating under the auspices of Himmler's SS. The armies would be followed by the *Einsatzgruppen* whose job, directed by Alfred Rosenberg, was extermination, but whose effect would be the alienation of a potential ally. For there waited in Russia a host of potential friends who longed for benevolent liberation.

Panzer Group 2's share of the spearhead forces, reinforced by an infantry corps plus two infantry divisions in the initial assault, was:

XXIV Panzer Corps, comprising a cavalry division, two panzer and one motorised infantry divisions.

XLVII Panzer Corps, two panzer and one motorised infantry divisions.

XLVI Panzer Corps, consisting of a single panzer division plus the motorised SS infantry division *Das Reich* and Infantry Regiment *Grossdeutschland*.

At a distance to his northern flank was to move Hoth's Panzer Group 3 with its two panzer corps. These two groups were to lead Bock's Army Group Centre whose mission, as finally stated by Bock, was to penetrate the Russian frontier-line concentrations between the Pripet Marshes and points north of Suwalki, to wipe out the enemy wherever he was encountered and to undertake a 400-mile thrust in the general direction of Smolensk, regardless of developments in neighbouring sectors. The instruction was necessarily somewhat vague because Hitler and OKH felt that Minsk, 200 miles distant, should be the first objective, while Bock, with the complete approval of Guderian and Hoth, favoured Smolensk. As a result Bock injected an element of subterfuge from the outset with the consequence that neither Guderian nor Hoth were fully aware of their

Leutnant Heinz Guderian—1908

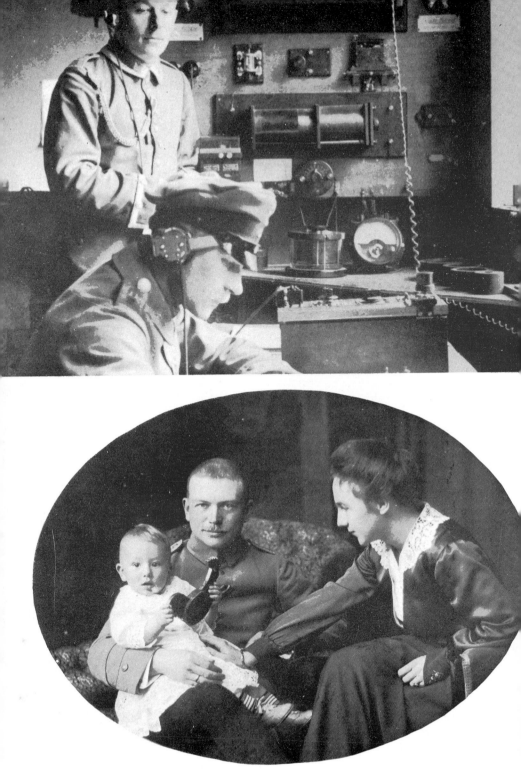

Above A wireless station of the German Army, 1914, of the type commanded by Guderian

Below Guderian in 1915 with Gretel and Heinz-Günther

Above Driving the Swedish derivation of the German LK II tank in 1928

Below The Inspectorate of Motorised Troops, 1932. Front row, left to right:
Nehring, Lutz, Guderian

Above The demonstration at Kummersdorf, 1934: on Hitler's right hand, Hermann
Göring, on his left, Guderian

Below The demonstration at Kummersdorf, 1934: Blomberg, Hitler, Göring, Guderian

Above The parade of exoneration for von Fritsch in August 1938. Guderian greets his old chief

Below The Polish Corridor, 5th September 1939. Guderian shakes Hitler's hand while Himmler polishes his spectacles

Above A German Pz IV tank in action in Poland

Below The Command Group in operation: orders on the march

The Command Group in operation: Guderian reads an incoming message

During the drive to the Swiss frontier: Guderian receives orders from the C-in-C, von Brauchitsch; Nehring watches (right)

Above Action in France

Below Products of the *Panzertruppe*

Right Franz Halder

Below With von Rundstedt after the French campaign

Action in Russia: after a journey to the front

Above Action in Russia: Guderian emerges from a ditch after Russian bombs
have exploded

Below The shock at Tolochino: first sight of the T 34s

'Anger gives you a thirst!'

Above With Panzer Regiment 35, 9th August 1941. The officers' expressions tell their own story of confidence in their leader

Below Kluger Hans and Schneller Heinz

Above Tiger

Below Panther

Above The Chief of the General Staff with Hitler Youth in 1944

Below Guderian in panzer uniform discusses operations with Wenck, autumn 1944

final objective. At the heart of the trouble was misunderstanding of the role and power of fast-moving units apropos slower horse and foot divisions, a fundamental split between those, like Halder, who still felt, regardless of France in 1940, mechanised forces should not get too far ahead of the marching masses. At the root of indecision was the irresolution of the C-in-C, von Brauchitsch.

Additional grit was thrown into the machine by a re-emergence of the old tactical chestnut that infantry formations should initiate the offensive across the River Bug near Brest Litovsk, leaving Guderian's Panzer Group 2 to exploit their bridgehead. The commander of the adjacent Fourth Army was Kluge, with whom, in the same vicinity, Guderian had had a slight disagreement over the dispersion of his corps in September 1939. Once more Guderian stood by his principles. Immediate and lasting success, he claimed, would depend upon the application of maximum surprise, shock, penetration and speed from the outset. This the infantry divisions could not guarantee whereas the panzer divisions could – a lesson that had been learnt on the Aisne in June 1940. Guderian gained his point though at the same time, and with common sense, he recognised the need for an infantry corps to reduce the fortress and vital communication centre of Brest Litovsk. For this purpose he was temporarily given command over XII Corps. Once more his willingness to give as well as take in a debate produced a genuine integration of ideas for, at the same time, Panzer Group 2 was attached to Kluge's Fourth Army in the initial stages, since they were operating in his sector. In the months to come Guderian's Group was to enter and leave Kluge's command on various occasions, though mostly he was to remain indirectly or directly under Bock at Army Group. Hence the personal relationship between these three men became crucial in the development of the campaign and of Guderian's fortunes – subject to the brooding influence of Halder in the interminable arguments with Brauchitsch and Hitler.

Throughout the Army Bock was rated as 'difficult' with his superiors and hard to serve as a subordinate, though in the latter respect Guderian had few problems. Together they produced outstanding results because they shared a routine General Staff approach to strategy while Bock, as the rules demanded, left Guderian to apply his own tactics. Frequently in his letters Guderian was to extol good relations with Army Group. And yet it tells us something about Guderian when he states a preference for Rundstedt despite that officer's apparent weaknesses as a commander. This generosity to Rundstedt can be explained by Guderian's natural response to men of warmth even when it cloaked obvious imperfections. Rundstedt was warm: Bock was chilly. Another cause of Guderian's reservations about Bock may have been the events of 1938, for Bock was among those who supported Brauchitsch in allowing Fritsch only a luke-warm exoneration: Guderian's loyalty to Fritsch never wavered.

131

But what Guderian's behaviour would have been had he known, in 1941, that Bock's headquarters had become the centre of a conspiracy against Hitler (of which Bock himself was aware) neither history nor Guderian records. Almost certainly Guderian was unaware of it, and had it been otherwise might well have taken action against the plotters, for his faith in Hitler was still unshaken. Bock's was not, but Wheeler-Bennett defines him as insignificant of character, a man who would not be drawn into the conspiracy despite his contempt for Hitler. Yet Bock was among those who resolutely refused to transmit the infamous Hitler order which encouraged the Army to kill Commissars and thus he saved Guderian the embarrassment of seeing it. Nevertheless Guderian, in his turn, declined to repeat another dangerous instruction absolving soldiers who committed excesses against the Russian population. In writing 'Both I and my corps commanders were immediately convinced that discipline must suffer if the order were published' he gave the military (as opposed to moral) reason that all German generals offered in declining such demands. But in *Panzer Leader* he wrote: '. . . German soldiers must accept their international obligations and must behave according to the dictates of Christian conscience'.

Generalfeldmarschall von Kluge was quite different from Bock in as much as he was even more energetic but also, according to Wheeler-Bennett, deceitful and not above taking bribes. On his sixtieth birthday, in 1942, while still on the active list, he received a letter of good wishes from Hitler enclosing a cheque for a substantial sum and a permit to spend still more upon his estate. Let it be added that, in due course, Guderian too would receive a gift of land from the Führer, though after his service seemed to be over, and that Rommel and List refused rewards. Whether or not these were bribes is another matter. If so a great many past military commanders of all nationalities should have suffered from uneasy consciences when their grateful nations bestowed awards upon them. But the unhappy relationship between Guderian and Kluge had nothing to do with bribery or politics, though each, whilst at first compliant to Hitler, was in due course to practise resistance in his own way. Their acrimonious disputes were personal and professional, commonplace among generals who seem to have a weakness that way. Kluge, the gunner, regarded Guderian, the panzer man, as a menace to orthodoxy who, in the interests of discipline, needed to be suppressed. Guderian felt ill-at-ease in Kluge's presence because of what he viewed as the *Feldmarschall*'s icy conceit and intolerance: pictures taken of Guderian shortly after meetings with Kluge show visible signs of strain upon his face. In Kluge (known throughout the Army as *Kluger Hans* – a play on words which, in modern parlance, can be translated as 'Tricky Dickie'), Guderian recognised a threat to the military principles which he upheld as the keys to victory when the prospects of ultimate victory were fading.

Guderian's strong dislike and burgeoning mistrust of Kluge, which turned to outright hatred along with accusations of incompetence against a soldier who was far from being that, simply represented a clash between two ways of thinking – between a daring commander who took undiluted, if calculated, chances and a prudent general who sought security of his personal well-being besides the safety of his army in battle, preferring to spread rather than concentrate the risks. But while, undeniably, the antipathy between *Der Schnelle Heinz* (or *Heinz Brausewetter* – 'Hothead' – as Guderian was also sometimes known) and *Der Kluge Hans* disturbed the smooth implementation of the central and principal thrust into Russia, disproportionate importance should not be attached to this squabble between Army Commanders. There were disruptive attributions of far greater magnitude than that in readiness to wreck the German machine.

The flicker of gunfire along a 1,500-mile front which, like summer lightning, preceded the thunder of renewed combat just before first light on 22nd June, need not have surprised the Russians. They had received ample warning of the coming storm but acted far too late upon it. As a result many of the Russian soldiers, who were befuddled by a Saturday night hangover, were swept into the German bag that Sunday morning without firing a shot in their own defence. Within a matter of hours the *Luftwaffe* had won an air supremacy it was rarely to relinquish throughout 1941, and the three mighty Army Groups, in one of the most proficient armies history had seen, were breaking strongly upon a temporarily stunned opponent.

A comparison between the activities in Russia of Panzer Group 2 (or Panzer Group Guderian as it was better known among the soldiers who took pride in the G painted on their vehicles) and of XIX Corps, the previous year in France, is revealing. In 1941, with five panzer divisions at half the numerical tank strength of the three he had commanded in 1940, Guderian actually led fewer tanks than in France (though the substitution of medium for light tanks redressed the balance of power), while in Russia he had more infantry formations, some of which had armoured assault guns attached to them when in the lead. Yet, in France, XIX Corps had been committed to a frontage which rarely exceeded 25 miles, whereas in Russia his frontage would expand to as much as 100 miles. And while French resistance was frequently immobile and increasingly feeble, that of the Russians grew steadily in fierceness notwithstanding the ineptitude with which their leaders handled numerically superior forces. Neither the wider frontage nor the increased enemy resistance made any difference to Guderian's conduct of operations. He handled a Group as he handled a Corps – by personal leadership at the front by wireless – and overcame the paucity of the roads by working his staff and drivers that much harder in his efforts to keep in touch with the tanks at the spearhead of action. Again and again he came under direct enemy fire and narrowly escaped. But a comparison between distances covered demonstrates a truly astonishing difference between the two campaigns, even allowing for the fact that there was far more space to trade in Russia than there had been in France.

In France XIX Corps had moved 149 miles from Sedan to Abbeville in 7 days, the maximum distance covered in a single day being 56 miles on the final day. In Russia, Panzer Group 2 moved 273 miles from Brest Litovsk to Bobruisk in 7 days, the maximum distance in a single day (again the last) being 72 miles – and by 16th July the Group had advanced 413 miles to Smolensk despite persistent Russian resistance and self-imposed halts for maintenance. In the course of this remarkable progress a vast haul of enemy equipment, including 2,500 tanks and 1,500 guns, was taken by Army Group Centre alone (the lion's share in tanks going to the two panzer groups). But the marching infantry also performed prodigiously by covering enormous distances, under the goading of Bock and Kluge, through appalling dust and in intense summer heat in their endeavours to catch up with the motorised columns and rope in hoards of Russians who had been by-passed by Guderian's and Hoth's spearheads. Once again, yet more perniciously than in France, the dilemma of gearing the pace of advance to the rate at which a by-passed and defeated enemy could be contained or captured, preoccupied the minds of the higher commanders. Guderian and Hoth were insistent on pressing forward, regardless of what went on behind. They reckoned to achieve safety by movement and believed that the disruption they caused would override minor enemy incursions into their rear. With a glaring torch of success drawing them forward they were blind to what went on behind. But reviving the precedent he had instituted in France, Hitler intervened in Russia and demanded that Guderian and Hoth should close the pincers at Minsk instead of Smolensk, as Bock, Guderian and Hoth wished – even though Guderian accepted that to stretch so far at a single leap incurred risks.

On 27th June Hitler's orders were implemented, trapping a seething mass of Russians within a steadily contracting circle. Yet, although Guderian writes in *Panzer Leader*, 'The foundations had been laid for the first great victory of the campaign', he was rather more reserved in his letter to Gretel:

'To-day, after six days of battle, a first short greeting with news that I am well. We are deep in enemy territory and, I believe, have had a very considerable success.

'A thousand thanks for your kind greetings at the departure and on my birthday, and special thanks for the cornflowers and marguerites. They gave me great pleasure.

'The battle started early on the 22nd where I left off in 1939. The first

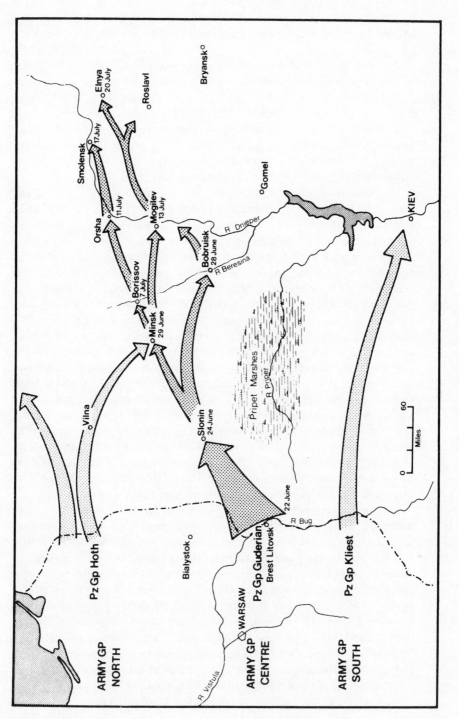

The Advance to Smolensk

Bryansk

Elnya 20 July

Roslavl

Smolensk 17 July

Gomel

Orsha 11 July

Mogilev 13 July

R. Dnieper

KIEV

Borissov 7 July

Bobruisk 28 June

R Beresina

Minsk 29 June

Pripet Marshes

R. Pripet

Vilna

Slonin 24 June

60

Miles

0

22 June

R Bug

Pz Gp Hoth

ARMY GP
NORTH

Bialystok

WARSAW

Pz Gp Guderian

Brest Litovsk

Pz Gp Kliest

ARMY GP
CENTRE

ARMY GP
SOUTH

R. Vistula

blow achieved surprise and had a devastating effect. A few strenuous days followed with little time for eating and sleeping and no time for writing . . .'

He went on to regret the losses including several officers who had been close to him and then wrote:

'All this is very sad. The enemy resists bravely and bitterly. The fighting, therefore, is very hard. One just has to put up with it.

'In addition there is some annoyance, one incident of some importance. But of that nothing in this letter. Troops and equipment again in good order, everything else is ship-shape too. Heat, gnats, dust. My caravan proves itself beautifully. But I am missing my bath.'

The 'annoyance' was caused, primarily, by his immediate superiors. On 1st July he told Gretel: 'Kluge has distinguished himself to good effect as a brake on progress' but in the same letter appears something far more significant, a sign of awakening insight into the perils of Hitler's misguided power: 'Everybody is scared of the Führer and nobody dares say anything. Regrettably, this is what causes a useless waste of blood'. This lack of sympathy with the difficulties being experienced by Brauchitsch, Bock and Kluge was, of course,.a common enough attitude by any leader of conviction to whom half measures were anathema. Ironically, Halder's diary on the 29th records a hope that Guderian would disobey the Führer and strike out on his own! Many Germans might have felt easier in mind had they understood the appalling confusion into which the Russians had been thrown. It was not until 30th June that Stalin and the Russian High Command came to hear of the Minsk encirclement (such was the state of their palsied communication system which never rivalled that of the Germans), and only then did they learn by monitoring a German communique. Not even General Pavlov, the Army Group commander, fully recognised the disaster. Indeed, he was never given the opportunity, for he was arrested that day, along with his principal staff officers, and shot. The Germans had not plumbed to depths such as those – as yet.

As it had been in France, so it became in Russia. Enormous panzer successes, which Guderian considered as reason enough for further advances, attracted instructions to slow down while the spoils of war and the still articulate, though isolated, Russian armies, were digested. In Army Group Centre (and in the sectors of the two flanking Army Groups, too, for that matter) three distinctly different kinds of battle, often widely spaced, took place. The infantry formations either grappled with or by-passed Russian formations until they were eliminated or had demobilised themselves among the towns, villages, forests and marshes. The mobile troops tried to make as much headway as restrictive orders permitted and as infantry formations caught them up. And in the ever enlarging zone of communications to the rear of the field armies' boundaries, the SS *Einsatzgruppen* began their work of suppression and extermination under the guise of anti-guerilla warfare – in a land where guerillas were, as yet, non-existent and where none need have appeared if humanity had been the rule. Several German generals were aware of the pogrom – though few, if any, its enormity. Nearly all, especially the engrossed operational commanders, ignored it. Guderian, for example, was not in the habit of visiting the lines of communication, but Paul Dierichs recalls his fury when two Russian civilians were shot by SS early in the campaign. And on the 29th Guderian wrote in hope and disquiet to Gretel, 'The people look on us as liberators. It is to be hoped they will not be disappointed.'

In conditions of fluid mobility the trend of German operations became highly volatile. Loosely formulated, pre-campaign instructions which lacked the discipline of clearly defined objectives were compounded into a series of tactical and strategic improvisations that were relatively simple to implement through the admirably flexible command and communication arrangements. At short notice Bock could decide, on or about 28th June, to place Guderian's and Hoth's Panzer Groups under Kluge and rename Fourth Army as Fourth Panzer Army. Simultaneously he placed the infantry formations (which, up till then, had been under Kluge) under Second Army. Thus Kluge, without a clear directive, had the unenviable task of controlling the eager Guderian and Hoth. The switch in command was easy but the formulation of directives suffered in continuity. Everybody wanted to move quickly to the east, but each at his own pace. The initial uncertainty of each thrust became further and perilously haphazard as Hitler's opportunism manifested itself in ill-co-ordinated, direct orders to individual Panzer Corps, instructions which, regardless of the central strategy, aimed them at specific enemy concentrations the moment intelligence claimed to have detected them. Thus, as Hoth was to point out, the panzer fist turned into an outspread hand – the converse of '*Klotzen, nicht Kleckern*'.

Guderian, short of orders, met trouble from Kluge halfway, and, even as Kluge was taking command on the 30th, flew to meet Hoth in an effort to pre-empt what he feared might come, to make private arrangements for their future collaboration in a continued drive to Smolensk as originally demanded by Bock. The evasive system that had evolved in the closing stages in France was re-introduced. While token panzer units were retained to satisfy extraneous demands from above, essential spearhead formations were kept motoring towards the River Dnieper and Smolensk. The Beresina had been crossed on the 28th and on 2nd July the Dnieper was reached at Rogachev. Progress was much slower, in part because of the brake applied by order, in part because heavy rain reduced the fields to quagmires and the foundationless roads to watery cart tracks – but also because the Russians were bringing up reserves and mounting a slightly more coherent resistance. As yet, however, there was nothing to persuade German intelligence that a properly co-ordinated enemy defence was being prepared – a supposition which was absolutely correct and daily typified by the piecemeal commitment and subsequent swift elimination of fresh Russian forces. Nevertheless Guderian and Hoth were threatened with court martial by Kluge when, on 2nd July, elements of their divisions made simultaneous advances that were quite counter to a halt order applied by Kluge.

More ominous to Guderian was a technical shock disclosed by the enemy. The swarm of Russian tanks that had initially presented itself for destruction came as no surprise, nor was their technical inferiority unexpected. These machines showed little advance upon those which the Germans had seen in 1932, at various subsequent Russian demonstrations and in Poland. But reports from Army Group North on 24th June began to tell of a very powerful heavy tank which, for hours on end, had resisted the fire of every gun except the 88 (this was the KV 1 with its new 76mm gun). On 3rd July 18th Panzer Division became involved in a heavy fight with Russian tanks and reported an entirely new tank of quite revolutionary design. Nehring was commander of 18th Panzer (he had been succeeded as Guderian's Chief of Staff in the autumn of 1940 by *Oberst* Kurt von Liebenstein) and thus was quick to appreciate the significance of the find. What was more he would soon present Guderian with two undamaged specimens – one an improved type of the other – where they lay in a bog alongside the road. On the 10th at Tolochino Guderian saw and photographed his first T 34s – tanks with well-sloped armour, the powerful 76mm gun and an excellent cross-country performance. At a glance these machines were superior to any German tank in service or planned for introduction. Not even the latest medium and heavy tanks, projected in 1937 and 1939 respectively, would match them in all departments.

The appearance of the T34s coincided with a mounting sense of crisis as the German situation on the Russian front began to deteriorate. If, on 30th June – the 9th day of the campaign – Guderian could claim that his Group's state was satisfactory, the fuel situation well in hand, ammunition, supply and medical services functioning smoothly, casualties light and co-operation with *Oberst* Mölder's fighters excellent, there were already reasons, in fact, for serious concern on technical grounds. On the 12th day of battle in France the first hesitations occurred because tank strengths were falling below the level of safety. Similar warnings came earlier in Russia where thick dust caused accentuated engine wear similar to that first experienced in the Western Desert by Rommel only three months before. Moreover the replacement and repair system was about to be exposed for what it was – an instrument suitable for short campaigns only. Spares were in irregular supply, facilities for major overhauls in the field non-existent; major repairs could be carried out by maintenance companies – only providing they received spares. After the brief encounters in Poland and France the tanks had been returned to the homeland for overhaul and rebuilding. This was impossible from Russia in 1941, not only because the Russians declined to stop fighting but also because the railway system, that had yet to be converted to the German gauge, could neither, in the summer of 1941, carry supplies forward nor backload shot-up tanks to Germany. In consequence replacement tanks were harder to come by as repairs fell behind wastage – and all this at a moment when it was clear that the Russians were receiving fresh machines.

Acrimony grew more vituperative between Kluge and Guderian when the latter, with Hoth, re-started the advance on Smolensk. On 9th July there was a row after Guderian, contrary to instructions, prepared to cross the Dnieper. Kluge was perfectly aware he was being manipulated and blatantly blackmailed when Guderian blandly produced the argument that arrangements had gone too far to be reversed and that to remain stationary was to invite destruction by the Russian Air Force. There were serious risks in what Guderian and Hoth were doing. The marching infantry was several days to the rear and Russian reserves were appearing in strength to front and flank. On the other hand it was well argued, from experience, that to leave the Russians undisturbed would merely allow them to establish strong defences where, for the present, none existed – a lesson which had been learnt all too often in the First World War. In effect Guderian was patronising to Kluge and snubbed him too openly for safety. Yet not always were they angry with each other and at times there was a grudging similarity of opinion. On this occasion Kluge, according to Guderian, 'Unwillingly gave his approval to my plan' with the remark 'Your operations always hang by a thread'. For a variety of reasons, therefore, it is interesting to read an account by Kluge's Chief of Staff, General Günther Blumentritt:

'In the period from 2nd to 11th July our Panzer Groups . . . drove into the difficult woodland and marshland of the Beresina – Russian resistance stiffened considerably . . . On the few roads we encountered the first minefields, numerous bridges which had been blown up, the enemy tenaciously holding out in the woods and swamp; as the result a unique phenomenum of this war occurred.

'. . . strong Russian elements simply stayed in hiding in the pathless forests away from the roads. The infantry corps of Fourth and Ninth Army . . . had to deal with these enemy forces and as a result furious engagements were fought in the woods day after day . . .

'The first doubts arose in our minds. No decision had been reached . . .

'*Feldmarschall* von Kluge decided to commit the two Panzer Groups . . . for an attack along a broad front towards the east . . . We planned to carry out simultaneous crossing of the wide Dnieper and

Dvina rivers at a maximum number of places . . . This great operation of von Kluge's Panzer Army will always be regarded as a strategic master-piece. To be sure he had two armoured commanders with outstanding qualifications. *Generaloberst* Guderian . . . in addition to all his other qualifications, possessed inexhaustible energy and enjoyed the absolute devotion of the units serving under him. He could be as hard as steel in his demands, and he was no pleasant subordinate, but he was a born armoured commander. In the eyes of the troops he was a kind of "Rommel of the Armoured Command". Guderian meant victory!

'*Generaloberst* Hoth was a modern armoured commander who adhered strictly to the techniques of the General Staff Corps. He applied a firm hand with circumspection and acumen. He was an obliging subordinate, a kind of Prince Eugène.'

In this short passage can be recognised the key to an appreciation of the operations which resulted on 15th July in the completion of another wholesale encirclement of Russian forces at Smolensk and the attainment of a crucial stage in the campaign. Kluge's difficulties with the Russians and with Guderian are plain to see, but one is left in little doubt from whence the strategic motivation came and to whom Blumentritt gave most credit – and Blumentritt was usually loyal to Kluge.

To *Oberstleutnant* von Barsewisch, Guderian's *Luftwaffe* officer, his commander was a 'superman, a ball of energy and brainy too . . .' Barsewisch wrote in his diary of the planning which took place on the 11th/12th, as he saw it: 'When Guderian makes decisions it is as if the War God himself rides above Walstatt. When his eyes flash Wotan seems to hurl lightning or Thor swings the hammer'. And in the evening he listened to a conversation with *Oberst* Rudolf Schmundt, the Führer's military assistant, when Guderian passionately exclaimed, 'It's not my fame but of Germany for which I care'. This was a protestation of some significance which Barsewisch may not have appreciated at the time, affecting, as it did, Guderian's rising sense of destiny.

The operations by Guderian and Hoth in the approach to Smolensk are among the most remarkable of the war – supreme examples of a mobile offensive in pursuit of a strategic aim against stiff resistance by a numerically inferior foe. For a month the Russians persisted in their piecemeal counter-attacks against Army Group Centre, yet the Germans, despite logistic limitations, maintained a steady rate of advance even though its pace was reduced compared with the early days of the campaign. Between 10th and 16th July Panzer Group 2 pushed forward only 75 miles from Krasnyi to Smolensk, but it covered countless additional miles through the necessity constantly to shift its stance to deal with Russian counter moves and to occupy successive nodal points in the battle of manoeuvre. Steadily it moved eastward, implacably the Russian groups were outflanked and isolated, invariably it was the Germans who were first to seize vital points with tanks and infantry and then hold them with anti-tank and machine-guns brought up in defence, while the tanks moved on to conquer fresh ground. Only when it rained, and the tanks sank to their turrets in slime, was there a pause, for rarely even by night was a standstill permitted. Men and machines began to wear out, fuel ran short and ammunition had to be used more sparingly. But Guderian was everywhere, coated in dust and tirelessly developing his schemes.

At the peak of his form he attained new heights in generalship and an even deeper understanding of his profession. Strategic, tactical and technical skills he supplemented with a lighter touch: he even managed to win the admiration of one of his more virulent critics, Geyr von Schweppenburg, the commander of XXIV Panzer Corps. 'We worked in a model way together, owing to the tact and skill of his Chief of Staff and to Guderian's own discretion and good will. During six months of daily hard fighting there was not a single row.' The same could not be said of the relationship with superior headquarters far to the rear: with them a bickering struggle to obtain enough reinforcements and supplies to sustain the failing panzer forces went on. Yet by the very persistance of their success the Panzer Group leaders belied each angry show of anxiety since they always somehow managed to stay mobile, to mop up over 300,000 trapped Russians along with 3,200 tanks and mountains of equipment besides stopping those Russian attacks which came in from the east. Hitler, OKW and OKH were becoming, in fact, dangerously spoilt and complacently accustomed to the seemingly automatic flow of panzer victories: they failed to realise that these good things were by way of being military miracles. Divorced from the front by space, as they were, it was hardly surprising that they shrugged off complaints from spearhead commanders who repeatedly conjured up triumphs despite their cries of alarm and despondency.

Neither OKW nor OKH could be genuinely aware of what von Barsewisch called '. . . the unbelievable deprivations and exertions imposed upon to-day's generals' since none of the senior officers in those remote places had experienced anything like it in their lives. Von Barsewisch gives a vivid impression of Guderian in a moment of crisis which was to occur on 5th August, a day in which his commander raced from place to place in attempts to prevent a large body of Russians from escaping encirclement. Information that a threat was developing against an important bridge at Ostrik came in. 'He rushed immediately to the point', relates von Barsewisch, '. . . full of rage, and closed the gap with a battery of anti-aircraft artillery which he led personally into battle. There was this fantastic man, standing by a machine-gun in action against the Russians, drinking mineral water from a cup and saying, "Anger gives you a thirst!" ' It was almost superfluous when Barsewisch wrote 'Guderian is well known by his 300,000 men. It is amazing the respect with which he is greeted everywhere he goes'.

Twice Guderian wrote commentaries to Gretel upon himself. On the 6th August he remarked, 'how long heart and nerves can stand this I do not know' and on the 12th, in a letter which wonderfully describes the stresses of command besides his own reactions:

'Have I not become old? These few weeks have imprinted their marks. The physical exertions and battles of the will make themselves felt. Occasionally I have a tremendous yearning for sleep which I can seldom satisfy. Yet, by and large, I am feeling very fit when something is going on – also quick and able. But as soon as the tension is relaxed comes the relapse.'

Notwithstanding the gallantry of the front-line troops, a dangerous crisis loomed over OKW and OKH. At the beginning of August it was apparent that the enemy, far from being broken, was strong and capable of prolonged operations. On July 31st Guderian wrote, 'The battle is harder than anything before . . . it will take some time yet.' Though vast areas had been occupied and immense armies smashed the capture of a major political or economic objective had not been achieved, nor had the Russians been annihilated. Indeed, in the Ukraine, the Russians had nimbly evaded Army Group South and still held Kiev, while Army Group North stood well short of Leningrad.

From the outset each Army Group commander had been eager to seize the principal objective that lay within the boundaries of his command. To Bock, Moscow was a prize beyond price even though he doubted its political significance. But now the difficulties of achieving their ambitions were accentuated by a belated appreciation of the tyranny of distance and the inadequacy of their resources to overcome that tyranny. Not only were the fighting vehicles breaking under the strain but so, too, was the machinery of logistics as well as the moral fibre of the commanders whose thoughts turned pessimistic again. The *Wehrmacht* was stretched to the limit: only one major objective could reasonably be pursued at a time. Bock, supported by Kluge, Guderian and Hoth, gave unified support to Brauchitsch and Halder in their endeavours to make Moscow the primary target. Almost perversely, it seemed, Hitler proposed instead that Leningrad and the Ukraine should be taken; thereupon, he claimed, Moscow would fall of its own weight. As his reasons for diversifying effort, he propounded the need to attack political and economic objectives rather than concentrate upon a purely military task – but Hitler chose convenient arguments to suit short term aims which, on this occasion, were ill-defined.

Nothing could be settled until Hitler had visited each Army Group headquarters in turn, seeking to test the opinions of von Leeb, von Bock and von Rundstedt while reimposing his personality upon them and sowing the seeds of dissention which could undermine their faith in

Halder and OKH. Insidiously Hitler worked upon the susceptibilities of the generals, aiming to dominate each one through personal fascination regardless of the integrity of the strategy he was promulgating.

Concerning Bock's headquarters, where Hitler arrived on 4th August, there has been gossip about some sort of plot by the Ia, *Oberst* Henning von Tresckow, and his ADC, Fabian von Schlabrendorff (a barrister) along with two more ADCs, to arrest Hitler in the hope that a chain reaction would be set off against him. This ludicrously amateur scheme (if it ever existed) was mentioned in Schlabrendorff's book of 1946, *Offiziere gegen Hitler* (but omitted from his subsequent book of 1965). It appears to have been abortive because, only at the last moment, did the plotters realise that Hitler was too strongly escorted. It is also said that Tresckow had tried to involve Bock in the plot and that Bock refused to give support unless presented with a proven success, and there has been a suggestion in Wheeler-Bennett's *Nemesis of Power* that Guderian was aware of the Tresckow plot and undermined it by falling in line with Hitler's aims. Guderian, who denied the truth of anything written about him by Schlabrendorff in 1946, has history on his side, whereas Schlabrendorff's book was riddled with inaccuracies and hearsay accounts. For example, Schlabrendorff asserted that Bock did not want to go to Moscow but asked to revert to the defensive, while Guderian was more interested in the Ukraine: both notions are substantially contradicted by contemporary diaries and personal accounts. Admittedly Hitler interviewed each senior commander alone and nobody can be sure what was said, but there is nothing to show why Schlabrendorff should be right and everybody else wrong. In fact Guderian's only public strategic disagreement with anybody else at this moment was with Hoth over the date of the start for Moscow – the former calculating he could be ready on 15th August, the latter more cautiously preferring the 20th – the critical factor being the repair of tanks. Meanwhile, in private, Bock and Guderian disagreed mainly upon what the fundamental effect of capturing Moscow might be, Guderian arguing that occupation of the capital would be sufficient in itself to bring about the collapse of Stalin's regime, Bock holding the much more political and sophisticated opinion that 'Russia can only be conquered by the Russians through a civil war and a national liberation government'.

Abstruse political theories come low in the priorities of a field commander at the height of battle. Guderian was consumed by combat and returned to the front after the conference eager to prepare his Group for the drive on Moscow which he reckoned must surely take place. A few swift orders to his staff and once more he raced to the front line to fight, an action he described to Gretel: '. . . I fought a battle at Roslavl, conquered the town, took 30,000 prisoners, 250 guns and much other material including tanks . . . A pretty success. But still somebody [Bock under

143

whose direct command he then was] interferes as before and endeavours to deploy the tanks in dribs and drabs, ruining them by useless journeys. One despairs! How I can overcome this stupidity I do not know. Nobody helps me . . . Three days ago I was ordered to the Führer to report on the panzer situation. The opinion at OKW and Army Group does not match my ideas despite the fact that the Führer was extremely understanding. What a pity! What a pity!'

At the higher headquarters, where the sound of gunfire was only rarely heard and time seemed to have lost some of its importance, the long debate about future strategy dragged on. As the campaigning season ebbed away the only immediate friendly beneficiaries of a pause were the German logisticians who thus found the opportunity to recuperate the formations' strength along with stocks at the front. The main long-term beneficiary was, of course, the Russian Army which at last had time in which to consolidate its positions. When the initiative is finely balanced, inaction is often more destructive of generals' composure than is the actual crunch of battle on soldiers. The strain upon Halder, who, best of all, knew that a moribund strategy tolled the death knell of Germany and who pondered and strove under well-nigh intolerable conditions, was appalling. He was caught in a vortex of proposals and counter-proposals but lacked the authority and ability to turn them into positive action. Frequently reviled and blatantly ignored by OKW, too often abandoned by his C-in-C whose credibility with OKW had sunk low, his consequential ineffectuality became apparent to worried colleagues at the lower levels, and they began to lose confidence. This highly strung staff officer, who would have welcomed a rigorous debate in straightforward terms, began to lose his sense of poise. An argument that shifted amid the sands of Hitler's tortuous political manoeuvres and intuitions was destructively exasperating to Halder.

Guderian merely wished to keep moving since this, to him, was the essence of panzer tactics, and the mainspring of victory. On 12th August he wrote: 'I would not wish to be in this area [Roslavl] in the autumn: it is not very pretty . . . waiting always brings the dangers of immobility and static warfare: that would be terrible.' That he knew only too well the troubles of the High Command, he showed in a letter on the 18th:

'This situation has a bad effect upon the troops, for everyone is aware of the absence of harmony. That is the product of unclear orders and counter-orders, absence of instructions sometimes for weeks . . . we are missing so many opportunities. But it is annoying when one knows the reasons. These most probably cannot be put right during this war, which we will win despite it all. That is human nature in great moments and with great men. Don't listen to too much talk about me. It is all much exaggerated and people make a mountain out of a molehill.'

For talk there was – about his intransigence, on the one hand, but ever more loudly about his virtue linked with a growing feeling among a small and influential caucus that he was wasted in the lower echelons of command. Or so it seemed to *Oberst* Günther von Below, Hitler's *Luftwaffe* adjutant, who was a fervent admirer of Guderian. It was clear to him, as many others, that the poor relationship between von Brauchitsch and Hitler was leading to disaster and that Guderian, for whom Hitler had much more respect, would be the right replacement. At this moment, in playing a hunch, he suggested to *Major* Claus von Stauffenberg, a staff officer at OKH, that he should visit Panzer Group 2 to assess for himself Guderian's fitness for the higher role. Stauffenberg, like most visitors after a stay with Guderian, returned enthused and the two conspirators sought ways of unofficially thrusting Guderian's qualities upon the Führer's attention. At about the same time von Below asked Guderian what his reactions would be if he were asked to be C-in-C, and Guderian, not surprisingly, had answered that he would 'follow the call'* Von Below says that Guderian's Chief of Staff, Liebenstein, probably knew of the scheme, though *Oberst* Schmundt was unaware of it. Through notes in his diary it is apparent that Barsewisch knew too** but whether or not Halder was informed is a matter for conjecture, although *Oberst* Heusinger, the Chief of Operations, was told and may have discussed it. I think it very likely that Halder did know. Certainly his subsequent relationships with Guderian and those who supported the panzer general assume a different character if viewed in the light of this positive assumption, for up to the middle of August Halder had little for which to thank Brauchitsch but good reason to feel gratitude towards Guderian, besides an increasing disenchantment with Hitler whose arbitrary behaviour was worsening.

For not only the Commander-in-Chief was losing – or had totally forfeited – prestige. The Führer too had begun to suffer from failing authority and was finding it more difficult, by sweet persuasion, to sway doubters. Ever more frequently he felt compelled to resort to bullying injunctions to over-ride contrary points of view. Increasingly he came to rely upon the thoroughness of Prussian discipline to bend the generals to his will. Each set-back and every revelation of weakening in Germany's situation was to lead to a coercive tightening of his lonely, dictatorial grip. And since he was never effectively opposed by his closest followers and

* Guderian gives no hint of this approach in *Panzer Leader* though in his correspondence there is ample evidence of his realisation that new horizons were appearing. Since he was repeatedly the target, after the war, of accusations of being a self-seeker, his reticence about this affair is at least understandable even if unnecessary. So far as I am aware, however, this highly significant factor has not been published before in books in English.
**The entry in Barsewisch's diary for 29th August is revealing in its reflection of the 'nothing we can do about the command situation now' view expressed by Guderian in his letter of 18th August mentioned above. While the entry for 15/16 September says 'Alone with Guderian on one of his serious themes – Clausewitz, Moltke and Schlieffen, appointments at OKH and in the General Staff – so that everything about us seemed to stand still for an hour'.

sycophants, and persisted in holding dissident factions at a distance, he was permitted to formulate and actuate warped ideas upon false or ephemeral premises which all too often were turned into faulty policy. For example, the limited operations mounted by Guderian in the interim period between his arrival at Smolensk and the construction of a revised strategy, are coincidental with Hitler's suggestion to abandon the principle of securing victory through sweeping mobile operations in favour of small local actions, analogous with static warfare, to take unimportant terrain. This concept, encouraged by Halder and adopted by Bock as a temporary expedient to maintain a limited mobility, led to an innocuous advance on Gomel by Second Army along with random requests to Panzer Group 2 for assistance – the requests which led Guderian to complain on the 18th about the plethora of unclear orders and counter orders. Liebenstein bitterly remarked 'The troops must think we are crazy' and he wrote in his diary on the 15th, that the moves '. . . cannot lead into the flank and rear of the enemy' and, again on the 20th in complaint in connection with tanks held in the line instead of being relieved by infantry in order to prepare for the next main task: 'After all, this Army Group appears to intend attacking on both sides of the road Roslavl to Moscow. Our further extension to the south is therefore no longer appropriate'. Guderian, though he knew that the order had come from OKW via OKH, resisted it – Liebenstein quotes Guderian as saying, on 22nd August, that to send the Panzer Group in this direction was 'a crime'. But as Second Army, under Bock's goading, edged southward, the seeds of decision at last germinated in Hitler's mind: he opted firmly to strike heavily southward in the direction of Kiev. At about the same moment, on 18th August, Brauchitsch and Halder put their names to a document demanding an advance upon Moscow.

The plan submitted by Brauchitsch and Halder nevertheless temporised in that it still allowed the flanking army groups sufficient resources to reach the main objectives within their boundaries. Hitler, in rejecting it, gave a politician's reply by accusing OKH of being too strongly influenced by the three Army Group commanders. Once more Halder asked Brauchitsch to join him in joint resignation, but again the C-in-C declined. He knew that a second-rate policy was promulgated, an offensive based upon pure opportunism in which a Panzer Group was to be peeled off Army Group Centre and made to collaborate with Army Group South in a gigantic envelopment of the Russian armies defending the Ukraine. In every sense he took the line of least resistance.

Halder stuck to his guns and called yet another meeting at Army Group Centre at which the Army and Panzer Group commanders were in attendance. With compulsive zeal and ability, Guderian argued the case against diverting his Panzer Group to the south, pointing out the logistic difficulties that would arise and emphasising the debilitation of men and machines. Some of the men, he said, had forgotten the meaning of rest. Then he raised the spectre of a winter campaign which had never been envisaged by the planners and for which, on the face of it, no apparent preparations had been made. In essence he said that, though the Kiev operation was feasible, it precluded a subsequent offensive against Moscow and made a winter war inevitable. This precisely coincided with Halder's and Bock's opinions. Now it was that von Below suggested to Bock that Guderian was the man to accompany Halder in a final effort to change the Führer's mind, a scheme to which Halder readily acceded – all the more readily, one feels, if he too was convinced, as possibly he was, that Guderian was the one man who might succeed where Brauchitsch had failed. Indeed, at this moment, it seems entirely reasonable to believe that Halder supported Guderian as the candidate for Brauchitsch's job.

Controversy surrounds every aspect of Guderian's visit to Rastenburg on 23rd August, as perhaps befits a turning point in the campaign. Liebenstein records in his diary for 23rd August (an entry obviously written shortly afterwards, perhaps with the intention of protecting Guderian's reputation):

'The commander flies with the Chief of the General Staff with the aim of preventing Panzer Group being sent into action in the south. As he says upon his return, he was met by the C-in-C [Brauchitsch] with the words. "The attack to the south has been ordered. Now it only depends on how".'

In *Panzer Leader* Guderian elaborates upon his meeting that night with Brauchitsch who, he wrote, forbade him to mention the question of Moscow to the Führer. One asks, did Brauchitsch know about the plan to depose him? Probably not, but Guderian goes on to say that the conversation with the Führer (at which neither Brauchitsch nor Halder were present) got round to an attack against Moscow and that he reasoned the case strongly for this strategy and against that of going to Kiev. Hitler, in the company of Keitel, Jodl and Schmundt, replied with reasons – economic, political and military – for entering the Ukraine and for neutralising the Crimea, adding the patronising phrase, 'My generals know nothing about the economic aspects of war'. Members of the entourage nodded their heads in agreement. In the face of this tirade Guderian, unsupported, took the view, according to Liebenstein's account, '. . . that he cannot debate a resolved issue with the Head of State in the presence of all his company'. It would have been as much to the point had he mentioned the inhibiting effect of knowing that his future prospects of becoming C-in-C and, perhaps, saving Germany were in jeopardy. A headlong row with Hitler at this moment would have damaged them beyond repair. By arguing only mildly at this point he could enhance the Führer's goodwill and turn the prospect of maximum influence in the near future into a probability. It is one of the sad commonplaces of relationship among senior German generals with Hitler that they tended always, when posed with the dilemma of mutual confidence, to bargain concessions in the hope of an improvement in their future relative status – and every time to see those hopes dashed. Each in his turn suffered and so, therefore, did the Army and Germany.

What now transpired was the complete destruction of accord and faith between Halder and Guderian, those two who were probably Germany's last hope in the struggle to curb Hitler's irrationality. Liebenstein wrote: 'The commander is being accused by the Chief of the General Staff of having given way'. And Halder commented scathingly on Guderian:

'Previously he said he could not go south. Now he declares that in view of the Führer's demands to move as soon as possible to the south . . . he has changed his mind. Guderian says that he gave this [original] explanation in order to hinder the operation to the south. Once the Führer declared his determination he felt it his duty to make the impossible possible. This shows in a shattering way how official reports can be used to serve an individual's purpose. As a result an order is being issued on how to make reports. But you cannot alter characters through orders.'

Guderian says that 'Halder suffered a complete nervous collapse' when he reported failure of his mission, and Bock confirms this collapse on Halder's part. It was reasonable for Halder to be disappointed, but an over-reaction on this scale needs a more convincing explanation than that. In the first place Halder, on the face of it, had been extraordinarily optimistic if he imagined that a relatively junior officer could change Hitler's mind in a few minutes when he and Brauchitsch had failed over the weeks – and more than hopeful if he believed that a resolved matter could be challenged in a way that was quite contrary to the code of Prussian discipline. For Halder had been less than straightforward with Guderian: he had omitted to tell him that orders had been issued already by OKH to Army Group Centre instructing it to co-operate with Army Group South using '. . . a strong force, preferably commanded by *Generaloberst* Guderian'.

If one admits that Halder knew of the move to replace Brauchitsch with Guderian then his behaviour becomes comprehensible since, for a start, he must have been fairly – if not strongly – convinced that Guderian had special influence with the Führer as well as the determination to succeed where others had given way. Moreover, if Guderian *had* changed Hitler's mind the chances of his becoming C-in-C would assuredly have been enhanced. On 23rd August, therefore, Halder could well have looked on Guderian as his future commander with all that implied. Therefore his fury and disappointment must have been redoubled at the outcome and hence the scale of his outburst of pent-up emotions along with accusations of disloyalty and remarks to Bock on the telephone that Guderian had let them all down. The fact remains that from this moment Halder was Guderian's enemy who, over the years, came to perpetuate the

legend of Guderian as a maverick at odds with the élite of the General
Staff, along with the notion, as he wrote after the war, that Guderian was
shallow. But Halder was also thrown upon the defensive when the king he
thought to have played turned out, in his opinion, to be a knave. For there
were those on the staff (among them *Oberst* Fritz Bayerlein, Guderian's
Ia) who contended that, as the result of the events of 23rd August,
Brauchitsch and Halder should have resigned, not Guderian whom the
Halder faction thought should have gone.

Be these things as they may, the soured future relationship between
Halder and Guderian can now be seen in a new light that looks still clearer
when one realises that the move to replace Brauchitsch gathered further
momentum while at the same time the adherents of Guderian came under
what almost amounted to persecution by Halder – as the ensuing train of
events demonstrates.

The drive into the Ukraine demanded every atom of Guderian's
ingenuity since his fight was against both the Russians and Halder's
obdurate opposition. Halder's diary states his opinion about the new
operation as tackled by Guderian:

> '24th Aug. The intention of the Panzer Group to strike out . . . with its
> left wing . . . leads too far east. Everything depends upon it helping
> Second Army across the Desna and then the Sixth Army across the
> Dnieper.'

In other words the 'fast units' were once more to have their effectiveness
curtailed by placing them in support of the slowest marching formations.
Yet within forty-eight hours, on the 26th, he was noting that 'the infantry
moves slowly forward in face of stiffening resistance' though he persisted,
on the 27th, in demanding of Bock, 'Not to let Guderian run south but
keep him in readiness for the Second Army's crossing of the Desna'.
Speed was far from being the essence of this operation.

Liebenstein registered his commander's protest at this splitting up of
the panzer group by the removal of XLVI Panzer Corps into reserve. But,
although deprived of one third of his force, Guderian resolutely ignored
Halder and Bock in an attempt to achieve dramatic results in the usual
way. This time, however, there was much more urgency than usual since
only by a rapid conclusion of the Kiev operation could a start be made
against Moscow in sufficient time before the onset of winter. The initial
advances struck an astonished enemy who had not expected an attack in
this direction, but the Russian reaction grew daily stronger and heavy
fighting stretched the two panzer corps to the limit. Halder recorded a
message from Bock on the 27th in which he said that 'Guderian rages
since he fails to make progress because of being attacked in flank and
demands reinforcement of his remaining fast units. Bock feels unable to
do so because he must keep a reserve. I am of the same opinion and

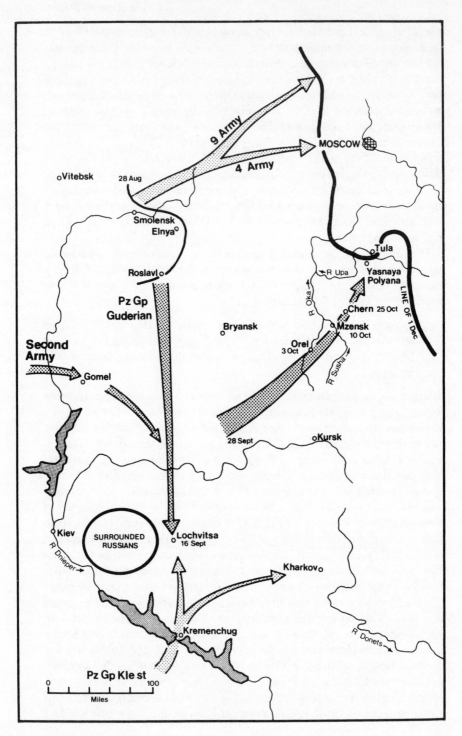

Kiev and Tula

request him not to give way to Guderian . . . In addition I ask him to keep a tight rein on Guderian . . .' And on the 28th – after Paulus, now Halder's chief assistant, had pleaded Guderian's case for support: 'I realise the difficulty of the situation. But in the final analysis all war consists of difficulties. Guderian will not tolerate any army commander and demands that everybody up to the highest position should bow to the ideas he produces from a restricted view-point. Regrettably Paulus allowed himself to be caught. I will not give way to Guderian. He has got himself into this fix. Now he can get himself out of it.'

Matters came to a head on the 31st when Halder wrote about the '. . . decidedly uncomfortable position of Guderian's Group (this day Guderian had to deploy a field bakery company to hold a threatened sector) . . . he throws out accusations and insults in a telephone conversation with Bock. He can only be helped by infantry but that will take several days, so he must sit tight as the result of a faulty attack. I consider it wrong to help him . . . Bock, however, intends to send forward two infantry divisions'. Later that day Halder mentioned a telephone conversation with Bock in which the latter complained of Guderian's tone, '. . . which he cannot in any circumstances tolerate, and demands, in order to have his way, a decision by the Führer. That is an unheard of insolence!'

Liebenstein's diary puts it another way on 1st September:
'It is a major mistake . . . that insufficient forces have been committed to achieve success quickly to reach our goals before the onset of winter. Repeated requests for the XLVI Panzer Corps are refused . . . The commander has the impression that Army Group, as well as the Chief of Staff, still cling to the old plan for a drive to Moscow. It is certain that the Führer is against dispersal of panzer groups, as he told the commander on the 23rd. Therefore the commander sends a message to Army Group Centre and points out that in view of Second Army's slow progress the operational goal cannot be reached without additional forces, and proposes support from XLVI Corps, 7th Panzer, 11th Panzer and 14th Mot. and requests decision by the Führer . . . As can be expected this wireless message created house-high waves . . . Result: The immediate placing of an SS division with us . . . The Chief of Army Group tells me in a private conversation "There have been errors . . ."' The next day *Generalfeldmarschall* Kesselring of the *Luftwaffe* arrived and confirmed to Liebenstein that the Führer supported Guderian's activities. On the 3rd Liebenstein wrote: 'Army Group refuses to state its objectives. Evasions.'

The plot intensified, on the 4th, when Halder persisted with what now looked suspiciously like a vendetta: with intrigue against Guderian through Hitler: 'Great agitation has taken place. The Führer very angry with Guderian who will not abandon his intention to move to the south . . . The order is issued to bring Guderian back to the west bank of the Desna. Tension between Bock and Guderian. The former demands that Guderian should be relieved of his command.' And on this day, when *Oberstleutnant* Nagel, Halder's liaison officer, repeated Guderian's views in conference, he was removed from his post for being 'a loudspeaker and propagandist'.* Liebenstein, lacking clear orders, was in the dark as to the reasons for complaint and wrote that Guderian was 'deeply affected' by OKW's apparent dissatisfaction with the Panzer Group and his feeling that '. . . a scapegoat is being looked for from above for lack of speed, whereas we are sure that, with sufficient reinforcement, we would have succeeded. He is of the opinion that the entire situation should be reported to the Führer.' Significantly, on the 5th, Liebenstein cried: 'When can we expect orders, not criticisms?'

And yet, although the roads were crumbling as the first deluge of autumn rain swept down and brought the motorised troops to the pace of the marching men in the glutinous mud, advances were made. For it was no easier for the Russians, of course. They too became mired whenever, in inclement weather, they strove to break the encircling German pincers which thrust southward from Smolensk and (not until 14th September) northward, under Kleist, from Kremenchug. Each despairing Russian thrust was beaten off, though not without moments of crisis and drama. German defensive localities, strung-out like beads in a necklace behind the advancing spearheads, were often rescued in the nick of time by tanks scurrying to their aid. On 16th September Guderian and Kleist joined hands at Lokhvitsa and the encirclement was accomplished. On the operational maps it was made to appear that 3rd Panzer Division completed the job, as indeed it had, but so far as its tank strength was concerned that was but a shadow – a mere 10 roadworthy machines of which 6 were the obsolete Pz IIs. Ten days would pass before the spoils of this achievement were harvested, days in which nearly half a million Russian prisoners, over 800 tanks and 3,500 guns fell into German hands. Few escaped.

Liebenstein began to piece together the tale of intrigue from above. On the 13th a repentant von Bock told him that he would have liked to send Guderian more divisions but Halder regarded the drive on Moscow as more important. Who then was disobeying orders? Later, on 30th September, it was revealed by Schmundt that '. . . the Führer's intentions were incorrectly executed. Army Group Centre had pursued their own goal towards Moscow. The Führer wants panzer groups to act in unison but he is shy to order it. He played with the idea of having panzer groups under himself as Göring has with the Air Fleets'. Of course it would have been almost a unique event in history if there had been total agreement

---

* It is, perhaps, noteworthy if only coincidental that a high proportion of Guderian's supporters were sent to North Africa about this time. Bayerlein had gone, Stauffenberg went in October, Nehring and Liebenstein in 1942.

among fellow military commanders over strategy, even surprising had there been a total absence of intrigue. The remarkable aspect of Halder's behaviour at this juncture was his apparent willingness to sacrifice German soldiers to the benefit of his own ambition. The fact that he did so and played a double game boded ill for Guderian. For Halder never forgave the alleged betrayal of 23rd August while his own ommissions he sought to conceal. Having delayed the completion of the Kiev operation he now hastened to restart the attack on Moscow, late as it was in the campaign season.

As the pincers closed in the Ukraine, orders were issued that the drive on Moscow was approved at last and was to start with the least delay. Tentatively, on 24th September, Bock fixed 2nd October for the start but withheld confirmation until the 27th when an inevitably complex regrouping and redeployment seemed assured. But there were even more fundamental matters to worry Guderian. On 27th August a liaison officer who had gone to see von Schell in Berlin in an effort to obtain spares for the wheeled vehicles, had returned with Schell's answer: 'We are on the verge of a catastrophe . . . There is a shortage of steel, therefore the production of several kinds of vehicle has had to be cut by as much as 40 per cent.' Liebenstein adds: 'Resupply is often senseless. For instance, sometimes we receive mortar ammunition which contains a high percentage of concrete bombs, or mudguards instead of spare parts for engines'.

The hours of daylight were getting short, the weather both colder and wetter. The forces Bock had been promised were spread, before redeployment, between the Leningrad front and Konotop in the south, their establishment was 15 per cent below strength and their tank strength at a bare 75 per cent – Guderian's was actually down to 50 per cent. But though infantry strengths were low the actual number of tank crewmen was sufficient since their casualties had not been heavy. Fuel stocks were down, transport – horse and motor – beginning to fail on the rough tracks, and, though the railheads were being pushed forward, a shortage of rolling stock was acute. Therefore regrouping was governed by the desire to reduce movement to the minimum: hence the headquarters of armies found themselves placed over formations with whose personalities they were unfamiliar. For example, Guderian whose command of XLVI Panzer Corps had been relinquished to Hoepner's Panzer Group 4, in the north, took over XLVIII Panzer Corps from Kleist's Panzer Group 1, in the south, because it was geographically convenient to do so. A mere twenty-four hours elapsed between taking command and sending them into action.

The shortest distance to Moscow was the 200 miles separating the city from Panzer Groups 3 and 4 where they formed up on either side of Smolensk. That distance represented five days combat motoring in June against a Russian Army which had yet to suffer its first defeat. In September, therefore, the likelihood of reaching the ultimate goal seemed within the bounds of theoretical feasibility, for the Russians were severely depleted, particularly in tanks, and were as badly directed as ever. It mattered less, to German minds, that the two Panzer Groups destined to drive from Yelnya to Moscow should be spread over a 150-mile frontage and that Guderian's Group, to the south, was separated from them by yet another 150 miles. The Germans were becoming accustomed to winning victories with isolated panzer groups which operated on a shoestring, and a measure of their confidence can be found in the nature of Guderian's contribution to Bock's plan.

Divorced as he was in space from Panzer Group 4 to his left, he opted to open the attack on 28th September, two days before the rest of the Army Group. Only in that way, since his was a subsidiary operation, could he obtain maximum bomber support, but principally he was concerned with fighting his way into closer company with the other formations since there was insufficient time to redeploy nearer to them while out of contact with the enemy. Moreover he gambled upon reaching the slightly better communication system at Orel before the autumn rains brought about a total collapse of the poor tracks between Konotop and Orel. He knew, as did everybody else, that they were engaged quite as much in a race against the weather and time as against the Russians.

As a feat of sheer brilliance in organisation, command, control and improvisation, Guderian's shift through 90 degrees in direction, from a posture of containment of the Kiev pocket on 26th September, to one of outright aggression on the 30th is almost unparalleled. The arrival of 50 new tanks was of assistance though the crews remained those same weary warriors who had fought without cessation for three long months. In fact the battle began even sooner than Bock intended, Guderian launching the newly received XLVIII Panzer Corps in an attack on the 28th to secure the flank of the main thrust that was intended to go north-eastwards from Gluchov to Orel. This preliminary operation failed. Nevertheless all three Panzer Corps began the main assault on the 30th and made useful headway despite a strong Russian counter-attack and early morning mist which prevented the dive-bombers taking off. The spearheads shot forward and the marching infantry toiled behind, but their progress had been made easy, for not only were the Russians thin to the front, but again they had been entirely taken by surprise since they too, quite logically, thought that the campaigning season was all but over.

Von Barsewisch gives a glimpse of Guderian in action, frightening '. . . some waddle papas of the Infantry who have now come to know us and think our kind of war terrible. He derives from it a quiet and warm-hearted pleasure. "You don't think you can secure 10 kilometres with a battalion? What a shame! Just think, I have 300 kilometres of open flank in which there is nothing and that does not bother me in the least.

So, therefore, please . . ." ' And on another occasion when their car became stuck in mud, 'Guderian grinned and said "Well, my dear Herr von Barsewisch, we seem to be in the shit" ' – the remark of a true tank man which immensely pleased Barsewisch.

Moving at its fastest through heavily wooded territory, Panzer Group 2 advanced 130 miles in two days to capture Orel, completely outpacing the Russian counter-moves and slaughtering defenders whose principal aim was escape. In the forests around Bryansk more Russian armies lay trapped and eventually this vital communication centre would be in German hands along with the customary collection of booty. Now Hitler began intervening again with characteristic diversionary directives aimed at taking quick pickings instead of persevering with the main strategic purpose: Kursk was to be taken and the Bryansk pocket squeezed dry even though this meant that the crucial advance upon Tula, once Orel had fallen, was to be denied essential support. Once more the capture of Moscow was to be delayed in favour of a resounding local victory. It was the same story at Vyasma after Bock's principal attack had got well under way and netted another gaggle of Russians.

First the Russians and next the weather conspired to change German fortunes. On 6th October Bryansk fell and Guderian's leading division (4th Panzer) ran into the 1st Russian Tank Brigade with its KV 1 and T 34 tanks at Mzensk, a quarter the way to Tula. This was an awesome moment. For the first time the Germans experienced in a big way the threat that Guderian and Nehring had apprehended when they made the discovery on 3rd July. The German tanks were out-fought and the advance brought to a halt through excessive losses. That night the first snows fell. It was a hollow distinction that Panzer Group 2 was renamed Second Panzer Army that day.

All at once the situation swung hard against the Germans and for the first time Guderian lost hope. The tale of woe which fills the pages of *Panzer Leader* sincerely reflects his feelings at the time. The advance died in its tracks and twitched only fitfully in the moments when the state of the roads and the surrounding fields permitted. After each snowfall the thaw would bring a standstill; in the aftermath of every standstill the enemy would be that much better prepared and the process of regaining momentum had to be primed all over again. Moreover options were no longer open for changes of direction and the achievement of surprise. The Russians easily read German intentions and skilfully sited their blocking positions.

With every day that passed Guderian's thoughts turned anxiously to his soldiers' predicament as opposed to the need for pushing them deeper into Russia. Each visit to the front produced evidence of worsening privations caused by a shortage of boots, shirts and socks – indeed of all kinds of winter clothing. Senior officers were beginning to show signs of exhaustion, though it might have been of himself when he wrote that their problems were 'less physical than spiritual'. For on 21st November at the beginning of a letter to Gretel, in which he wrote of the duties of a commander as 'a misery', he displayed that same extraordinary mixture of hope and despair which had governed him in 1919 at Bartenstein. Even in the dying spasms of the German advance on Moscow he could somehow recognise the smallest trend of a development in his favour – 'step by step'. And yet: 'The demands on the troops are enormous and their performance is admirable. There is no support from above. I must muddle along on my own. Yesterday I was on the brink of despair and my nerves were at an end. To-day an unexpected battle success by the brave panzer divisions has given me new hope. Whether it continues remains to be seen . . . If the battle allows I intend to go to Army Group to explain our situation and to find out their intentions for the future . . . I cannot imagine how we can have things straight by next spring. Here we are, close to December, and no decision has yet been taken.' This was not the letter of a general whose viewpoint was restricted but that of a commander who thought like a commander-in-chief.

In *Panzer Leader* he caustically refers to 'the high spirits in evidence at the OKH and at Army Group Centre', though this was a little hard. It is true that Halder's diary reflects confidence: it is also essential that any superior command should maintain an outwardly confident mien to its subordinates. Guderian did no less himself. But Halder was aware that his belated drive on Moscow was in danger and his reputation with it. Von Barsewisch recorded how 'Guderian is outwardly composed but inwardly worried about the bad weather', and quotes Guderian's persuasive encouragement of the troops when he spoke to them: 'Comradeship depends upon mutual frankness . . . a big effort now, if we press on, will save far greater suffering in the year to come'.

Von Brauchitsch had recently suffered a heart attack, while at Army Group, von Bock was down with stomach cramps, though driving himself to the limit. In due course, with 30 degrees of frost reducing the combat worthiness of men and machines to a mere 20 per cent of efficiency (if that), he would come within sight of Moscow in the north. But Guderian's Second Panzer Army (even though it made far more progress, at this time, than the other armies) was stuck near Tula and a count of destroyed tanks on the battlefield revealed that, for the first time, more German than Russian tanks had been destroyed. The KV 1s and T 34s were deadly.

The moment for something stronger than straight talking to Hitler had long since passed and when, at last, a *Generalfeldmarschall* lost patience, it was too late. Rundstedt's Army Group South had taken Rostov-on-Don on 20th November, but at once its salient came under intense Russian pressure from both sides. Without seeking permission, Rundstedt did the prudent thing and withdrew – the first retrograde strategic step in German military experience since 1919. And when OKW had instructed him to rescind the order he told them, in a moment of weary exasperation, to find somebody else to do it. Reichenau stepped into his shoes – but the withdrawal continued, and the effect of Rundstedt's resignation only whipped up a wave of resistance to Hitler's authority. Even the SS leader, Sepp Dietrich, told Hitler his approach was wrong. On the eve of a major Russian counter-offensive before Moscow on the 6th December Guderian, Hoepner and Reinhardt presented Bock with a *fait accompli* and withdrew their leading troops into shelter. Almost simultaneously they came under mounting pressure from the Russians and had to begin a withdrawal. Inevitably equipment, stores and some of the wounded and frost-bitten had to be left behind. Yet the German soldiers continued to fight back and there were no signs of disruption even in the face of defeat.

Faced with impending disaster, Guderian is on record for his efforts to gather support from those with influence to bring a halt to the offensive and a withdrawal to refuge. Always, for him, there was safety in move-ment whether it was forwards or backwards. At the crux of the matter was the need for adequate supplies to sustain the mobility of machines and the well-being of his men. On 23rd November he had detected incomprehen-sion at Army Group and had asked his old comrade-in-arms Balck (who was on a visit to the front from his office job in Germany) to give his pessimistic views to Brauchitsch. The telephone log of Second Panzer Army is a record of Guderian's struggle with Bock to end the winter campaign – a poignant document. On 8th December he was lobbying visiting generals and on the 10th sending written reports to Schmundt, and to Bodewin Keitel in an effort to reach the ear of Hitler. At a meeting at Roslavl on the 14th with Brauchitsch, Bock and Kluge (whose Fourth Army had already made withdrawals) he asked for and received permis-sion to withdraw towards the Susha/Oka river-line covering Orel. At this meeting he was entrusted with the unified command of the southern wing with Second Army as well as Second Panzer Army incorporated into the 'Provisional Army Guderian'. Next day Brauchitsch, reiterating what Guderian had said, told Halder that he saw no way out for the Army.

On the 16th Guderian met Schmundt near the front 'at my urgent request', and then wrote to Gretel. 'I am now awaiting the Führer's call to report to him, first hand, about our state and the measures I think essential. I hope it is not too late . . . I do not know how we can get out of it. At any rate the administration must be taken quickly and energetically in hand . . . I am glad that the Führer knows the situation and I hope he will intervene with his customary energy to rectify the administrative failures amid the railways and so on. I can never remember being so dominated by my task as now. I hope I can last out. My old sciatica is causing me trouble again. At night I lie sleepless and torture my brain as

157

to what I can do to help my poor men who are unprotected in this crazy weather. It is terrible, unimaginable.'

At 0300 hours on the 17th the call from Hitler came through on a bad line. In that it set yet another pattern for the future it was historic. There were sumptuous promises of forthcoming aid by air and then an order – repeated – to stand fast. Germany's fighting generals would get used to such words and harsh demands in the days to come, but Guderian was among the first to hear them – and in the prime knowledge that he listened to the man who was about to downgrade the Army one step further. For Schmundt had told Guderian that Brauchitsch was to be retired and his place taken, not by Guderian or even another soldier, but by Hitler himself. In this way the true spirit of National Socialism was to be injected into the Army and the Head of State and Supreme Commander empowered to give orders to himself. Just then, however, Guderian cared only for those things that were. Liebenstein wrote, apropos the telephone call, 'The Führer's order to halt, forbidding all evading actions, does not correspond in any way with reality, as it does not correspond with our insufficient strength. Despite all claims and reports it has not been understood by those above that we are too weak to defend ourselves'. Guderian proceeded with the withdrawal – Hitler's order notwithstanding. But at last he could see for himself from whence so much of the trouble originated, though he held the belief that Hitler was being misinformed by the optimists in OKH. With his Provisional Army in controlled retreat under corps' commanders who keenly felt their peril, Guderian, on the 17th, asked Bock's approval to fly to Rastenburg for a personal interview with Hitler. Noncommittally Bock let him go; his stomach ailments were worse and he had made up his mind to report sick the next day and take no further part in the campaign.

On 17th December Halder began to nag, knowing Guderian was restive, but on the 19th the whole atmosphere changed. Halder was called for by Hitler who informed him that Brauchitsch had been replaced and that, henceforward, operational command would be in the hands of the Führer himself. Bock was to be replaced by Kluge. From now on the Chief of Staff was to be responsible for the Eastern Front, alone, while the other theatres of war were to be controlled by Keitel and Jodl from OKW. Hitler reserved to himself the right to give orders as far down the chain of command as he chose while hiving off to others the chores of a C-in-C which did not interest him. Halder could – perhaps should – have resigned there and then. But he did not and for the reason of old – he felt his first duty was to the Army. So he soldiered on in closer proximity to Hitler, executing orders in which, frequently, he did not really believe.

Skirmishing began at once between Kluge and Guderian as soon as Kluge took over from Bock. On the 17th Kluge had told Guderian that the Führer's standstill order must be carried out '. . . in such a way that as much as possible is preserved of the Army. No area is to be given up unnecessarily but neither is it to be held if troops are to be wiped out as a result'. There was flexibility in this, but Guderian replied, ten hours later after talking to Hitler on the telephone, 'I know the Führer's mind. I will do everything I can . . . I need freedom of action and cannot ask whenever I want to move a division'. He continued gently to withdraw before the Russian pressure, in compliance with Brauchitsch's earlier directive but contrary to what Hitler demanded.

The five-hour meeting with Hitler, when it took place on the 20th, was totally unproductive. Each time Guderian produced evidence of appalling conditions at the front, Hitler brushed it aside with impracticable solutions. When Hitler refuted Guderian's fears of impending doom with an historical analogy, Guderian had a prompt historical retort. A claim by Hitler that winter clothing had actually reached the troops was denied by Guderian with irrefutable proof that it had not. The slightest imputation that OKW did not understand the situation at the front stimulated the Führer's indignation and anger. Suggestions that Hitler should bring battle-experienced officers to replace the OKW staff were anathema. Neither convinced the other of his sincerity and purpose and Guderian was compelled to return to the front to make the best of a bad job – to hold where no defensive localities were prepared, to employ equipment that was falling apart and to drive men who were jaded and depressed – though not yet broken.

The burden of Kluge's telephone call to Halder was to complain about Guderian's continued withdrawal, and say that Guderian had lost his nerve. Kluge was securing his own position, and so, too, was Halder against any possibility of blame by Hitler. They guarded against Guderian's habit of circumventing authority, a habit from which Kluge had often suffered in the past. And almost at once Guderian was making local withdrawals, although, as the Second Panzer Army telephone log shows, they were within the terms permitted by Kluge on the 17th and with Kluge's expressed authority. The log shows how Guderian meticulously asked Kluge's permission for each redeployment, their exchanges sounding almost comic by comparison of minute detail with the expansive freedom of the past. Wielding his power Kluge became more than usually patronising:

'You have a sack full of reserves . . . what do you intend to do with them?' he asked on the 24th. 'Haven't you kept an eye on the roads from Bryansk?' 'Why move again?' And to each provocative question Guderian answered calmly, explaining in detail but warning 'that a 25-kilometre gap had opened which had to be filled', to which Kluge blandly replied: 'The sector must be held . . . after speaking to the Führer and Halder I will let you know.'

A few hours later the town of Chern was reported as lost and Kluge instantly took this opportunity to accuse Guderian of having ordered its evacuation twenty-four hours previously. Guderian denied it and there were hot words. But next day Kluge felt fully justified in his primary suspicions when the units, which had been holding Chern, arrived back escorting several hundred Russian prisoners. Kluge blankly accused Guderian of sending a deliberately falsified report and announced that the matter would be reported to Hitler. At that Guderian impulsively asked to be relieved of his command. But Kluge, who recorded in his diary, 'I am basically in agreement with Guderian but he must obey orders', beat him in the act and recommended at once that he should be removed.

There was no hesitation on Hitler's part either. To him, at that moment, Guderian was just another rebellious senior product of the General Staff who, as Goebbels put it, '. . . are incapable of withstanding severe strain and major tests of character'. Over thirty more generals were categorised that way in December and relegated to the ranks of the disaffected. And yet, ironically, Guderian, at this moment of ugliest adversity, had performed at his best – never before or again does he appear to such advantage by force of personality in leadership or with such innate comprehension of what operationally had needed to be done. Under his hand the troops of Second Panzer Army demonstrated that a flexible withdrawal in winter conditions was within their capacity – and thus he refuted the Hitlerian contention (so willingly approved by a large body of German generals both during and after the event) that if the troops had been permitted a wholesale withdrawal, a rot that transcended French experience in 1812 would have set in. Surpassing even his ability in the techniques of command, however, was his willing cutting of losses that led to the sacrifice of his own career in the service of what he believed to be right. In this way he led his contemporaries and became set upon a course of resistance that converged ever more sharply upon collision with the Führer. Indeed, Paul Dierichs says that in his farewell address to his staff Guderian included hard criticism of Hitler's decision. But for the time being he had no option but to retire from the fray and look on in anger.

9 The Road to Lötzen

Gradually the world and, last of all, Germany became aware of the wholesale dismissal of the military leaders who so recently had won such terrific victories. Among the thirty who went only Brauchitsch's removal was given much publicity, and that in order to boost the Führer's reputation as the new C-in-C. Guderian's sacking, announced almost at once to his own Second Panzer Army by an Order of the Day and repeated with distress by successive lower formation commanders, was withheld from the public, so that by the time more people came to hear indirectly that one of their heroes was no longer in office, fresh champions had been elevated by the propagandists. One of these was Erwin Rommel whose riposte in Cyrenaica in January 1942, after a serious set-back at the hands of the British at the end of 1941, did much to distract attention from those things which had gone wrong in the Russian theatre of war.

Guderian cared little about the loss of personal publicity. When a journalist began research for a potted biography, he had written words of caution to Gretel, in September 1941, asking her to withhold intimate material: 'I would not under any circumstances like becoming involved with propaganda à la Rommel'. But when one has become accustomed to working at full throttle and living expensively upon nerves and physique in conditions of high tension and discomfort over a period of years, a sudden relaxation along with inactivity can be as physically damaging as if full stress was maintained. In Guderian's case a heart condition appeared in March and got worse the following autumn. Simultaneously strains of another sort were substituted for those of battle and persuasion which had buffeted him most. Alongside a nagging patriotic concern over the waning state of Germany's fortunes, grew knowledge of a new peril, the realisation that he was being watched by several kinds of inquisitive people – by the agents of Nazidom, on the one hand, as they investigated his reactions to punishment; by historians who searched for information of an academic kind; and later by the emissaries of a resistance movement who probed his willingness to join their conspiracy. Furthermore Gretel caused him worry when she was confined to bed for several months in the spring with malignant blood-poisoning. In this state of anxiety Guderian half-heartedly hunted for repose in the sun, for a small house near Lake Constance. There seemed little else to do since, in September 1942, he was told that Hitler looked unfavourably on a suggestion by Rommel that he was the best man to take command of Panzer Army Afrika. But since there was no intention of employing him again Hitler, by recompense, offered him land in the Warthegau, once part of Prussia, and retaken from the Poles by conquest in 1939. This was put forward as a national donation to one who, when the Russian campaign seemed all but won on 17th July 1941, had been honoured with the rare Oak Leaves to the Knight's Cross. He accepted and in October 1942 took possession of 2,500 acres of good farmland at Deipenhof. Post-war accusations as to Guderian's cupidity led him to justify the deal in *Panzer Leader* on the grounds that, since his home in Berlin had been bombed, he had nowhere else to go. His son is more explicit in denying any suggestion of profit but frankly stating that the return of the family to the homeland and the policy to strengthen the German population in the Warthegau were problems of which the family was conscious.

It is instructive to observe the fervour with which he approached the traditional role of a land-owning *Junker*. Partly, it seems, he wished to occupy, and thus relax, an active mind, but additionally the change in occupation was welcome for the opportunity it gave of indulging in family life. With the barest rudimentary knowledge and little enough preparation, apart from study in books, he began stock holding and breeding, throwing in the same wholehearted enthusiasm that he had given to soldiering – projecting his objectives far into the distance and planning with meticulous thoroughness. His letters of instruction to Gretel abound with administrative directions. Sheep and cattle were to be the staple of Deipenhof's economy. The presentation of a prize bull (named *Panzergrenadier*) by the farmers of Schleswig-Holstein got him off to a good start. He learned the basic rules and, as usual, was filled with optimism. It is endemic that soldiers, the world over, tend to harbour a sublime belief in the value of a military career for teaching good husbandry. Though the statistics of bankruptcy show grimly against them, there are always retired Servicemen ready to try their luck. Whether or not Guderian would have prospered where others had failed neither time nor events would allow. The war intruded.

He never quite gave up hope of a recall to command – hope, after all, was the last thing he ever abandoned. In September, in the course of final negotiations about Deipenhof, he called wistfully on Bodewin Keitel. But once more Gretel's kinsman told him that the chances of re-employment were poor, worse than ever. Bodewin might be the brother of Wilhelm, but his influence counted far less than before and within a matter of a few days he was to be replaced by Schmundt. As Germany's fortunes slipped into decline, power fell into the hands of men who were hostile to the old order. The revolutions of 1919 and 1933 were at last bearing full but sour fruit. By this time, moreover, it was well known that, within the inner circles of Government, the slightest false move in opposition by an Army officer could lead, at the very least, to instant dismissal. Jodl had experienced a narrow escape in September 1942 and, after a painful rebuff by Hitler, had confided to Warlimont that '. . . one should never try to point out to a dictator where he was wrong since this will shake his confidence . . .' And Warlimont himself had been temporarily relieved of duty by Wilhelm Keitel in November 1942 for an intervention in support of a Duty Officer, a *Major* who had withstood Hitler in an effort to defend Rommel's integrity: '. . . only by the skin of his teeth' did that major 'escape being shot within ten minutes', writes Warlimont.

Henceforward the slightest direct resistance to Hitler by an Army officer was fraught with dire retribution. Therefore common sense stood on the side of those who, like Guderian, chose mainly indirect methods of opposition, seizing rare propitious moments for direct confrontation. What use was there, they could argue, in needless self-sacrifice when, by currently playing softly, they might later find an opportunity to influence affairs by subterfuge? Gretel's advice 'The Fatherland will need you later on, the moment has not come' held as good in 1942 as it did in 1919.

An overriding fear among the generals was the growth of Himmler's SS. The original *Waffen* SS units had sprouted into a large private army composed of divisions which soon would compose corps and eventually armies. Even Göring's *Luftwaffe*, though it faced eclipse in the air because its technology was falling behind that of its opponents, continued to benefit from immense prestige. The SS and *Luftwaffe*, rich in the favour granted to Nazi-orientated organisations, absorbed the best of the manpower and had first pick of industrial resources. Only towards the end of 1941, when the catastrophe prophesied by von Schell was imminent, was the Army given equal production priority with the *Luftwaffe*.

The eventual defeat of Russian and British offensives in the winter of 1941/42 revived German hopes, of course, and led to further deep German penetrations the following summer which carried them to Stalingrad, into the Caucasus and to within a few miles of the Suez Canal at El Alamein. But none of these achievements brought a conclusion – quite the opposite. A universal halt in the autumn was rapidly followed by reverses in winter. First the British blow at El Alamein, conjoint with Allied landings in north-west Africa, threw the logistically impoverished Axis forces back into Tunisia. Then a Russian counter-offensive led swiftly to the isolation of the Stalingrad garrison and the eventual evacuation of the Caucasus. These catastrophes, accompanied by minor Hitlerian repressions, such as those mentioned above, and by his perpetual vacillations, threw a heavy strain upon the Staff. Life for Halder became unbearable and it was a relief to almost everybody when he was sacked on 25th September and replaced by the very junior

Generalleutnant Kurt Zeitzler. Zeitzler was reputed to be sympathetic to Hitler and undeniably possessed a virtue much prized by the Führer – supreme optimism. Almost at once he gave to Hitler what all new Chiefs of Staff felt bound to do – a concession by the Army. In his case it was the promulgation of the Hitlerian qualifications for a staff officer:

'I require the following from every Staff Officer: he must believe in the Führer and in his method of command. He must on every occasion radiate this confidence to his subordinates and those around him'. Nobody challenged it.

Also in the manner of his predecessors Zeitzler rapidly came into collision with his Führer over both operational and administrative policy. Hitler decided personally to influence key Army postings and took direct charge of Bodewin Keitel's Personnel Office. But although Bodewin was no longer able to help Guderian, this was not cripplingly disadvantageous. Guderian remained on good terms with the powerful Schmundt, whom he rated a genteel and sound officer, and continued to enjoy useful relationships with influential members of the *Waffen* SS and *Luftwaffe*. In 1942 Sepp Dietrich, an old *landsknecht* and *Freikorps* man, had gone out of his way to tell Hitler that Guderian had been unjustly treated in December 1941 and, early in 1942, had publicly demonstrated feelings of respect for his old commander. Guderian reciprocated. Dietrich, to him, was the personification of the men whom, in 1919, he had regarded as 'the real fighters' and 'Germany's last hope'. He cared not at all if this contributed to his reputation as a Nazi sympathiser.

So Guderian had friends as well as enemies at court, though it is doubtful if the enemies were anything like as all-powerful as sometimes, without stating names, he implies in *Panzer Leader*. Inevitably there were those with vested interests who resisted him: he was uncomfortable company among traditionalists and the memory of his single-minded assault on Cavalry, Infantry and Artillery sensibilities besides his rudeness to those, such as the members of the Training Department, who had obstructed him, were never forgiven. Officers whose susceptibilities had suffered and who, at last, had seen what they took to be his back, were not in the least bit anxious for his return. Besides, the gunners, quite sincerely, believed they had at last discovered a way to recover their old predominance. Not only had they equipped themselves with a kind of tank – the armoured assault guns – but they were in possession of a new type of low-velocity anti-tank shell, that worked on the hollow charge principle, which, they told Hitler, might make the tank obsolete overnight. They overlooked, somewhat, the problem of hitting pin-points with low velocity projectiles – but Hitler was enthused and that was what mattered.

Tank production and development reacted as much to the seesawing of Hitler's whims and uneducated assessments as did strategy and tactics.

Like a great many politicians he was content to leave well alone until something obviously had gone wrong. Crash-remedial action was then demanded to solve the crisis. Foresight was at a premium. That the appearance of the Russian T 34 tank in July 1941 had hardly registered its danger is recorded above. Not until these machines appeared in large numbers, three months' later, was serious notice taken of Guderian's initial warning and a concentrated effort made, in November 1941, at Guderian's desperate insistence, to hasten the current, lethargic programme of re-equipment. He had pressed for more powerful tanks and, in addition, for self-propelled anti-tank guns – *Panzerjägers*. This brought an astonishing retort in a letter from OKH, 'I only regret that the demand was not made six years ago. We should now be in a different position'. This, as Liebenstein wrote, was received by Guderian as a personal insult: 'There is no other officer who has fought harder than he for better tanks. His demand for 40mm armour was refused years ago and the same can be said over armament – 50mm guns were demanded before 1934'.

The rebuff before Moscow galvanised Hitler in all manner of ways, tank development being but one of them. Being Führer he now demanded instant miracles – increased production and a new, much more powerful tank to defeat the T 34. In January 1942 he was presented with the design of a tank that, it was hoped, would outmatch T 34's *successor* – a new medium tank, known as VK 3000, a machine which eventually would weigh 45 tons and, with its long 75mm L 70 gun, be called 'Panther'. In addition the heavy tank, based upon Guderian's pre-war conception of a 'Break-through Tank' and projected in 1939, was hastened into production: this would be 'Tiger', weigh 56 tons, and be armed with the 88mm L 56 gun. But long before these heavily armoured tanks could be put into production (a few Tigers were ready by the autumn of 1942, the first Panthers in the spring of 1943) something had to be done to restore the tank balance in 1942. This, in fact, was quite easily achieved by increasing the armour – in 1943 80 mm was barely sufficient on the original Pz IIIs and IVs – and re-arming them, respectively, with a long 50mm (L60) and a long 75mm (L46) gun. In addition the number of self-propelled guns – *Panzerjägers, Sturmgeschütz* and artillery – were to be increased to give closer armoured assistance to the infantry and to stiffen anti-tank defence. These machines were based on existing chassis – both obsolete and new.

This vast programme – the sort which had been rejected as impracticable in the summer of 1940 – incurred enormous outlay since increases in the production of existing tanks progressed alongside the development of new machines with radical specification. But introducing new models meant disrupting and then stopping present production. In December 1942, as the panzer divisions came under intolerable pressure in Russia and the Allied effort built up to unprecedented heights in what was, predominantly, a tank war in North Africa, Pz III was taken out of production. At first Hitler followed the advice tendered to him by the officers who represented tank interests at the higher levels of command and by the leading industrialists. They laid down the philosophy that tank design should be based, in order of priority, on armament, speed and armour. This in no way contradicted Guderian's beliefs, even though he worried that many of the army officers involved 'did not have a clear conception from their own experience of the development of modern panzer forces'. Unfortunately neither these officers nor the industrialists were complete masters (or mastered) within their own house. On 8th February 1942 Dr Todt had been killed in a crash and his place as Minister for Armaments taken by Hitler's favourite – the architect Albert Speer. Speer was a remarkable man and a superb organiser, but he knew nothing about tanks or any other sort of weaponry. He had to lean on experts, and the experts had vested interests. For example, industrialists vied with each other to favour their pet concepts and designs. In a competitive trial between two tank types anything might happen: it was quite customary for materials of ridiculously high quality to be used in a test vehicle, well knowing that the production machine could not be similarly supplied. And if a maverick designer of the verve and ambition of, to quote the supreme example, Dr Porsche, did not get his way in committee or by trial he was perfectly capable of making a direct approach to Hitler, whose susceptibilities to the gigantically dramatic were familiar.

In consequence, throughout 1942 and despite the agreed order of priorities laid down in January, Hitler indulged in the habitual game of digression. Some off-hand mention of a new threat or idea would stimulate fresh fears. The product might be discussions about a host of counter-projects, some sound, many fanciful and useless, with the danger that bad things could be initiated. Yet by the skin of its teeth and the dedicated efforts of the commonsense few, the central programme was maintained and improved. Battleworthy tanks began to reach the troops at the front. Even so, in October 1942, total production of Pz IVs was only 100. Appalling wastage in an overstrained and badly organised industrial base was compounded by a multitude of different permutations of self-propelled gun. An extraordinary number of variations, along with redoubled armour thicknesses, were tried in efforts to defeat every sort of enemy attack. Work went ahead on a tank weighing well over 100 tons and there was talk of a truly bizarre monster weighing 1,000 tons. While Speer successfully carried out a rapid and amazingly effective reorganisation of industry, he was quite unable to control its products because nobody could curb Hitler's military intuition at its most fantastic. A moment was to arise in February 1943 when the panzer divisions in Russia, recoiling before the storm of the Russian offensive, could muster, on average, a mere 27 tanks each. And yet by common consent, and despite the gunners' fond expectations, the tank obstinately provided the key to survival in mobile warfare fought over vast frontages.

Guderian writes in *Panzer Leader* that '. . . the few men of insight in Hitler's military entourage began to look around for someone who might be capable, even at this late hour, of staving off the chaos that threatened us all. My prewar writings were placed on Hitler's desk and they managed to persuade him to read them. It was then proposed to him that he send for me. Finally they succeeded in overcoming Hitler's distrust of my person to the extent that he agreed to listen to me at least once.' A slight mystery surrounds the names of the officers concerned but all, in fact, is made clear by an entry on 28th February 1943 in the official diary of the Chief of the HPA – by now Schmundt who had taken over from Bodewin Keitel:

'Chief HPA has for some time recommended *Generaloberst* Guderian to the Führer giving as reason that he is one of his most faithful followers in the General Staff. During long discussions on 25th and 26th February . . . the Führer has convinced himself that he could trust *Generaloberst* Guderian with this responsible post.' General Engel also helped, but it was Schmundt, quite obviously, who carried on where von Below had failed in 1941. Guderian is right, therefore, to give the impression that it was difficult to persuade Hitler to take him back – the Führer's deep-seated mistrust of anybody who had once challenged him was never completely dispelled. Yet Hitler was capable of a semblance of forgiveness if it suited him: Rundstedt who had been retired by him in 1938 at the time of the Fritsch crisis, had been brought back in 1939 – and Rundstedt had been forgiven in 1942 for his temerity in 1941. Moreover Hitler now felt in need of something more potent than advice. His confidence had been shaken by the failure of the operations under his personal direction. His intuition had proven fallible. He needed independent executives. On the Eastern Front he all at once gave Manstein unusual freedom of action to stem the advancing Russian armies in the Ukraine. On 20th February Manstein hurled them back upon Kharkov when their fuel ran out.

That same afternoon, Guderian, having stated to Schmundt the terms for his reinstatement in an appointment of his own design – to be called Inspector General of Armoured Troops – had an interview with the Führer. Guderian perceived Hitler's mood of uncertainty and reports him as saying 'Since 1941 our ways have parted: there were numerous misunderstandings at that time which I much regret. I need you.' It is possible that, in a troubled moment, this most insincere of politicians, for once, spoke the truth. It would be equally likely that he won his way back into Guderian's trust in the innate knowledge that a man he had previously failed to convince could be persuaded to help only by a display of warm humility and abnegation.

As the product of this meeting and a round of talks with key personalities, Guderian drafted a charter for Hitler's signature embodying the authority which had been denied in 1938. In the opening paragraph Hitler was made to state that the Inspector General '. . . is responsible to me for the future development of armoured troops along the lines that will make that arm of the Service into a decisive weapon for winning the war. The Inspector General is immediately subordinate to me, has the status of a Commander-in-Chief of an Army, and is the Senior Officer of the Panzer Command.' Guderian's responsibilities, as drafted, were to include organisation and training not only over Army units but also, where appropriate, those of the *Luftwaffe* and *Waffen* SS. Close collaboration with Albert Speer was called for in the technical development of weapons, along with the creation of new formations and tactical doctrine. He was given direct command, too, over all Replacement Units of mobile troops including the home-based schools. Finally he was authorised to issue regulations. In effect he had at last achieved the aim of making a self-sufficient combat force within the *Wehrmacht*, endowing it with much of the military status already enjoyed by the SS and the *Luftwaffe* and even, as one day would prove, a small measure of political power.

Guderian's charter looks remarkably similar to a document which had been drafted by his opposite number – Percy Hobart – in England in the autumn of 1940 when the state of Britain's Army and armoured forces was as parlous in the wake of Dunkirk as was Germany's in the aftermath of Stalingrad. Hobart had suggested to Winston Churchill the creation of a Commander of the Royal Armoured Corps with status equal to that of an Army Councillor and powers almost identical to those attained by Guderian. Winston Churchill's most senior generals – Generals Dill and Brooke (both of them gunners) opposed the idea. But the Prime Minister was not prepared to override them in the same way as Hitler, though he was later to express regret at not having done so. In Britain a system similar to that which had evolved in Germany in 1938 was the result. There was also a difference in approach between Hobart and Guderian. Whereas Hobart did not feel himself fitted (for reasons of abrasive personalities) to the supreme task, Guderian never for one moment doubted that he alone was the man for the job, regardless of the opposition. Commenting on his charter after the war he wrote: 'Disadvantageous results from this organisation are unknown to the author.'

Not everybody would have agreed with that profession of faith. The artillerists grumbled and managed to snatch the anti-tank units from Guderian's clutches – to his unspeakable rage – but for the most part the fighting soldiers heaved a sigh of relief that Guderian was reinstated. So too did Speer who at last found himself teamed with a man with sole responsibility whose sense of urgency and system braced him in standing firmly by rational ideas and commitments. Very soon the fighting soldiers, those who mattered so much, would know that '*Schnelle Heinz* was back' and with him the hope that the changes they had asked for would be implemented. He took post on 1st March. In a document, prepared for the Americans shortly after the war, he described the methods and organisation employed. 'Training and organisation were each controlled by a General Staff officer and each branch of the Panzer Command was represented by war-experienced officers, most of whom were not fit for active duty because of serious injuries . . . The duty of these specialists was the development of their branch and the issue of regulations written by special commissions composed of officers with fresh experience at the front. These commissions worked under the supervision of the agency for regulations at the Panzer Command School.'

By his insistence upon employing war-experienced officers, Guderian practised what he had been preaching regularly to the OKW and OKH whose senior staff officers, he maintained, were hopelessly out of touch with reality since they were innocent of active service since 1918. For his Chief of Staff Guderian selected *Oberst* Wolfgang Thomale, 'an ardent tank man' and a staff officer of immense capability. Their partnership was complete – far more, perhaps, than is generally realised. The sub-division of their duties was precise. Upon his appointment Guderian said, with a grin, 'One of us must travel and the other run the office. I will travel!' It is fairly obvious that Guderian regarded his appointment as of wider scope than anybody else intended. Speaking to the Americans after 1945 he said that he '. . . considered it his mission to obtain personal insight into the character of his superiors and co-workers and to make immediate proposals based on his own experience with the troops as circumstances required. Therefore the staff was billetted in the vicinity of the Führer's headquarters and that of the Chief of the General Staff in order that he might remain in constant touch with the command of the *Wehrmacht* and the Army.' At the same time Thomale set up an office in the Bendler-strasse in Berlin, and began one of the most intensive spells of activity any chief of staff could experience, working with enthusiasm for a man he describes as 'Germany's best and most responsible general'.

These are not the achievements of a man who was unduly crippled by ill-health, although this factor, in connection with Guderian, has to be examined. Ill-health, frequently incurred through fatigue and a rugged determination to remain in office regardless of the consequences, has diminished the performance of many senior officers, and statesmen too for that matter. It will do so again. Hugh L'Etang, in his study *The Pathology of Leadership*, cites Guderian's heart condition as a weakness, remarking, in general terms, that 'Fatigue tends to be the fate of the ambitious, the conscientious or the idealistic. It is rarely experienced by the astute, the lazy or the clever . . . who may go to considerable trouble to avoid the condition'. The reader is at liberty to categorise the mildly hypochondriac Guderian, but there is little evidence to suggest that a heart condition, real as it was, detracted from his performance. When he occasionally collapsed it was usually *after* some marathon performance in conference when he had excelled himself. Possibly he reached this state as the result of burning himself out over the previous decade and perhaps this heightened the violence of his choler. But the production of choler in the presentation of his policy of 'absolute frankness' had by now become part of an act. His elder son, who was very close to his father, does not believe that the heart condition had much effect and believes, too, that his father merely performed as he would have done whatever his health. Incidentally, Guderian did not eventually die of a heart complaint.

In less than a week of feverish work a policy for tank construction and the reconstruction of the panzer forces had been hammered out for presentation to Hitler. Rationalisation was its keynote. Bizarre projects were set aside and an extraordinary scheme to stop production of the Pz IV as well as the Pz III, before the Panther and Tiger were either in full production or proven, was rescinded. In essence it proposed revised establishments for the panzer divisions, to take account of the new equipment that was coming into service, and attempted to prevent the formation of *Luftwaffe* and *Waffen* SS panzer divisions. Whereas Army panzer divisions, in theory, were to possess only 190 tanks (of which most were Pz IVs), those of the SS would be well above 200. Yet eventually all sorts of variations were implemented since the combination of war and Nazi anarchy defied a uniform system.

Without reservation Guderian supported the introduction of the long 75 and the 88mm guns. Almost any sort of increased armament was welcome to him, including the provision of 20mm and 75mm guns on armoured personnel carriers – the outcome of talks with the troops at the front. The most controversy surrounded assault artillery (*Sturmge-schütz*). Now that Guderian himself was convinced of the need for these machines, he wished only that their design should be regularised so that tank production would not suffer (rightly he appreciated that the tank with its rotating turret was a far more potent all-purpose weapon system than a vehicle with a gun that had only limited traverse), and that the whole lot should come under him. To all intents and purposes he had his way over design but the matter of command led to difficulty.

The presentation of Guderian's plan took place before Hitler and a large gathering of interested people on 9th March – clean contrary to Guderian's hope that he would be able to push it through a select group and thus avoid a prolonged debate with hostile, vested interests. Bureaucracy and sectionalism won after four hours of dialectic battle. At the end he collapsed and in the outcome lost control of the assault guns and failed in the attempt to veto the *Waffen* SS and *Luftwaffe* panzer divisions – his main aim being consolidation of the old and tried Army divisions instead of a proliferation of new, inexperienced ones. (It is of interest to observe Guderian's reaction to this defeat in the pages of *Panzer Leader*, for while he rails at the gunners and Schmundt, he defers mild criticism of the SS and *Luftwaffe* who also frustrated him. In fact, he gives the impression at this point in the book that they fell into line: only later does he mention an unavailing attempt to save his point with both Himmler and the *Luftwaffe* Chief of Staff).

So, once more, he had to make do with second best, and then begin a long round of visits to training establishments, factories, experimental stations and, of course, the units at the front. From these numerous and all-embracing contacts, plus the flow of information accumulated by his staff, he assembled a clear picture of Germany's failing position and the irrational methods that were being employed to counteract it. Most of all he came to understand as never before, even in the closing days of 1941, the utterly pernicious effect of Hitler and his close entourage. Though not at once admitting it, there is little doubt that, with this profounder understanding, came a delayed realisation of the reasons for much else that had gone wrong in the past. At last he could appreciate the difficulties suffered by Brauchitsch, Halder, Rundstedt, Bock, Kleist and the rest – he might even have spared passing sympathy to Kluge. But whereas Guderian made peace with most of his past opponents, unhappily he was never able to bridge the gap with Halder and Kluge. After the war, when he and Halder were in American custody, an attempt (on Guderian's initiative) to bring a reconciliation failed because of Halder's refusal. Death prevented a reconciliation with Kluge, though it is doubtful if an understanding was ever possible. In May 1943, in an atmosphere of latent hostility, they met for the first time since their clash of December 1941. Guderian, with bluff indifference, told Kluge – 'my special friend', as he once called him! – how deeply he felt about his dismissal and that he had never been given satisfaction despite the subsequent clarification of the situation as it had really been. Kluge interpreted the word 'satisfaction' in its strictest Prussian relation to 'honour' and wrote asking Hitler for permission to challenge Guderian to a duel, with Hitler to act as his second. Hitler told them, by implication, to stop behaving like children and settle their quarrel – and instructed Guderian to apologise.

Guderian's tendency to overtrust some people, contrasting sharply with his implacable enmity with anybody found seriously wanting, was a sharp cornerstone of his character – and, in one instance in particular, has a distinct bearing upon history. As a member of the unemployed in 1942, he was tentatively sounded by the resistance conspirators asking if he would join them. *General der Infanterie* Friedrich Olbricht was all at once very attentive and tried to enmesh him in the plot though, at the time, Guderian could not understand why since their previous association had been distant. Schlabrendorff in his 1946 book correctly indicates that approaches were made by Dr Carl Goerdeler, von Tresckow, and *General der Artillerie* Friedrich von Rabenau, though Wheeler-Bennett, who leans quite heavily upon Schlabrendorff in *The Nemesis of Power*, is mistaken when he states that Guderian made '. . . no mention of these earlier approaches'. In *Panzer Leader* the contacts with Goerdeler and Tresckow are described in some detail, and that with Rabenau implied. The substance of the meetings with Goerdeler are the subject of a post-war affidavit sworn by Guderian. However, if Guderian is correct when he says that Goerdeler asserted, in April 1943, that the assassination of Hitler was not contemplated, this was an important contradiction by the conspirators. According to Schlabrendorff an abortive attempt had already been made in March, one in which he had been deeply involved – and of which he was, by 1946, the only surviving witness.

More repellant than anything else to Guderian was the disclosure by Goerdeler that the controller of the conspiracy was none other than Beck – an officer whose Christian character Guderian did not impugn but whose procrastination and incapacity for taking quick decisions seemed at variance with the requirements of a risky *coup d'état*. Goerdeler, who is described by Schlabrendorff as a man with '. . . ability to talk to people from all walks of life and in each case find the right words to win them all over . . . ' singularly failed to charm Guderian, besides several more hard-headed, serving senior officers, including Manstein. Officers, such as Witzleben and Hoepner, who had been harshly treated by Hitler, joined the conspiracy in 1943, while, of those in office, Kluge hopped off and on the fence to their support. Guderian makes his position at that time perfectly clear:

'The weaknesses and mistakes of the National-Socialist system and the personal errors that Hitler made were by then plain to see – even to me: attempts must be made to remedy them. In view of the dangerous situation as a result of the Stalingrad catastrophe and of the demand made [by the Allies] for unconditional surrender . . . a way would have to be found that did not lead to a disaster for the country and the people . . . I came to the conclusion that Dr Goerdeler's plan would be harmful . . . and was, furthermore, incapable of being put into practice; I therefore declined to take part in it. Like the rest of the Army, I also felt myself bound by the oath of allegiance . . .'

Even so Guderian claims that, at Goerdeler's request, he undertook to sound various generals at the front. Eventually he was compelled to report no support, but adds that he gave Goerdeler his word not to divulge their conversations, and maintains that he kept it until 1947 when he saw the matter mentioned in Schlabrendorff's book. Schlabrendorff, for his part, in 1946, stated that Rabenau had felt the need to threaten Guderian with disclosure of his involvement in the plot in order to prevent a leakage – though he did not repeat this allegation in the 1951 edition or in the 1965 book. Gretel told her elder son that Rabenau threatened Guderian's life. In any case it shows how little the conspirators understood Guderian if they imagined he could be silenced in that way – or that it was necessary to threaten once he had given his word.

None of those generals who were contacted, and who refused to commit themselves, divulged the threat to Hitler. This was hardly surprising in the aftermath of Stalingrad, for by then the writing was plainly on the wall – even to optimists like Guderian. Each in his own way was trying to find a solution to a desperate situation – but the vast majority preferred constitutional and non-violent methods. And, being disciplined soldiers, they reasoned that their part was to create the conditions of military stability from which the politicians could negotiate in strength. It is unlikely that a single senior officer, apart from sycophants like Keitel, would have wept many tears if Hitler had been deposed – legally or illegally – and it is an essential aspect of Guderian's story that he was among those who tried to bring that about by a gradual process of limitation through reduction of the Führer's responsibilities. He is no more to be criticised for his failures than the conspirators are for theirs; the latter's ineptitude in implementing plans had, until then, been pusillanimous. While they plotted, Guderian was compiling new and irrefutable evidence of the need for changes in methods and among the actual leadership – and coming to realise the almost wholly insuperable problem of bringing this about. Yet a desperate moment might come, even for him, when almost any release from perfidy would seem blessed.

Tapping the loyalties of field commanders cannot have absorbed very much of Guderian's time as he toured Europe in his endeavours to find quick solutions to a thousand problems, many of which had awaited an answer far too long. Everywhere he encountered an atmosphere of omnipresent crisis. Though a measure of stability had been achieved on the Russian front, the failure of the Russian logistical system, quite as much as German prowess, had brought it about, and here the steady refurbishing of the armoured forces was constantly inhibited by prodigal waste. The formations at the front were too weak and had been only parsimoniously refitted with new tanks. Those tanks in service were hampered by lack of spares because, as Speer writes: 'Hitler insisted upon giving priority to new production which could have been reduced by 20 per cent if we had made provisions for proper repairs'. As it was the field workshops stripped everything from tanks which broke down with the result that, when that tank's carcass arrived back in Germany for reworking, practically nothing of value remained and a total and costly rebuild was inevitable.

A fruitful and crucial relationship sprang up between Guderian and

Speer, both of whom were bent upon making better use of Germany's resources for what they saw as the common good. So seductive was Guderian's persuasiveness that he actually managed to obtain for the *Panzerwaffe* materials and manufacturing capacity that previously had been exclusively *Luftwaffe* property. Hence the *Luftwaffe*, plagued by misguidance from Göring and the errors of some among his favourites, found itself shorn of facilities as the air attack upon German industry mounted in intensity. To airmen sold on the dream of air power, this seemed a pernicious blow to Germany's hopes of survival though it is equally certain that, now as always in the past, they also exaggerated their case.

Far more destructive than administrative chaos, however, was the irrevocable and repeated commitment of Army formations to lost situations. To within a few days of the final collapse of the Axis forces in North Africa in the first week of May, fresh troops were still being sent across the sea. A last minute plan to evacuate the key personnel of the tank forces by air, strenuously supported by Guderian, came to nothing with the result that what could have been cadres for many fresh units and formations were needlessly lost. At about the same time the plans for an offensive against the Russians were in course of discussion. The Chief of Staff, Zeitzler, had proposed to Hitler an enveloping attack against the Kursk salient where it invitingly jutted out towards the west. When the idea had been mooted in April by Manstein, for implementation on the dried-out ground in early May with the relatively weak panzer forces then available, the Russian defences were still weak enough to proffer a reasonable chance of success. Early in May, however, it seemed apparent that the Russians were forewarned (as they were) because the defences were being vigorously and noticeably strengthened. But by then Hitler had become enthused and was demanding, with political, propaganda motives, a dramatic victory that employed as many as possible of the new Tiger and Panther tanks. This requirement imposed delays to enable these machines to be brought forward in large numbers straight from production. At once Guderian was drawn into a direct confrontation with Zeitzler and Hitler, pointing out not only the continuing and inevitable mechanical deficiencies of the new tanks with their unfamiliarised crews, but also the pointlessness of striking at Kursk: 'How many people do you think even know where Kursk is?' he claims to have asked Hitler. And Hitler – who once said that he knew 'with whom of my people I can allow myself this [scornful disregard] and with whom I cannot' – had actuated his Guderian-deflection device by appearing to agree while persevering unheedingly with what he instinctively preferred.

As was his policy, Guderian struggled to penetrate the places of decision in order to influence overall strategy. Though once more he could drive to the front, speak to the crews, and watch the tanks in action – as he did when the Kursk offensive at last began, after repeated delays, on 4th July – essentially he had risen above the battlefield environment and was bent on changing Hitler's habits along with those of OKW and OKH. At Kursk the tired and grimy crews described what he had feared and expected. Failure. The Panthers, in particular, had given trouble with running gear that broke down and optics which did not allow the tank gunners to make full use of the excellent, long 75mm gun. The Tigers, too, broke down while a number of the latest most heavily armoured self-propelled guns, the Ferdinands, suffered tactical reverses because of their inability to fend off Russian infantry once they became separated from their escort: invulnerably armoured and heavily armed with an 88mm gun, they had only one machine-gun for close defence. But, fundamentally, the failure at Kursk was due to the employment of a faulty plan which lacked the element of strategic as well as tactical surprise.

In the high courts of power he met men whose aims and methods were often quite contrary to his own. In Guderian's judgement the defeat at Kursk was decisive because '. . . it damaged the German Army to an irreparable degree and the loss of the war dates from this defeat even more than from that at Stalingrad. The Russians had comparatively small losses and struck back after the German attack, leading to renewed breakthroughs and retreats on the part of the Germans'. It would, he said, '. . . affect the establishment of a defensive front against invasion in the West . . . ' The primary target for his disappointment at the defeat at Kursk was Zeitzler, but Zeitzler merely suffered from the ailments wished upon him by his predecessors – and this Guderian now came to realise. Albert Speer, who supported Guderian through thick and thin even in his attempts to curb the members of Hitler's entourage, was now instrumental, at Guderian's request, in setting up a meeting with Zeitzler in his own house at Obersaltzburg. Ostensibly it was to settle '. . . some disputes . . . springing from unresolved jurisdictional questions . . . But it turned out that Guderian had more in mind than the settlement of minor disputes. He wanted to discuss common tactics in regard to the matter of a new Commander-in-Chief of the Army.'

Speer continues: 'The differences between Zeitzler and Guderian quickly dwindled to nothing. [It is certainly noticeable that, from the late summer onwards, Guderian's attitude to Zeitzler softened.] The conversation centred upon the situation that had arisen from Hitler assuming command of the Army but not exercising it. The interests of the Army as against the two other branches of the services and the SS must be represented more vigorously'. In essence the two soldiers agreed that Hitler should become less partisan and that he ought to relinquish the post of Commander-in-Chief and appoint somebody who would maintain personal contact with the army commanders and take care for the needs of the troops. It was agreed that Speer and Guderian should speak independently on the subject to Hitler, but unfortunately neither knew that both Kluge and Manstein had recently done precisely the same. Hitler drew the false conclusion that all four were in collusion – as, to all intents and purposes, was so. Tresckow had already sounded Guderian, ostensibly on behalf of Kluge, to see if a reconciliation could be effected between the old antagonists as a first step in a joint approach to Hitler in an endeavour to arrange a diminishment of his powers. Guderian had declined because of 'My very exact knowledge of Field-Marshal von Kluge's unstable character . . .' It may well be that Tresckow, as one of the principal plotters, had pushed Kluge hard into making the offer (as he had invariably to do in pushing Kluge towards any sort of resistance) but Guderian, none the less, may have been wrong to decline even though he was shrewd in his judgement of the hesitant Kluge. At that moment a combined effort by the most senior commanders might have averted the tragedy to come, forlorn though the hope could be. Guderian, however, was playing a lone hand from a sense of necessity. Accustomed to being rebuffed by his seniors and contemporaries he scarcely hoped to achieve lasting alliances among the hierarchy.

The oppressive atmosphere of intrigue and circumlocution which pervaded Hitler's court stimulated its mood. Within those walls, personal relationships fluctuated with the same frequency as policy. Loyalty and continuity were at a premium. Conflicting judgements were the rule rather than the exception. In 1943 there was, in the innermost circles of power, a fairly strong consensus of opinion that Guderian, as Warlimont put it to me, 'politically sought a closer association with the Party than was customary among the officers'. To a large extent this is confirmed by Goebbels in the pages of his diary. On 6th March 1943 he quoted Seyss-Inquart as saying that '. . . our generals sometimes get weak in the knees' and added: 'This view is confirmed by a long talk with *Generaloberst* Guderian . . . We discussed the abuses prevalent in the *Wehrmacht*. Guderian is a very sharp critic of these obvious improprieties. He impressed me as an exceptionally wide-awake and alert commander. His judgment is clear and sensible and he is blessed with healthy common sense. Undoubtedly I can work with him. I promised him my unstinted support.' According to Guderian he attempted to have Goebbels persuade Hitler to replace Wilhelm Keitel with an officer '. . . who understood how to function as an operational commander', but nothing of importance came of this meeting. Goebbels was never among those to offend the Führer. Nor was Guderian successful in another meeting with Goebbels on 27th July when again, according to Goebbels, 'He told me about his grave concern over the present status of the war. He pleaded for concentration at some point since we cannot afford to be active on all fronts. He complained about the inactivity of OKW which does not contain a single leader. Guderian made an excellent impression. He is certainly an ardent and unquestioning disciple of the Führer.'

It is possible that the normally forthright Guderian was engaged in a delicate attempt to split the Nazi ranks by administering mild doses of the Hitlerian virus – a little sweetness here, a little poison there, with the intention of bringing general pressure to bear on Hitler while enhancing his own standing. He even tried to influence Himmler, though Göring, who 'disliked working', he left alone. Within a year Goebbels, at a vital moment, would adopt a strikingly different opinion of the Inspector General of Armoured Forces, but that was at a moment when the whole Nazi house of cards was shaking. It is undoubtedly true, as will be seen, that Guderian envisaged himself as the man who might yet save the Army and the nation.

In the meantime any hope there might ever have been of Germany 'concentrating at some point' had evaporated. Germany had forfeited the initiative long before the disaster at Kursk. The annihilation of the last bridgehead in Tunis had provided the springboard from which, in July, the British and Americans had launched the invasion of Sicily, an event which had led Hitler to call off the attack at Kursk. The fall of Mussolini followed and, in September, the invasion of Italy as Germany's major ally sued for peace. A guerilla war which, since 1941, had spluttered in the Balkans, broke into flames and attracted large German forces in efforts to pacify a vaste area, as well as deterring an Allied invasion. In Russia the waves of an almost irresistible flood of offensives rolled westward, engulfing formations and units whose combat prowess had been stabilised but whose higher direction was permanently hampered by Hitler's vetoes on yielding ground. An incipient inability on Hitler's part to comprehend that mobility was as much part of defence as it was of attack, inhibited Hitler from permitting his commanders to exercise the full potential of the panzer divisions which, given the opportunity, had shown outstanding defensive powers.

The panzer divisions were forced to perform the defensive role which Seeckt and Guderian had originally envisaged for Germany's limited forces – manoeuvres in depth with the flexible aim of destroying enemy forces on ground of the defender's choice. What was more, the German Army in Russia, throughout the mid-period of 1943, possessed a far better capability to achieve what had been dreamed of in the 1920s. They not only had ample space in which to play an infinite number of tactical permutations, but a superior mobility and hitting power far in advance of anything seen before. The new regulations, then being issued by the Inspector General's staff, were couched in terms of the defensive offensive battle based, initially, upon careful reconnaissance. In this respect the run down of the reconnaissance troops after 1941 was a matter of deep regret to Guderian who was busily trying to rehabilitate them. These units could find and track each enemy thrust in co-operation with aircraft.

When the strength of direction of each threat was confirmed it would be for the infantry divisions, backed up by self-propelled guns, to hold vital points. Then the panzer divisions could move at speed to key, and preferably flanking, positions from which they initially blasted the enemy, as in an ambush, and next drive among the shattered remnants to deliver the *coup de grâce*. Finally the panzer divisions would withdraw in readiness to deal with the next threat as it developed. Unfortunately Hitler frequently intervened to hamper preliminary operations, and either delayed them too long or began them too soon, thus mitigating their effects. Command of tanks can only come from the front. Alternatively he would allow success to be won and then sacrifice the advantage by vetoing a subsequent redeployment or persisting too long in the face of a subsequent stalemate. Invariably he turned economic plans into profligate waste.

In Guderian's summing up: 'The unfortunate and ruinous combat of 1943 had defeated all schemes to increase the fighting power of the panzer divisions. Only the quality of the individual tanks could be improved, but the total number dwindled steadily. By September 1943 there were fourteen divisions with one panzer battalion each, eight with two, and two with three. In addition there were ten *Panzergrenadier* divisions each with one panzer battalion armed with assault guns. The authorised strength, per company, though stipulated to be 22 tanks, was actually only 17.' On the other hand Guderian understates the vastly improved striking power provided by the new, more accurate high-velocity guns, and that, in training, infinitely more trouble was taken in profitably improving the gunner's skill. Before 1939 tank gunnery had been rudimentary. Now much more time and trouble was given to shooting techniques with great emphasis on live firing on realistic practice ranges. Henceforward German tank gunners scored far more hits than their opponents and it was this capability, allied to improved equipment and the existing tactical skills, that was the greatest achievement of the Inspectorate under Guderian. Without this amazing feat of organisation and inspiration the German Army would have collapsed much sooner than it did.

Increasingly Guderian came to worry about the functioning of the higher leadership and strongly to doubt the Führer, though he was far from first to do so. For example, Erwin Rommel had lost faith in Hitler as long ago as November 1942 when Hitler had forbidden him to abandon a broken position at El Alamein. In the aftermath of incurring quite unnecessary losses, Rommel had been frankly outspoken in his criticism of Hitler and, in consequence, had been extracted from Africa. He now posed an embarrassment to the Führer who, nevertheless, felt compelled to keep his most highly-prized, propaganda general in the public eye. Rommel was given sinecures – a job on the Führer's personal staff and then the task of up-dating plans in the event of an Italian surrender. But once more Rommel disappointed Hitler by demanding that Italy be abandoned and that the defence of Southern Germany should be based upon the Alps. So Rommel was denied the post of Commander-in-Chief of Italy: instead it was given to Albert Kesselring of the *Luftwaffe*, a more amenable character.

These things Guderian interpreted in his own way and linked them with yet another awful blunder that was in course of preparation by Hitler – an ill-prepared counter-stroke at Kiev in November. On 9th November, the day Hitler proposed this operation, Guderian wrote a letter to Gretel in which he clearly indicates his forebodings and, incidentally, corroborates the tone of disenchantment in *Panzer Leader*. Referring to the seriousness of things at the front and the fact that '. . . insight into the situation does not keep pace with it, resulting in a continuous lagging behind of decisions . . .' he went on:

'How long I can continue in my command under these circumstances I cannot say. I am not very optimistic. When I consider that Ro [Rommel] had to hand over his Army Group because, in essence, he gave correct advice . . . then I am not very hopeful that I shall fare better. Nevertheless I feel compelled at this hour to express myself critically in order not to be guilty of neglecting the troops, for which I could never forgive myself later. Keep your fingers crossed that things turn out right.'

This was the Bartenstein spirit of 1919, the sentiments of one who had resolved to offer himself as a sacrifice in his country's cause. If his adoption of this attitude seems delayed (apparently a whole year after Rommel), it can only be said that, whereas Rommel had suffered for 18 months under Hitler's direct command before loosing faith, Guderian required barely six to reach the same state. A comparison between the performance of Rommel and Guderian is certainly appropriate. Each had been raised to the heights of public adulation in exploitation of their dashing achievements in battle; each in his way was photogenic and an evocative subject for the propagandist; neither objected to a place in the limelight. But Rommel, the fighting soldier *par excellence*, had inferior foresight to Guderian and still less organising and administrative ability. Before the war, as Ronald Lewin says of Rommel in his *Rommel as Military Commander*, 'His record . . . is one of steady but conventional progress'. Rommel, in fact, could never have conjured up and pushed throught the imaginative *Panzertruppe* in all its ramifications and with the need for such deft negotiation. But Rommel had not been trained as a General Staff officer and his operations at war hung much more on a string than did Guderian's. Each, of course, had peerless insight into the demands and opportunities of the battlefield and was a superb tactician, though the better trained Guderian calculated the risks more thoroughly and, in endeavours to win his way in negotiation, cultivated diplomatic skill and, when necessary, the patience to give here or wait there for a more propitious moment. As Guderian once ironically and sadly reflected about Rommel (whom he admired), 'He *always* wanted to have his own way'. They were as one in their ideals, a Prussian and a Swabian in complete accord over the integrity of the oath and of honour, committed to criticism of Hitler (though Rommel was by far the more indiscreet) but opposed to removing him by violence. Both totally rejected assassination.

Guderian's negotiating methods are well illustrated in his relationship with the top men in the attempt to diminish Hitler's authority over the Army. Like his strategic and tactical approaches, they were indirect to begin with but finally looked like hammer blows, aimed straight at the target. Feeling sure of Speer and Dietrich, and at least on good terms with Goebbels (while dismissing Göring as of little assistance by reason of his laziness) he began by tackling Himmler but 'received an impression of impenetrable obliquity'. This was hardly surprising from the man who was the Army's deadliest enemy. Probably Guderian had not realised this before. Nevertheless, in approaching Himmler first he exhibited political realism by recognising in the Head of the SS the most powerful figure next to Hitler. Having failed at the top he moved a rung further down. A few days later he approached Jodl and laid before him a plan for the reorganisation of the Supreme Command of which the vital part lay in the scheme that Hitler should cease to control the actual conduct of operations and confine himself to '. . . his proper field of activities, supreme control of the political situation and of the highest war strategy'. Believing that these proposals were bound to reach Hitler's ears and being fully aware what the reaction must surely be, Guderian boldly placed his own head on the block. The outcome may have come as a surprise. Jodl, who was a devotee of outright control by OKW and who was unshakeably loyal to Hitler, merely put on a boot-face and asked, 'Do you know of a better Supreme Commander than Adolf Hitler?' Guderian says that he put his papers back in his brief case and left the room, but though this represented angry impetuosity there was nothing impetuous about his challenge, although there is no doubt that many in the hierarchy figured it as such – that being their customary assessment of Guderian's normal behaviour. He was extraordinarily naive if he did not assume that a report would be made to Hitler; therefore he now sat back to await dismissal. But nothing happened at once: he was allowed to continue with the restoration of the panzer forces and assert whatever influence he could upon a system in decay. Whether or not Himmler or Jodl passed on Guderian's remarks, there was only silence from Hitler.

In fact there was no other general than Guderian from whom Hitler took such affrontery and yet retained in his service. In January 1944 he actually created the opportunity to allow an airing of the subject of a readjusted command system by inviting Guderian to a private breakfast.

The discussion opened with a quarrel as to the desirability of building a strong, lay-back defensive system covering Germany's eastern frontier. Hitler argued, with a wealth of figures he had learnt by heart, that it was not feasible. Guderian claimed it was. The subject shifted to the question of the High Command. We only have Guderian's word for what transpired but it appears that he desisted from telling Hitler to his face that he should limit his powers 'since my indirect attempts . . . had failed'. Instead he proposed that a general Hitler trusted should be appointed as Chief of the Armed Services General Staff. Naturally Hitler recognised this thinly disguised attempt to whittle away his own powers: predictably he turned it down. Guderian drew the conclusion that there was not a single general whom Hitler did trust and began to ask himself the question, 'To whom would Hitler turn eventually for help in running the Army? Would it be a soldier, an airman or a totally unqualified member of the Nazi Party? Could it possibly be a soldier who was outwardly loyal to Hitler but wholly committed to Germany?'

An appalling atmosphere of doom hung over Germany. Air raids made both night and day hideous with death and destruction while news of the contracting frontiers threatened a more dreadful fate when invading armies reached Germany, as surely they must that year unless a miracle occurred. With invasion imminent in the West, the number of fronts would be increased at a time when Germany's resources were already stretched beyond the limit. Faced with these horrors and the knowledge that the man at the helm was incorrigible, those who sought his removal went more desperately to work in their different ways to bring this about. The most active party of conspirators, led by Beck, had taken fresh vigour when they were joined, as manager in May 1943, by the man who, in 1941, had tried to make Guderian C-in-C, the fanatically anti-Nazi *Oberst* Claus von Stauffenberg. Despite wounds received since 1941, this excellent staff officer put purpose into the detailed planning of a *coup d'état* which would embrace a take-over of Government by the Army, preceded by the assassination of Hitler and the arrest of the principal members of the Nazi Party and, of course, the SS. As cover for the putsch, a plan – called Operation Valkyrie – for the Army to deal with a mutiny by the SS or with unrest by the foreign workers in Germany was concocted. Inevitably many more people than those few behind the plot had to be brought in on the periphery. In consequence the risks of discovery were increased in the interests of achieving widespread effects: those generals who were infected with Nazism had to be excluded. It is instructive that, whatever Goebbels may have thought, the plotters did not believe Guderian to be that way politically inclined. He was kept aware of their presence not only by random contacts with Goerderler but also through Thomale. For although neither Guderian nor Thomale admit to complicity, Thomale is quoted as saying, in August 1943, to one of the inner ring of plotters, *Generalmajor* Helmuth Stieff, that Guderian 'explicitly desisted from taking part because direct action against Hitler would be demanded'. Moreover it was Thomale who arranged the meeting between Tresckow and Guderian at the latter's home and he who warned Tresckow not to mention Kluge's involvement with the plot. But to quote Guderian's son, 'Tresckow named Kluge and my father exploded in his bed . . . Thus the discussion was finished'. Clearly, therefore, Thomale was to some extent in the know and also aware of his chief's dilemma – the difficulty implicit in conscience concerning his oath to Hitler and the propriety of being complicit with murder, the application of judgement as to whether the conspirators' plans would work and, if they failed, the horror of what damage would be done. It would have been surprising and impossible had things been otherwise between Commander and Chief of Staff.

Regularly Guderian was coming into collision with Hitler. His disapproval of 'witch hunts' directed against generals who had failed – or had appeared to fail – at the front was made plain. Thus he contributed to resistance (without perhaps intending to) by delaying inquiries of that nature for which he was made responsible. With regard to strategy in the field, he was not only in sharp disagreement over the conduct of operations in Russia, but also with defensive preparations in France where Hitler backed Rommel in his desire to position the mobile forces close to the coast. Guderian agreed with Rundstedt who, urged on by von Geyr, wished to have them located centrally. The outcome was a compromise between the two lines of thought, both of which had pronounced merits and demerits since the argument for holding the armour forward was based on Rommel's fear of Allied air power. Of this Guderian had far less experience than Rommel, even though he admits to seeing for himself the impunity with which enemy aircraft in the West flew above the training areas and bombed as they chose.

Tragedy was in the making for Rommel. He was already committed in mind to an attempt at arranging separate armistice terms in the West and opening a gap for the Allies: and he had also been in contact with the principal conspirators. While somewhat ambivalent in his replies, he had stated to them: 'I believe it my duty to come to the rescue of Germany'. From this the conspirators assumed that he would be prepared to accept a senior appointment in some future government and, though there is conflicting evidence in the matter, it seems almost certain that he was aware of this development and did not reject it out of hand. What he was unaware of until too late was that this damaging evidence had been put in writing by Goerdeler. Finally Rommel committed himself to a confrontation with Hitler by sending the Führer a flatly challenging report on 15th July. The Allied invasion had been launched into Normandy on 6th June and, through the most desperate efforts, had been contained within a relatively small bridgehead. To Hitler he now declared, with Kluge's endorsement (as the new C-in-C West): 'The troops are fighting heroically everywhere, but the unequal struggle is nearing its end'. To his Chief of Staff he said, 'I have given him [Hitler] the last chance. If he does not take it we will act' – by this meaning a separate armistice in the West. It is not clear, however, if Kluge was compliant to this part of the scheme. This far Guderian would not have gone on his own – and certainly not in company with Kluge.

Yet already in the first few days of July a separate and final decision had been taken by the leading exponents of assassination. Pressure, that accumulated from threats of disclosure, was heavy upon them. Allied attacks on all fronts seemed likely to cause a total collapse of the *Wehrmacht* and even more senior officers were now convinced that the war was lost. These officers, whose company included Rundstedt (who had handed over to Kluge), Kluge himself and Fromm, the Commander of the Replacement Army in Germany, prudently adopted Bock's original attitude: 'If you can pull it off I'll join you but until then I'll not help: if you fail, Heaven be your help because I will not.'

On 17th July Rommel was eliminated from participation in the plot when he was seriously wounded by an air attack. This removed a key figure, one who as a propaganda idol might have rallied popular support behind the conspiracy. Guderian, of course, was another such figure. He says that on 18th July a *Luftwaffe* officer 'whom I had known in the old days' came to inform him that Kluge was contemplating arranging a separate armistice in the West. That much is true, but it is not the whole truth. His informant, in fact, was none other than von Barsewisch, his *Luftwaffe* liaison officer in Russia in 1941; the man who had flown Guderian forty-eight times at the front and who, therefore, had a special relationship with him; an officer of panache and principle who, at his peril after Guderian's dismissal, had criticised the Führer by holding – in Guderian's absence – a parade in his honour and by extolling him in a speech in Berlin; who had kept contact with Guderian ever since and knew of his old commander's opinion that Hitler was leading Germany to destruction. Barsewisch now came to Guderian as the emissary of the conspirators (in response to a request from *Major* Caesar von Hofacker) in a last effort to persuade Guderian to adopt outright resistance. News of the impending assassination, of which Barsewisch now told him without revealing its date (since the final decision had yet to be taken on the 19th), thoroughly shook Guderian. It was of no avail. Admitting the validity of Barsewisch's reasoning, after a four-hour tramp and talk in the woods out of earshot, Guderian held firm to his original contention that he could not break his oath and must do his duty as an officer. All mention of assassination at this meeting is excluded from *Panzer Leader*. Only the subject of the armistice is ingenuously discussed on the lines that if he informed the

Führer and the information proved false he would be '. . . doing *Feldmarschall* Kluge a grave injustice . . . Should I keep the information to myself I must share the guilt of the evil consequences that were bound to ensue.' He adds that he did not believe the story and decided to stay silent.

This aspect of the Bomb Plot story, concealed up to now, throws a flickering light on Guderian's part. In one respect – his omission of the whole truth from *Panzer Leader* (perhaps from a tortured conscience but as likely from true political reaction) – he emerges at less than his normal standards of behaviour. From another angle he becomes fully implicated in the plot. He knew Hitler was doing awful damage and he did nothing to stop the assassination either by arresting Barsewisch on the spot or reporting the whole matter. Instead he pursued a well-thought out policy adapted to the new circumstances.

At only a few hours notice, and clearly in a state of unusual tension, he set out next day, the 19th, on a hastily arranged tour of inspections to units which (by coincidence?) were within reach of either Berlin, his home at Deipenhof, Hitler's headquarters with OKW at Rastenburg, or OKH at Lötzen. When visiting anti-tank troops at Allenstein, Thomale called him on the telephone to seek agreement to a request by Olbricht (now among the leading plotters) to delay the despatch of a panzer unit from Berlin to East Prussia in order that it might take part in an exercise of Operation Valkyrie – an operation Guderian thought covered action against enemy air landings or internal unrest. He gave his 'reluctant approval,' as indeed he might since this virtually told him that the attempt upon Hitler's life was fixed for the morrow. At any moment he would be faced with decisions of quite appalling consequence.

Next morning, the 20th, he inspected more troops and then went to Deipenhof. At 1250 pm a bomb, planted by Stauffenberg, exploded in Hitler's conference room killing a number of officers (including Schmundt) but scarcely injuring the Führer. Without checking, and on the assumption that Hitler was dead, Stauffenberg flew to Berlin and at 4 pm started the conspirators putting the plan into action with telephone calls through the Reich and occupied territories, calling for the arrest of the Nazis. Unfortunately for them the most important telephone exchange of all, the one at Rastenburg, which should have been crippled by General Fellgiebel (the top OKW Signals Officer whose work in raising signal communications to such a high level had won Guderian's highest praise), was still working. Fellgiebel, on finding that Hitler was alive, had bungled the job without passing on the truth to his fellow conspirators and, incidentally, by his incompetence, revealed the incompatibility of General Staff officers for this sort of work besides ensuring the doom of the enterprise.

184

At 4 pm* Guderian, too, was out of communication, on a long walk far from the house, hunting roebuck in the course of inspecting the estate. From solitude he was summoned home by a despatch rider who told him to expect a telephone call from Supreme Headquarters. A few minutes later, over the radio, he heard of the attempt on Hitler's life.

Too much weight should not be placed on surmise (of which there is plenty), though that is all there is concerning much that took place on the 20th. But it must have been well known to Guderian that, in moments of crisis when he did not wish to be contacted, a revered past commander of his used to take a walk for evasive action. That commander had been Rüdiger von der Goltz. On the assumption that Guderian was forewarned of an impending and dangerous event and with it the implication that he might soon be required to take a fatal decision, it was essential that he should preserve for himself the maximum time in which to allow the plot to resolve itself: thus the lonely walk was loaded with precedent and provided an excellent pretext for a useful safety measure. When at midnight Thomale came through on the telephone, the conspiracy had been crushed and a decision was unnecessary. Beck, Stauffenberg and some of the others were dead, with several more under arrest. From the Führer's vengeful rantings it was obvious that anybody connected in the slightest way with the plot need expect no mercy; but then, there never had been much doubt that the price of failure would be a holocaust. Rommel had taken no direct part, but in due course his involvement would be revealed and he would pay with his life. Kluge, too, had stood back, filled with doubts, but he was fatally implicated and within a few weeks committed suicide. Possibly by luck, but much more likely as the result of exercising prudence and careful management over the past year or more, Guderian had isolated himself from contamination and yet, by keeping in touch and well informed, provided himself with an unshakeable alibi. If it had been his aim to preserve himself for a sacred task – the defence of Germany and of the old Army – he could not have gone about it more thoroughly and astutely. He saw no need for a martyr and positively declined to offer himself in that role.

Even so his fate, for one dramatic moment, hung accidentally by a string. When the news reached Speer at his Berlin office, his first assumption was that: 'It did not occur to me that Stauffenberg, Olbricht, Stieff and their circle might be carrying out the revolt. I would rather have attributed such an act to a man of Guderian's choleric temperament'. Speer recalls Goebbels and a *Major* Remer engaged upon crushing the revolt with whatever loyal troops could be found, and a melodramatic event at 7 pm when '. . . all was thrown into question again when he [Goebbels] learnt shortly afterwards that a tank brigade had arrived at

*Guderian's times are extracted from his sworn affidavit.

Fehrbelliner Platz and was refusing to obey Remer's orders. General Guderian alone was their commander, they had told Remer, and with military terseness had warned him: "Anyone who doesn't obey will be shot". Their fighting strength was so superior to Remer's that the fate of a good deal more than the next hour or so seemed to hang on their attitude'.

These troops, of course, were acting in the spirit of the Valkyrie operation to put down an SS mutiny. Also they were perfectly correct in saying that they acted under Guderian's orders since all home-based panzer units were, by Charter, under his command, and the commander of this unit had been told by Thomale only to follow orders from Hitler, Keitel or Guderian. In this moment of confusion, when nobody knew friends from foes, sudden false conclusions were inevitable. Speer writes: 'Both Goebbels and Remer thought it likely that Guderian was a participant in the Putsch. The leader of the brigade was *Oberst* Bollbrinker. Since I knew him well I tried to reach him by telephone. The message I received was reassuring: the tanks had come to crush the rebellion'. They did not, of course, say what sort of rebellion because they were unaware of the circumstances. This raises the important matter of loyalties. The panzer officers, at that moment, were willingly engaged in an operation on behalf of Hitler but they gave their initial allegiance to Guderian, all the more willingly, probably, in the belief that he was the Führer's agent. This not only underlines the conspirators' essential need for support by credible military leaders, other than forgotten and discredited men of Beck's standing, but shows how correct were those who evaluated Guderian as a potentially key personality in the crisis. It also goes to substantiate Guderian's contention that '. . . at that time the great proportion of the German people still believed in Adolf Hitler . . .' Without troops personally loyal to themselves the conspirators never had a chance. Yet, even Guderian's weight, thrown behind the plot at the last minute, as Barsewisch had asked, would have saved nothing. Still there would have been a bungle and as a result Guderian, too, would have been destroyed and deprived of the task he saw for himself on Germany's behalf.

At Rastenburg Hitler was picking up the pieces and giving the orders that were to lead to the slaughter of dissidents and infliction of the final indignities upon the Army. So far as Guderian was concerned this was neither the first nor the last time he benefited from the services of a Chief of Staff who was as meticulously loyal as, for example, Nehring had been. It was Thomale who, at 6 pm on the 20th, was the first to be asked to account for Guderian's absence and he who was called to see the Führer an hour later to answer, satisfactorily, further questions.* He was told to instruct Guderian immediately to go to OKH at Lötzen and take over as acting Chief of Staff. Fate had a hand, for Hitler had earlier decided to be

---

* Reference to a post-war affidavit sworn by Thomale.

rid of Zeitzler, whose objections had become too strong for comfort, and replace him with *General* Buhle. Zeitzler had retired on grounds of ill-health but Buhle had been wounded by the explosion and was temporarily incapacitated. Quite by chance, and as second choice, Guderian reached what Warlimont called 'the summit of his ambitions' – in which judgement Warlimont may well have been right in connection with an ambitious man, except that, as Guderian writes: '. . . even the rumour-mongers must admit that voluntarily to tackle the situation on the Eastern Front in July 1944 was no very enticing proposition.' For there were those who gave credence, as did Schlabrendorff, to the gossip that 'All those in the plot were convinced that Guderian had given them away to Hitler in order that he would be made Chief of Staff'. The fact that Buhle was already the Chief of Staff designate disposes of these accusations without the need to hear Guderian's defence that he was ordered to comply and that, in any case, 'I should have regarded myself as a shabby coward if I had refused to attempt to save the eastern armies and my homeland, eastern Germany'. These were reasons enough, but there was one more which he later confided to his family, to Strik-Strikfeld and close associates. That was the need to prevent an SS man becoming Chief of Staff, the vital necessity to curb the excesses of Heinrich Himmler and his minions as they closed in for the kill of the old Army.

There is a revealing clue to the innermost thoughts and intentions of Guderian in a letter from Gretel on August 20th. In it she wrote: 'We have often talked about this dreaded development and the task that would be set for you. That is how it has turned out! Also that we would be parted in this most serious hour and have to make independent decisions was clear to us. So now each must stand at his post and hope that we will be happily reunited quite soon . . . Our unique understanding gives me the strength to see things through . . . The forbidden emotions you will not be able to avoid in the future. I get panic-stricken sometimes when I think of all that is piling upon you. May God maintain for you his [the Führer's] close confidence. That is the foundation of all. If that is lost so is everything else.'

The letter, carried by hand, is of necessity guarded in its obliquity, for every communication was dangerous, but it seems quite apparent that together they had visualised, with a sense of forboding, a day he would be called upon as Chief of Staff. The reference to 'forbidden emotions' requires interpretation, but almost certainly concerns medical instructions that he must avoid emotions and excitements under stress. The references to Hitler's confidence do not, however, imply a close allegiance to Hitler, but suggest instead the need to cling to any straw for survival. This letter, however, could be read in the context of abiding loyalty to the Führer, had it been intercepted. Never before, let it be remembered, was the urge for survival more strongly stimulated in Gretel.

10 The Last in the Line

The task awaiting Guderian as acting Chief of Staff was gigantic beyond belief and, of course, preposterous in its enormity. An analysis of his duties, to which those of Inspector of Panzer Forces were now a subsidiary part, gives the barest indication of the absurd state to which the role of Chief of Staff had been reduced. Operationally, and primarily, he was responsible, subject to aggravating supervision by Hitler and OKW, for the conduct of operations on the Eastern Front. As a painful secondary task he was made a member of the Court of Honour set up by Hitler to examine the dossiers of officers who were said to be responsible for acts in connection with the Putsch and to expel them from the Service in order that they could be brought to trial by the People's Court. As self-appointed duties were his efforts to attempt to maintain the status of the Army and that of the General Staff, along with resistance to further encroachment by OKW and the SS in the province of OKH, and such endeavours as could be made to save innocent or only marginally implicated men from the Gestapo or any other form of summary justice. As guarantee of his presence he was expressly forbidden to offer his resignation, as had Zeitzler no less than five times!

Hercules, compared with Guderian, had a relatively easy task in cleansing the Augean stables, for at least there had been a nearby stream for his assistance, whereas the resources available to Guderian were drying up. Moreover Hercules had a free hand while Guderian's were tied, and his authority impaired. Ask as much as he liked to be '. . . permitted to give directions to all General Staff Corps Officers of the Army on such subjects as concerned the General Staff as a whole', Hitler, Himmler, Keitel and Jodl were bent on the General Staff's abolition and had no intention of relenting. Instead Guderian felt compelled to make larger concessions than any of his predecessors. On 23rd July, in a broadcast to the nation, he said, 'A few officers, some on the retired list, have lost courage and by an act of cowardice and weakness preferred the road to disgrace to that of duty and honour . . . The people and the Army stand closely behind the Führer . . . I guarantee the Führer and the German people the unity of the generals, of the officer corps and of the men in the Army in the single aim of fighting for and achieving victory under the motto created by the venerable *Generalfeldmarschall* von Hindenburg, "Loyalty is the essence of honour".' And on the 29th he issued a notorious order (one which Goerlitz says, with exaggeration, 'produced a division in the ranks of the General Staff which could never be bridged') saying: 'Each General Staff officer must be a National Socialist officer. That means he must show and prove himself by way of exemplary conduct in political questions, through active instruction and advice to younger comrades on the thoughts of the Führer in the political field as well as a member of the "selected few", and also in the area of tactics and strategy.' At this time, too, the Nazi salute, at Hitler's demand, became obligatory for the *Wehrmacht*. That a division was produced is undeniable though it is probably more correct to say that it was the cumulative effects of the 20th, not just the order of the 29th, which did it.

Neither the broadcast nor the order of the 29th are mentioned in *Panzer Leader*. It is likely the former was made at the request of Goebbels (whose activity was dynamic) and the latter under pressure from Hitler, whose fury with the Army was uncontainable. By means of silence in his memoirs Guderian transmits his disquiet at the measures to which he was reduced: if he had chosen to comment he would probably have elected to justify the ends being worthy of the means. His was to be a Micawberlike holding action, a bargaining of status for time in pursuit of a military stalemate from which a bearable peace could be negotiated. Quite deliberately he put country before self and the Army – and in so doing performed what may have been his greatest service to Hitler. For though the Führer and his henchman Himmler (who was appointed commander of the Replacement Army instead of Fromm) were well on the road to substituting the *Waffen* SS for the Army, they were not yet completely ready. Meanwhile the officers, rank and file of the Army cordially disliked and mistrusted their 'comrades' of the Party. By identifying himself as one with the Army and the Party Guderian, for the time being, guaranteed the Army's loyalty to Hitler. It is unlikely that there was another officer then serving (other than Rundstedt) who had the prestige to do so. As it was, Guderian felt the need for a complete restructuring of OKH, the disciplining of officers who were already (under cover of the new National Socialist atmosphere) taking liberties, and the incorporation of faithful followers who had served him in the past – among them Praun as Chief Signals Officer, and the enthusiastic *General der Panzertruppen* Walter Wenck (who had collaborated with him in developing minor panzer tactics in 1928 and had urged him on at Sedan) as Chief of Operations. After the Bomb Plot staff officers who, as Guderian demanded, 'should have three good ideas a day', were at a premium.

The customary initial renouncements were the price paid for the consolidation of Guderian's position with Hitler. Clearly he believed there was a slight chance of retrieval. On 30th July Gretel, in a letter which dealt mainly with the farm, had written: 'My feeling that one day you would be called to the top position in the Army has been proved right. May you succeed despite the most devilish difficult situation in keeping the Red hordes from invading our beloved land . . . May the Führer's trust stay with you and give you the opportunity to achieve your aim'. Well might the Führer's faith be in question: nobody, by this time, took him at his word and he trusted nobody. And Guderian had replied to her on the 18th August: 'Difficulties have to be overcome and that is my daily work. Because of this, much has to be done and successes are few. I hope by holding firmly to my goals we will survive, but it is difficult to catch up with years of neglect'. Hope was about all that did remain. Guderian, though not yet prepared to concede total defeat, realised that victory was impossible. As he took office, the front in Normandy was on the eve of rupture, that in Italy in steady recession, while in the East the Russian armies had overrun vast areas and were advancing into the Baltic States in the north, towards Warsaw in the centre and Rumania in the south. All three Army Groups in Russia were in the process of destruction along with those in the West. At the same time German cities and industry were being ripped apart by aerial bombardment. In this heart-rending position it is indicative of Guderian's innermost conviction of impending doom that he called upon a precedent of desperation to bolster his optimism – taking as model the events of the year 1759 and the calamity of the Battle of Künersdorf and its aftermath. On that occasion Frederick the Great had contemplated abdication but eventually had saved the situation through hanging on until there occurred the almost miraculous death of the Russian Empress with her successor ending the war when Prussia was at the last gasp. In essence Guderian's private and hopelessly optimistic war aim amounted to stabilisation of a fortified front in the East and the achievement of peace in the West – the latter helped, perhaps, by a local success.

Epitomising the stresses and strains, from within and without, that were imposed upon rehabilitation and operational measures, was the struggle for Poland where it centred through August and September on the Battle of Warsaw. On 1st August, as Russian armies, at the end of their tether, came close to the city after a 300-mile advance, the clandestine Polish Home Army rose up and cut vital German communication links with the armies fighting at the front. The insurrection was not, in fact, aimed against the Germans who, it was assumed, were utterly defeated as they evacuated Warsaw: if that had not been so the uprising would never have been ordered. The Poles were really attempting to win a prestige success with a view to establishing a political presence prior to the arrival of the Russians. Nevertheless the Germans could not stand by and let them do so, particularly since Guderian was assembling forces for the defence of the River Vistula: he stopped a panic evacuation that began after 22nd July and poured reinforcements against the flanks of the Russian spearheads. He also requested that the city be declared part of the Army's zone of operations and therefore should be handed over by the Governor General and the SS, who were the responsible agency, under Himmler, for all anti-partisan operations. But Himmler, encouraged by Hitler, refused to hand over and instead, on 5th August, sent his chief of anti-partisan operations, SS *Obergruppenführer* Erich von dem Bach-Zelewski, to lead the fight against the Poles. Thus there was divided command between the SS inside the city and the Army on the perimeter.

The fighting which engulfed Warsaw contained all that was worst in partisan warfare and attracted the fiercest of combatants whose forebears were the Reds of 1917 and the *Freikorps*. It had repercussions for Gretel too: in mid-August she received warning that some of the people on the estate might be of the 'Warsaw Organisation' and be plotting to do her harm. She wrote: 'I am not frightened, darling, and I sleep alone downstairs' – and went on living there until the Russians were at the gates in January 1945. Hitler demanded the extermination of the Poles and the destruction of Warsaw, instructions which Bach-Zelewski saw fit to disobey. Guderian, of course, knew about the merciless partisan operation which undermined, in varying extent, almost every corner of enemy-occupied territory, but this was his first experience of dealing with it in all its ramifications from High Command. If he had been unaware of the ruthlessly repressive and murderous anti-partisan instructions which, from time to time, had been issued by Hitler and OKW, he was left in no doubt now of the depravity which ruled on both sides. At the post-war trials of war criminals the perpetrators of horror at Warsaw were to appear and pay penalties. Guderian, as Chief of the Army Staff, was to be among those upon whom the Poles would have liked to lay hands. It is true that Army units fought in the streets of Warsaw under the direction of Bach-Zelewski and, of course, it was the Army under Guderian's command that stopped the Russians on the outskirts of Warsaw, so preventing the link-up with the Polish partisans that led to the eventual collapse of the uprising. Guderian, in *Panzer Leader*, is at pains to emphasise his interventions in mitigating the depradations by some of the cruellest anti-partisan forces under Bach-Zelewski's command and in seeking withdrawal of Hitler's demand that prisoners should not be granted full rights by International Law. He also underlines that the worst retributive orders were sent through SS channels and not those of the Army. The SS, eager for credit, took pride in this victory. Guderian could claim innocence of a crime and, after the war, the Americans declined to hand him over to the Poles.

While conducting the battle which led to the defeat of the Russians at Warsaw, Guderian began developing his technique of 'holding firmly to his goals' with Hitler. On 15th August they had a flaming row when

Guderian, in his capacity as Inspector General of Armoured Forces, remarked, apropos conditions in the West, 'The bravery of the panzer troops is not enough to make up for the failure of the other two Services – the Air Force and the Navy'. Warlimont wrote that '. . . he went about his new job with characteristic energy; he did not, however, as Zeitzler had done, waste any effort trying to get the other theatres of war back under OKH . . . In his impetuous and vivacious manner he would often use strong language even at the briefing conferences. From his general outlook and the consequential personal animosities it soon became clear that, even under the extreme pressure of the situation, the change in Army Chief of Staff was unlikely to bring any change in the unhappy relationship between the two top levels of the *Wehrmacht*. Although we were franker in our dealings with each other, it did not enter the head of any senior officers concerned with the overall direction of the war to make common cause with OKW or co-operate in opposition to the continuance of a war already lost'. This statement is somewhat misleading, bearing in mind the attempts which had been made by Army officers to present a unified front and the memory of those many occasions when OKW had preferred to follow its own inclinations contrary to OKH advice. Warlimont merely makes a case for OKW's infallibility. Whether or not Guderian's methods were realistic is a matter for argument; in fact he probably deluded himself when writing that he thought he had brought about an improvement. But he had always been a convinced advocate of unified command and, from the earliest days under Blomberg and Reichenau, had supported the attempts to merge the various, and often competing, agencies of the *Wehrmacht*. The effectiveness of the OKW was, in his opinion, diminished because of the inadequacy of Wilhelm Keitel who, in practice, was compelled to use it as nothing better than Hitler's military secretariat. After the war Guderian laid the blame for military failure on Hitler's declining health, added to the 'mental irritability . . . which led to a further splintering of the military command authority'.

Nevertheless Warlimont's reference to 'general outlook' and 'the consequential animosities' was apt. All men have blind spots and among Guderian's was the tendency to persist in his indignation with Kluge: others he could forgive, but never Kluge, not even in *Panzer Leader*. Within hours of becoming Chief of Staff Guderian was endeavouring to remove Kluge from command in the West by suggesting to Hitler (without avail) that he should be replaced because 'he did not have a lucky touch in commanding large armoured forces'. Guderian's reason, regardless of Kluge's implication with the plot, was less than just at the time and still more unjust when, after the war (and long after Kluge's suicide at the end of August 1944), Guderian persisted in denigrating Kluge's handling of the armour. To his interrogators he complained about Kluge splitting panzer divisions, committing them piecemeal into action and utterly failing to concentrate more than half the armoured force available for the counter-stroke against the Americans at Mortain. While it was true that, at times in the East, Kluge had split formations, conditions in the West were different. The crippling effect of Allied air attacks upon lines of communication and the consequential difficulties in achieving concentration of forces of any sort precluded Guderian's old tactics of concentration. It must be remembered that Guderian was not present in Normandy during the battle: nor was he responsible for operations there. In any case Kluge suffered from the Führer as much as every other C-in-C and the record of his courageous resistance to Hitler's maniac insistence upon suicidal counter-attacks by the panzer divisions at Mortain is valedictory of a desperate man.

To obtain an alteration to one of Hitler's preconceived notions demanded hard wrangling and endless patience at a moment when time was at a premium. Kluge's operations in Normandy were ruined by Hitler's interventions. Guderian, for his part, quotes the Führer's obdurate resistance to his own proposals for the construction of a system of fortifications along Germany's eastern frontier and his strenuous efforts to build them in the autumn in accord with begrudging permission from Hitler. It was some feat to get that much, for Hitler shut his mind to the threat in the East once the Russian offensive came to a halt at Warsaw, and dealt only with the current threat presently in the West where the Siegfried Line was being probed by the Anglo-American armies, and the main industrial complex of the Ruhr threatened. As fast as Guderian built up fresh fortress units in the East, Jodl, anxious for the Ruhr, had them transferred to the West: when Guderian asked for the release of captured enemy equipment from store, Keitel and Jodl denied that these weapons existed. But once Guderian proved them wrong, Jodl seized the best and then sent them westward too. Guderian had no part in the offensive projected in the West. He could only stand and hope in the East, deprived of reserves, and be witness to gathering Russian strength, on the one hand, and, on the other, Himmler's combing out of manpower from industry to create yet another German army – a People's Army imbued with National Socialist ideals and banded into so-called '*Volksgrenadier* Divisions' and the like.

Once he came to realise that direct opposition to Hitler and his entourage was likely to be abortive, Guderian resorted to methods which had stood him in good stead on the battlefield when senior commanders thwarted his designs. He either ignored the orders or tried to circumvent them. Sometimes it worked, sometimes not. For a while he was able to evade attending the Court of Honour, which sat under Rundstedt, until Keitel insisted that he at least put in an appearance. It was good for him that he did attend since he was able to hear, first hand, the methods to which the Gestapo had descended in order to condemn Army officers. There was little enough that could be done to save those against whom there was the faintest evidence of conspiracy or those whom the Führer was determined to punish. And as a last resort, Hitler employed *General* Burgdorf, Schmundt's inferior replacement, an officer reviled by Guderian for his bad behaviour and whom he called 'the evil genius of the officer corps'. This man was instrumental in aiding Himmler in his schemes. This 'fanatical adherent of the National Socialist Party' (Guderian's words) was the Führer's personal emissary to Rommel with the message and the poison which brought about that officer's suicide in October. Guderian did what he could* and some of the conspirators could be saved, among them Rommel's Chief of Staff, Hans Speidel, whose stolid pleas of innocence (even though he was implicated with the Putsch) could not be broken: he one day would play a leading part in reforming the extinct German Army.

Germany's allies were deserting her as the Russians approached or entered their countries. In turn, Rumania, Finland and Bulgaria changed sides as August turned to September and the autumn foreshadowed far worse to come. Hungary was in disarray but her regent, Admiral Horthy, had something to teach Guderian about political expediency on the eve of his nation's collapse: 'Look, my friend, in politics you must always have several irons in the fire'. It is instructive that Guderian quoted that remark in *Panzer Leader*, as an indication, no doubt, of his own mind's working.

The Western Allied air forces began concentrating their attacks upon the plant manufacturing oil as the Ploesti oil fields fell into enemy hands. The fuel of mobile defence drained rapidly away and the German motorised troops gradually came to a halt. In any case the panzer divisions were shadowy organisations of improvisation: rarely in the summer could the latest, reduced establishment of barely 120 tanks be made good. Meanwhile a flood of Russian, American and British armour did much as it pleased except where it met well-fashioned, static defences covering vital localities. But nothing that was German could last for long and the next line of defences to be breached were those tenuously defended by Army Group North. This was territory that protected the Prussian homeland and, with its past associations, was dear to Guderian. In August he prised a quick decision out of Hitler by playing upon his habit of delayed reaction until a threat became disaster. Permission was given to switch reinforcements from the southern front in Rumania (where the battle had yet to become catastrophically critical) to the north. This was the only alternative since nothing could be taken from the west (where the planning of what was to be the December, Ardennes offensive would

---

* Corroborated to the author from a private source.

soon be in progress) and OKH reserves were non-existent. But having, as a result, forced the Russians to pause near Riga and having opened a corridor through which the large German forces, trapped in Estonia and the rest of the Baltic States, might escape, the opportunity to evacuate completely was thrown away because Hitler forbade it. Early in October the Russians attacked once more and, this time, reached the sea near Memel, effectively locking the remains of Army Group North in the Kurland peninsula, whence they could only be supplied by sea. Also Russian forces set foot, for the first time, on the sacred soil of East Prussia. The sound of the guns was audible in Lötzen and Rastenburg. Soon Hitler would be forced to withdraw to his last headquarters at the Chancellery in Berlin.

The encirclement of Army Group North in Kurland, tragic though it was, merely wrote an incidental paragraph in the history of Hitler's mismanaged strategy. Its effect upon the outcome was militarily insignificant in the context of a chapter of total disaster. So far as Guderian was concerned it provoked him to the heights of indignation, not simply through the utter waste of strong, badly needed forces in holding too long a line, but as a subject for demonstrating his sympathy and devotion for the soldiers whose fate, a quite appalling one at Russian hands, was sealed. It mattered little that a further pause would now take place in the fighting in the East and that fortifications could be strengthened. Hitler's eyes were fixed upon the Ardennes and the out-moded dream of winning a victory of diplomatic as well as military consequence. He deluded himself, and a few dupes, that the Western Allies could be intimidated. But the delusion was ironically, in part, the making of Speer and the Inspector General of Panzer Forces for it was they who produced the flood of new armoured vehicles which filled the panzer division establishments almost to capacity. The remaining irony was the fuel shortage that hampered them.

In common with almost every other senior officer, Guderian saw little hope of anything worthwhile coming from the Ardennes project. Denied a hand in the planning he had only to bear with the loss of soldiers taken from his command to fill the ranks of the armies in the West and read the daily intelligence reports which told of oncoming failure. 'For the sake of my country I had hoped,' he wrote, 'that it would lead to a complete victory. But since, on December 23rd, it was clear that it could no longer result in a great success, I decided to drive to Supreme Headquarters to request that the battle, which was causing us heavy casualties, be broken off . . .' This he did on the 26th.

This request, like so many of those he made, was, according to Guderian, rejected and the angry atmosphere which regularly clouded his meetings with Hitler grew more intense. But he did obtain a few rein-

195

forcements.* These meetings were monuments to time wasting and irrelevance such as few cabinets can ever have had. They would go on for hours at a time, a grotesque mixture of discussion on high policy interspersed with trivial interjections when Hitler aired his knowledge of individual weapon performances, or gave the minutest examination to some local deployment or reminiscence about the triumphs or sins and omissions of years gone by. The transcripts frequently make bizarre reading, filled as they are with the phobias of Nazidom in its dying throes. The rise and fall of voices is lost in flat transcript, but the provocation of the Army by Hitler and his adherents stands out along, somewhat astonishingly, with Guderian's patient and persistent efforts to guide the discussion back to essentials. Warlimont quotes, with italicised comments of his own, an attempt by Guderian to have implemented, in September, a ruling by Hitler in July that the Navy, Air Force and civil authorities should relinquish badly needed lorries to the panzer divisions.

Guderian: All that's necessary is for the *Reichsmarschall* to give his agreement.

Hitler: I am giving the agreement now. We have got a Defence Staff. We have got an organisation the envy of every country in the world, OKW. No one else has such a thing. It hasn't been much talked about merely because the Army Staff didn't like it.

Keitel: *(as usual using stronger words to express the same idea)*: Has in fact fought hard against it!

Hitler: *(taking up Keitel's expression)*: Has in fact fought hard against it! After we had fought for years to get this organisation.

Guderian: Air Fleet 3 has such a large number of lorries.

Thomale: We must flush them out.

Kreipe: (Chief of Staff *Luftwaffe*): We've already lost so many using them on Army jobs *(refuses)*.

By the first week in January, when Hitler still persisted in trying to revive the offensive in the West and incontrovertible evidence accrued of an imminent Russian offensive, the tone of the meetings deteriorated. In an effort to achieve the essential concentration of resources along Germany's eastern frontier, Guderian doggedly endured the conferences, entering into asperity only when the main issue was under consideration or when the welfare of officers and soldiers was being harmed. He visited the fronts to gather a consensus of Army Commanders' opinions and from these drew the conclusion that the war was hopelessly lost. Not only

---

*Recently it has been suggested that Guderian did not make his request to transfer the main defensive forces to the east until *after* the Russians attacked. The evidence is academic and too thin to be persuasive.

was Germany overwhelmingly outnumbered but 'We had neither commanders nor troops of the 1940 quality any more . . .' On January 9th he
resolved upon a show-down and produced a detailed intelligence report
that proved beyond doubt the imminence of the Russian offensive and
the impossible odds mounting against the German Army in the East.
Hitler lost his temper and rejected the report, declaring that the man who
made it, *General* Gehlen, was a lunatic and should be shut up in an
asylum. Guderian says that he, too, lost his temper and told Hitler that
Gehlen was '. . . one of my very best General Staff officers . . . If you
want *General* Gehlen sent to a lunatic asylum then you had better have
me certified as well'. He refused to sack Gehlen and the row subsided. But
Gehlen's conclusions were not converted into remedial action so that,
when the Russians attacked three days later (precisely as Gehlen and
Guderian had predicted), there was another disaster among troops whose
deployment Hitler had refused to change to meet the conditions. At the
end of the conference Hitler had once more tried to placate Guderian
with soft words of gratitude and flattery, but these no longer availed.
Guderian says that he told the Führer, 'The Eastern Front is like a house
of cards. If the front is broken through at one point the rest will
collapse . . .' And so it proved to be, though it would probably have
happened whether or not reinforcements had arrived from the west.

Disaster at the front impelled, all too late, the counter measures which
should already have been taken. Either reinforcements were tardily
moved to localities where the situation was out of control, or transferred
by Hitler to places where they were least required. The Sixth SS Panzer
Army was sent from the Ardennes to Hungary, there to be wasted as yet
another diversion of strength on a front of lesser importance. This made it
all the easier for the Russians to take Warsaw and flood through Poland
and East Prussia, their spearheads thrusting towards Deipenhof where
Gretel persisted to the last minute in her attempts to run the farm.
Guderian was driven to distraction, but protest and intrigue were the only
levers remaining since real power was long ago lost. When he confronted
Jodl and angrily pointed out, for the umpteenth time, the iniquities of
Hitlerian strategy, all that officer did was shrug his shoulders. Jodl, too,
was baffled and must surely have realised the hopelessness of it all when,
on 21st January, Himmler was given command of Army Group Vistula.

The depths to which debate in council had descended – if that is the
way to describe fiery protests against intransigence – reached rock bottom in February when Guderian once more tried to persuade Hitler that
the forces locked up in Kurland must be withdrawn by sea. Prior to the
meeting he had taken a few drinks with the Japanese Ambassador. Speer,
who was present, takes up the story:

'Hitler disagreed . . . Guderian did not give in, Hitler insisted, the tone
sharpened, and finally Guderian opposed Hitler with an openness unpre-

cedented in this circle. Probably fired by the drinks he had had at Oshima's, he threw aside all inhibitions. With flashing eyes and the hairs of his moustache literally standing on end, he stood facing Hitler across the marble table. Hitler too had risen to his feet.

' "It's simply our duty to save these people and we still have time to remove them!" Guderian cried out in a challenging voice.

'Infuriated, Hitler retorted: "You are going to fight there. We cannot give up these areas!"

'Guderian held firm: "But it's useless to sacrifice men in this senseless way", he shouted. "It's high time! We must evacuate these soldiers at once!"

'What no one had thought possible now happened. Hitler appeared visibly intimidated by this assault. Strictly speaking he really could not tolerate this insubordination which was more a matter of Guderian's tone than his arguments. But to my astonishment Hitler shifted to military arguments . . . for the first time matters had come to an open quarrel in the larger circle. New worlds had opened out . . .'

But Hitler did not alter his decision. A week later battle was joined once more over the marble table, this time in connection with a quick counter-attack which Guderian deemed it was essential Himmler's Army Group Vistula should make. Himmler wished to postpone the attack, pleading shortage of fuel and ammunition. Guderian felt convinced that this was merely an excuse to hide the incompetence of Himmler and his inexperienced SS Chief of Staff. This time, however, he was doing far more than arguing for the saving of life or for an operational expedient. He was standing firm against the principle of SS men taking charge in the Army's province. The row developed over a petty wrangle concerning Himmler's competence, as Guderian stated his demand that Wenck should be attached to Himmler's staff '. . . so that he may ensure that the operations are competently carried out'. For two hours Hitler, in a fury, resisted, while Guderian, apparently stimulated as well as calmed by having provoked the Führer into losing his temper, kept his – and won.

It was, as he wrote in *Panzer Leader*, 'the last battle I was to win'. The attack, launched by Wenck on 16th February, enjoyed initial success, but on the 17th, after Wenck was seriously injured in a car accident, the momentum was lost. Wenck's replacement, *Generalleutnant* Hans Krebs, was of lower quality, lacking in high command experience and the sort of creature Hitler preferred to employ. He was thus a natural choice for Burgdorf. But the loss of Wenck came as hard blow to Guderian though, in the final analysis of doom, it was of little account. Such rare accomplishments as came to his credit, like the attachment of Wenck to Himmler, were ephemeral and rapidly made negative: always he was engaged in the attempted reversal of bad measures without the privilege of initiating constructive ones. But the spectacle of an Army Chief of Staff at last meeting the Führer's fire with fire of greater heat inevitably raises the questions as to what might have happened if, in 1938 – or even so late as 1940 – Beck or Halder had employed similar methods? Or what might have been the result if Guderian, in the mood of 1945, had been made Chief of Staff in 1938, as unbased rumour suggested might have happened? Or supposing Below and Stauffenberg had succeeded in 1941? At last it had been demonstrated, in the eleventh hour, that Hitler could be overborn. In that case, might he not earlier have been overthrown by men of implacable determination and personality? All too obviously the scrupulous Prussian soldiers had never been a match for unscrupulous Nazi cold-bloodedness: an established system of disciplined ruthlessness had fallen victim to anarchic, modern gangsterism.

True to his conclusions that the war was lost, Guderian, in collaboration with Speer, opened a defective campaign to limit its effects on Germany, and a major effort to bring it to an end with the connivance of anybody else in the Nazi hierarchy who might help. Speer's efforts to circumvent the programme of industrial destruction which Hitler wished to wreak upon the German homeland and economy was of only marginal use: what damage he managed to prevent with the aid of all manner of military and civil leaders was as nothing to the destruction wrought by the enemy who bombed, shelled and burnt at will – and often without discretion. Likewise Guderian's efforts to restrict the demolition of bridges and communications were doomed to failure. So, too, were his diplomatic advances, though these are a revealing commentary on Government circles and his own disenchanted and sulphurous attitude to those in power.

On 25th January he had a private meeting with the Foreign Minister, Joachim von Ribbentrop, to whom he described in detail the hopeless state of military affairs along with the recommendation that they jointly see Hitler and propose the initiation of steps for an armistice. Ribbentrop dared not face the Führer with such a request. Moreover, although Ribbentrop asked Guderian not to mention their talk to Hitler, he at once wrote the Führer a memorandum explaining what had taken place. Guderian comments, 'So much the better'. One more row in the midst of so many was of little importance to him, as the record shows. Almost recklessly, day by day at every opportunity, he was attacking Hitler and his systems as well as pleading for Army officers who had been demoted to the ranks for some petty indiscretion. These were attacks upon Hitler's kind of Reich: for himself he did not care any longer; in loyalty to his subordinates he was unbending.

A phantasmagoria of horror overlaid the scene. In February the lines to the West drew close to the Rhine and in early March lapped the river's banks. To the East, half of Prussia was overwhelmed and Berlin threatened as the incompetent Himmler tinkered with command.

Deipenhof had long since been lost to the Guderians and the homeless Gretel now kept her husband company at OKH in its last resting place at Zossen. Here she shared the final days of his power along with the bombing which wrecked the place on 15th March and wounded Krebs.

On or about the 16th Himmler, faced by the spectre of disruption at the front opposite his Army Group Vistula and depressed in the knowledge that, as a military commander, he was completely unsuited – thus disproving again the Hitlerian notion that anybody could manipulate armies – had taken to his bed with a simulated attack of influenza. A plea from his Chief of Staff to Guderian, 'Can't you rid us of our commander?' was received with the bland reply, 'That's a matter for the SS'. Nevertheless Guderian took an opportunity to visit Himmler and suggest he give up his command. This Himmler was unprepared to do in person but, taking a leaf from the Army's book, agreed to the ever-willing Guderian's suggestion that he might do it on Himmler's behalf. Taking advantage of surprise, Guderian made the proposal to Hitler along with the suggestion that one of Germany's best surviving commanders, *Generaloberst* Gotthard Heinrici, should take Himmler's place. Hitler grumbled and would have preferred one of his sycophants, but once more Guderian had his way and Heinrici was appointed on 20th March.

In the meantime Ribbentrop had, in secret, followed Guderian's earlier suggestion and was transmitting peace-feelers, indirectly bringing Guderian into his confidence as he did so, while mooting an approach to Himmler to see if he would add weight to their efforts. This Guderian did on the 21st, though with no apparent result, for Himmler, as usual, brushed an uncomfortable subject aside. But Guderian was mistaken in thinking that there was 'nothing to be done with the man'. Himmler was about to make his own choice, triggered by Guderian's initiative, and a few days later was engaged in private peace negotiations through Swedish contacts. Since Wheeler-Bennett calls Guderian's attempts at peacemaking 'half-hearted' and writes that '. . . certainly not Guderian himself was prepared to make this proposal to Hitler', the question must be put why Guderian did not take the plunge. To the Americans, after the war, he said he had been forbidden to do so, but that is insufficient. The answer probably lay in recent history and had nothing to do with Guderian's proven moral courage. In the previous July before the Bomb Plot, Rundstedt, in a moment of fury, had addressed Keitel with the celebrated words 'Make peace you fools', and had been sacked. In practice in March it was fruitless and conceivably suicidal for an Army officer to become involved in anything the slightest bit remote from military affairs. So Guderian, whose resignation was forbidden by Hitler, soldiered on and probably was denied an ultimate attempt to end the holocaust only because Hitler, Keitel, Jodl and Burgdorf were determined to be rid of him. Reading between the lines it is easy to detect what they may have guessed: Guderian was beginning, in the tradition of Chiefs of Staff of old, to manipulate the Government.

Nobody who gave the impression that the war was lost, as did Guderian, was wanted. Even Speer, once the Führer's favourite, was pushed aside because he flatly wrote to say that the war was lost. What little remained of law and order was being thrown to the winds. Nevertheless Guderian found Jodl arguing at his side when they successfully resisted an attempt by Hitler to scrap the Geneva Conventions governing the Conduct of War. But, although Hitler's visions of defeat clarified themselves into a pattern of ultimate extinction, Guderian and the vast majority of the Army Staff, along with the bulk of the German people, were blinded as to the depravity to which the state had been led. For example, the Propaganda Ministry managed to persuade Guderian to make a broadcast on 6th March in which he rebutted Russian accusations of German infidelities that included extermination camps with their gas chambers which had been found as the Russians advanced. Guderian said: 'I have myself fought in the Soviet Union but have never noticed gas chambers and the like.' This evaded the question. Mostly the major extermination camps were on German or Polish soil. He was almost certainly entirely honest, however, when he denied seeing these places and it is most unlikely he guessed as to their outright genocidal purpose. The pitiless people who ran the camps went out of their way to hide them in inaccessible parts of the land. Idle chatter about such matters was strictly curtailed by the fearsome penalties which were exacted upon rumour-mongers. Moreover, almost any interchange of information was thoroughly proscribed by the efficient censorship of news and the careful compartmentation of the members of the population, a compartmentation which extended through the government and military machine so that as few people as possible were aware of what was happening overall or even in their immediate vicinity. Nevertheless, in his position he must have known something. For example, von Barsewisch, who claims he heard of the extermination scheme in 1939 and that it was this which turned him from National Socialism to resistance, can hardly have failed to mention the subject when trying to persuade Guderian to join the resistance during the four-hour debate on 18th July 1944. Maybe it was this matter which Guderian did not, simply could not, believe – the whole horrible subject was certainly inconceivable to a normal imagination.

After a conference immediately following Guderian's plea to Himmler, Hitler spoke in private to Guderian and suggested that, in view of Guderian's heart having apparently take a turn for the worse, a spell of four weeks' convalescent leave should be taken. This Guderian rejected on the grounds that the loss through injury of Wenck and Krebs left nobody capable of doing the work of deputy. There seems to have been no warning of an imminent demotion and Guderian omits comment as to its possible inner purport. But it is reasonable to speculate that Hitler, once more apprised of Guderian's manoeuvres behind his back and sensing that too much influence revolved around the Chief of Staff, was determined to put an end to them. Pleas of ill-health were, by then, the standard excuse for terminating the appointments of men who had become irksome. Hitler himself was in appalling shape, his judgement warped by the depredations of physical and mental decay. In conference on the 23rd Burgdorf raised the matter of Guderian's future, indicating that he was in a hurry and he had a candidate for the job. Again no decision was taken because the doctors would not pass either Wenck or Burgdorf's nominee, Krebs, fit.

That day, in the West, the Allies crossed the Rhine in strength and, in the East, the Ninth Army under *General* Busse began an attempt to relieve a garrison cut off at Küstrin. At Küstrin there was failure at heavy cost. According to Heinrici, reported by Cornelius Ryan in his *The Last Battle*, Guderian insisted upon another attempt. Hitler wanted it. When Heinrici suggested that it would be better for the beseiged forces to break out 'Guderian flared at the proposal: "The attack must be mounted", he had shouted'. On the 27th it was and Küstrin was actually reached after a display of sacrificial courage by the soldiers, though within hours the relieving force was driven back by the Russians who were overpowering in artillery and tanks. In the West, at that same moment, Frankfurt-on-Main fell to the Americans who, with the French and British, were moving almost unchecked into central Germany.

Guderian states that he tried to prevent the final attempt at Küstrin and that during the conference on the 27th there were hard words from Hitler as to the troops' performance and about Busse's competence. Guderian assembled irrefutable evidence proving that all that could be done was done and wrote a memorandum to that effect. It is evident that he recognised the threat to his appointment and was making every effort to retain power. Seeking further information he asked permission to visit the front and examine the situation in person. This was refused by Hitler who, instead, instructed Guderian and Busse to appear before him at the next conference on the 28th.

What followed at that meeting is obscure – and that is hardly surprising since, from the outset, tension was high and emotional stress predominant. In essence, Hitler accused Busse of negligence and Guderian angrily refuted Hitler's every word. It is doubtful if the scene was more turbulent than that which attended the earlier direct confrontations of the Führer by his Chief of Staff. It is equally obvious that Hitler was primed. As soon as it became clear that Guderian had no intention of backing down, Hitler cleared the room of everybody except himself and Keitel. Those who left must either have dreaded or longed for a violent end. They knew Guderian had taken his life in his hands. As Warlimont writes, he had shown '. . . for the second time exemplary "moral courage" in protecting his subordinates'. It matters not that Warlimont (who had left OKW in September and therefore did not witness the major period of Guderian's days as Chief of Staff) was unaware of the other numerous occasions when 'moral courage' was displayed. What matters is that the last great Chief of Staff kept faith with the calling and fought for his beliefs to the end.

There was anti-climax. Hitler mildly told Guderian that he should take six weeks' convalescent leave and then return because 'the situation will be very critical'. Indeed it would be; by then Hitler would be dead and Germany-in-arms extinguished. They parted at the end of the conference, neither regretting to see the back of the other, Guderian fortunate to escape with the freedom to choose where he wished to go. As the one general to win the Führer's respect in the last days of the Third Reich he certainly earned the privilege. He had sacrificed many ideals. Remembering how lack of an intact Army in 1919 had totally undermined Germany's bargaining power in the peace negotiations, he had tried and failed to keep the Army safe. In the process he had acted out of character, had played politics and thus fallen below the nobler principles which were normally his guide. But politicians' standards, as so often he had noticed, were different from those of soldiers – and Germany came before self.

After taking leave of the staff at Zossen, the Guderians made their way to Munich where he underwent a few weeks' treatment for a heart which was fatigued rather than weakened. Then, on 1st May, he rejoined the Headquarters of the Panzer Inspectorate where it had found refuge in the Tyrol and on the 10th, while still by title Inspector General, entered American captivity.

11 The Final Stand

Among the most traumatic paradoxes of Guderian's experience was the sudden and cataclysmic reversal of his mode of life which took place within the few weeks after his dismissal as Chief of Staff. From being the holder of one of the most prestigious offices in Germany he became, almost overnight, a fugitive and then the captive of foes who planned his prosecution for war crimes. At one moment he was engaged upon tasks which legally demanded an aggressive outlook and the next he was thrown back entirely upon the defensive in justifying the propriety of his previous employment. It was far from the least of his achievements that he adapted himself to these swift changes in fortune with relatively good humour and assured dignity. Precedent may have come to his aid: it was not the first time he had experienced abject defeat.

The intention of the victorious Allies, to bring both the persons and organisations of their late opponents to trial, threatened members of the General Staff with a double chance of standing in the dock either for such criminal acts as they were deemed to have committed as individuals or as the servants of organisations – the Great General Staff and OKW – – which were to be tried en bloc. It was as a potential war criminal in his own right and as a member of the General Staff that Guderian found himself incarcerated by the Americans along with many of his past colleagues in triumph and tragedy – among them Halder, Thomale, Milch, Praun, List, Weichs, Blomberg, and Leeb. Initially their treatment was overbearingly that to be expected by the vanquished from an arrogant conqueror, and the generals were submitted to many humiliations. Strik-Strikfeld records that, 'In general Guderian's bearing was dignified and soldierly, particularly when the American guards started to play tricks. I remember an American sergeant pointing a carbine at him and he stood there calmly facing him. I was close at hand and we managed to get the sergeant to drop his carbine'. And later Strik-Strikfeld recalls a day when a number of Russian officers who had fought on the German side were being made ready for transfer back to their homeland – and certain death for treason. 'List, Weichs and Guderian went across to a young American captain who had always been correct and even friendly. "We must protest against the handing over of our Russian comrades to the

Soviet authorities." The Captain said he was merely carrying out his orders . . . I can still see them standing there, the two field-marshals and the general, once so powerful, now helpless and pleading . . .'

Gradually conditions for the generals improved. Interrogation followed by interrogation helped pass the time, and to describe their experiences to their captors (even though the threat of following their Russian comrades was rarely far from their thoughts) was a fruitful way of reliving past glories and defining their part in creating one of the most remarkable military machines the world had known. Guderian, as the architect of the key *Panzertruppe* and a past Chief of Staff, was at once recognised as a star turn and he, too, at first, gave freely of his knowledge.

A revealing glimpse of Guderian is obtained through the American officers who interrogated him. On 26th August, 1945, Major Kenneth Hechler, an infantryman, sat down to question him on the subject of the employment of panzer forces in Normandy. The entire exchange was friendly and in English and came as a pleasant surprise to Hechler who was aware that, previously, Historical Division officers had not found Guderian too co-operative. Guderian greeted Hechler genially with: 'Aha! A fellow armoured officer!', which Hechler sceptically adjudged as '. . . just so much soft soap, but I did not have the feeling that he twisted any of his real opinions in order to say what he felt an American would like to hear. He responded quickly to all of the questions and I do not believe that he was trying to make any particular impression or grind an axe.'

Guderian's attitude waxed and waned in relation to the treatment he received and the aptitude of his intelocutors. For a prolonged period he withdrew all co-operation because it came to his ears that the Poles were demanding he should be handed over to them for trial. But the timing of this refusal was in some ways unfortunate since it coincided with a creative idea being fomented by the Americans. Dr George Shuster, the head of the War Department Interrogation Commission, is quoted as saying that '. . . after talking with General Guderian he could think of nothing more calculated to produce a good, strategic history of the German General Staff than to bring Guderian to the United States and install him on somebody's porch up in Connecticut for a summer of casual conversation'. Shuster's impression bore fruit in early 1946 when the Americans began to concentrate more than 200 former German generals and staff officers in one camp at Allendorf in order to gather as much information as they could from their previous enemies. In their opinion the two men with outstanding qualifications who should act as co-ordinators of the German writers were Halder and Guderian, but this was at once rendered impracticable because Guderian was moving through one of his periods of non-co-operation and in any case he and Halder were not on speaking terms. So Halder became co-ordinator in one of the most remarkable historical research projects ever attempted, while Guderian, when finally he decided that it was safe and in his better interests to help (he was told on 18th June 1947, his birthday, that all charges had been dropped), made contributions on the periphery and commented upon the major studies and those upon which he could focus his special expertise. As much for the insight they give into his way of thinking as in the nature of their contribution to the matters with which he dealt, his commentaries are valuable reading: prejudices and pride are intermingled with the caustic shafts which won him a special recognition among the Americans. But Guderian was far from being alone in expressions of pique: factions gathered round Halder, with the traditionalists on the one side, and the progressives, including Guderian, on the other. Thus *Generalfeldmarschalls* von Blomberg and Erhardt Milch (the master-builder of the *Luftwaffe* under Göring) suffered from a form of ostracism in company with Guderian. Halder, for example, declined to shake the hand of Milch when it was offered and repeatedly declined even to discuss the quarrel with Guderian. In this military university the members of rival academic factions, in the process of relieving the tedium of captivity, hurled verbal darts at each other while they refought – on paper – the battles of the past. A passage at arms with *General der Infanterie* Edgar Roehricht provides a good example of Guderian's invective when roused. Roehricht, in a paper describing, somewhat inaccurately from memory, the training organisation of OKH, had seen fit to criticise the methods employed by the Panzer Command, and to resurrect the infantry's fundamental distastes for the tank men. As an opening retort Guderian wrote: 'The study shows that the author had just as little peacetime training experience as wartime combat experience' – a tart piece of defamation since Roehricht had much experience in many capacities, as Guderian should have known. Guderian went on to object to remarks such as, 'The arbitrary manners of the armoured forces from the very beginning . . ' and summarised his views (to the satisfaction of the American editors who deleted Roehricht's offending passages) with 'The contributor . . . also knows nothing about the Inspector General of Panzer Troops. Who was "disturbed" by the Inspector General? The work of the Inspector General did not lead to any "duplication of effort" nor did it cause any lack of uniformity in tactical views. It certainly had no "fatal consequences".'

The principal articles written by Guderian for the American project were a long paper describing the training of General Staff Officers and a study giving his personal concept of the structure of joint command in the future. In the latter he developed an expansive and controversial line of thought, tackling the problem from a joint service angle instead of narrowly from that of *Army* High Command, and demonstrating his grasp of the essential need for such a concept in substantiation of his long-standing belief in unification. Halder treated the paper to some typically acetic, though by no means invalid and unconstructive, comments. Unhappily the exchanges between these two were injurious to their reputations and productive of factions. Among Halder's loyal adherents, an insinuation that Guderian was shallow, as Halder, with unworthy insincerity, made him out to be, became current. And Guderian, to the world at large, was to present Halder as of lesser calibre than, in fact, this remarkable man was. Halder the cool intellectual with a schoolmasterly manner, and Guderian, the dynamic man of ideas and action were worthy of better things.

Throughout this academic period behind bars in the unaccustomed role of comparatively passive inactivity – a style of secluded intellectual activity which had eluded him since the 1920s – Guderian was at last to find a relaxation which previously would have been inconceivable. To his elder son, who as a General Staff officer was his fellow prisoner, he appeared as something of a revelation in that he began to play bridge for the first time – and did so light heartedly. Moreover, he tended the camp vegetable patch with immense enjoyment. Heinz-Günther recalls those days with a sense of keen enjoyment. In 1948, too, the Americans were registering his father as a 'very kindly man, cheerful . . . with an excellent sense of humour', but, by then, of course, Guderian already knew he was not to be abandoned to the Poles, or any other court of justice. 'The straight road', as he wrote to Gretel, 'proves right in the long run.' And when captivity at last came to an end on his 60th birthday in June 1948 (he was the last to be released from the camp at Neustadt although, during the last six months, Gretel was allowed to be with him), it was to move to a small house at Schwangau, there to begin work on the memoirs for which he had laid foundations while in prison and to start gardening with characteristic enthusiasm and a quite astonishing knowledge. And, as old men will, he planted trees. The garden of the home he later bought at Wurnburg is, to-day, a miniature forest!

Battles there remained to be fought, though none with much relish. In 1948 it came to his notice that Schlabrendorff's book, *Offiziere gegen Hitler*, which had already been published in Switzerland, was about to be serialised in a Munich newspaper. The serious allegations against Guderian's conduct had to be combated, particularly the assertion that he had betrayed the 20th July plotters in order to become Chief of Staff. A prolonged wrangle took place out of court and resulted in what, in some respects, amounted to a Pyrrhic victory. Nevertheless the documents and sworn affidavits by Guderian and Thomale stimulated and provide an important contribution to the history of resistance against Hitler. When Schlabrendorff recanted in the pages of the *Münchener Abendzeitung*, saying '. . . much new material has been found. Due to this a rewrite of the book has begun . . . For this reason I have asked the editor of the

Münchener Abendzeitung to stop publication of the old edition', his letter appeared under the headline 'The End of a Legend'. The paper added its own comment to the effect that, already, the case at that moment being heard against Halder showed that there could be no talk of a substantial political resistance to Hitler among the General Staff.

Guderian was never brought to trial because there was nothing of substance against him. The remainder of his life was spent mostly in a backwater, although he was constantly engaged in correspondence with journalists all over the world and in caring for the interests of his old comrades of all ranks. Yet occasionally his name cropped up as a shot fired in the cold war being waged between East and West. In October 1950 he wrote a booklet about European defence called 'Can Western Europe be Defended?', its appearance timed to raise alarm at a moment of appalling weakness of the West's defences as NATO began to seek new teeth to make its task credible. The booklet caused a stir, the London *Times* referring to people's bewilderment at the authoritative ring of a voice from the recent iniquitous German past and the general's acceptance of an estimate that the Russians had 175 divisions at readiness which they could raise to 500. And in 1951, at the invitation of his publisher, another evocative little booklet appeared – *So Geht es Nicht* (This cannot be the Right Way) – in which he unflinchingly and predictably stated the view held by so many people, that Germany could not remain divided and that there was a danger that NATO, in rearming the Germans, wished only to use them as the principal defenders of a unified Europe against the threat from the East. Looking farther ahead he added the fear that the Western Powers would exhaust themselves by the struggles in the Far East to the detriment of the essential defence of Europe. In that year, too, the Poles, searching no doubt for political advantage, exploited the name Guderian with its old symbolism of naked German aggression: they complained to the USA that Guderian was in charge of an alleged intelligence organisation which 'established the so-called Guderian group for smuggling American agents into Poland' – an accusation which lacked foundation.

These mild forays and minor disturbances ruffled him but little, while the intense interest of Germans and foreigners in *Panzer Leader* (which the critics gave a fair if not exuberant reception) was exhilarating. It starred among the best-sellers of 1952 in the USA (where he was made an Honorary Member of the International Mark Twain Society in March 1954) and was translated into ten languages including Russian, Polish and Chinese. Within a few months of its publication his health fell into decline and on 14th May 1954 he died.

Above his grave members of the Frontier Police fired a last salute, for military honours he could not receive since the German Army had yet to be reborn. But in the final days of his life he was aware that the organisation that had absorbed his career must soon be recreated. The negotiations to rearm Germany were in train. In October she was to be admitted to NATO and the *Bundeswehr*, a unified defence force of which he might have approved, became a certainty.

It was part of this man's final tragedy that the new Germany and its *Bundeswehr* still finds it impossible to pay him the official honour which is his due. A plan to name barracks after him in the 1960s remains unfulfilled.

12 Seer, Technician, Genius or Germany's best General?

It has to be left to the imagination whether Guderian could have fulfilled all the demands that can be placed upon a high commander for he never held a completely independent high command. Therefore it is impossible to assess fully his qualities at this level by the standards of Field-Marshal Lord Wavell when he declared that he would only consider the high-commander in history who had ' . . . handled large forces in an independent command in more than one campaign and who had shown his qualities in adversity as well as in success'. Wavell's qualifications as a judge are undeniable: among modern commanders he is almost unique in his record of endurance of the vicissitudes of independent command in many campaigns – in success and in adversity – and, also, respected as a writer with profound insight into the problem of generalship. Let it be recalled that Erwin Rommel carried a copy of Wavell's lectures on campaign with him, though Guderian seems hardly to have felt the need for a foreign mentor – except, perhaps, Fuller. Nevertheless Wavell's criteria are useful in evaluating Guderian as a Great Captain, even if the field-marshal's requirements have to be adapted because Guderian had, perforce, to filch independent command of large forces by circumventing the restrictive orders of his superiors.

It is, in fact, by his propensity to walk alone, divorced from traditional orthodoxy, that Guderian must be judged, for he cannot be assessed by the standards of his more obedient contemporaries from whom so frequently, with calculated dissent, he stood apart. Guderian was that rare combination of a man of ideas equipped with the ability and verve to turn inspiration into reality. No other general in the Second World War – and few in history – managed to impress so wide and intrinsic a change upon the military art in so short a time, and left such a trail of controversy in his wake. And so the questions about this maverick general which have to be answered concern the impact of his unorthodoxy (if unorthodoxy it was) upon events as well as those concerning wisdom and stability of character. Was he seer or empiricist, a mere technician or a radical genius? Above all, in a profession which abides by strict discipline and standardised behaviour, could he be damned as an instrument of negative disruption or upheld as the harbinger of a new kind of military unity? By creating a unified *Panzertruppe* within the German Army was he a cause of fragmentation within that army? Or was it automatically productive that, by forging a system that parallelled the first attempt at creating a consolidated Defence Force, he introduced conditions which eliminated the burden of a long attritional war, such as ended in 1918, and made feasible, once more, campaigns of swift, economic viability?

Under the headings by which Wavell tested a High Commander, there is abundant evidence in support of Guderian's strategic insight. The confident stroke against the rear of the entire Polish Army at Brest Litovsk in the culminating phase of the 'Great Manoeuvres' of September 1939, when his execution and verve far exceeded in practice his superior commander's expectations, was explicit of the feasibility of a military practice Guderian had been developing, almost in isolation, for fifteen years. The exploitation to the Channel coast after crossing the Meuse in May 1940, including Guderian's suicidal gesture of resignation when his intentions were frustrated, is confirmation that his boldly publicised concept of mechanised warfare contained strategic applications that far exceeded simple military demands; whole nations bent before a system based on élitist principles that, historically, were the essence of orthodoxy. The astonishing speed and purposeful direction of the drive to Smolensk and into the Ukraine in the summer of 1941, along with a skilful juggling of inadequate resources to achieve an outstanding series of envelopments, was further proof of his aptitude in devising a true economy of force – even though its outcome turned into an experience of major personal adversity along with defeat for the Army. Finally, as an example of strategic competence in retreat, there was the halting of the Russian forces at the gates of Warsaw in August 1944 – a brilliant husbanding of minimal resources in ending a rout.

By the same token the subtle tactical handling of units and formations which, at the beginning of each campaign, were so often out-numbered, and in frequently producing by surprise that overwhelming concentration of strength at the crucial point, puts Guderian on a par with the Great Captains. Though the original strategic plan to break through the Ardennes into northern France in 1940 belongs to Manstein, it was Guderian who reinforced the High Command's nerve by confidently pronouncing the feasibility of infiltrating massed mechanised armies through intricate terrain (a genuinely original concept in its day) and he whose pre-war preparations engineered the techniques that made the movement possible not only by his own corps but by that of every other part of the German Army. For he had developed the unique logistic and communication systems which enabled mechanised troops to operate independently for up to five days, and to respond rapidly and flexibly to the commands of its leaders. Without this system in perfect operation nothing would have prevailed.

However, the tactics which the Germans employed with such panache throughout the Second World War (except when untutored influences intervened) were only made possible by superb training. In this connection Guderian also satisfies Wavell. To whatever level – section, company, battalion or any one of the higher formations – that Guderian addressed his creative mind in the search for innovation and the improvement of efficiency, new heights of excellence were reached. Not only did he dream, study and synthesise, but he built practical organisations and expounded his ideas with a crisp phraseology that epitomised his irresistible enthusiasm and sense of practical purpose. He was omnipotent, a trainer and director of training rolled into one who so rationalized new methods that he left himself ample time to tackle, with asperity, those in authority who – in reality or imagination – stood to bar the way to the future. He had a remarkable facility for drawing the best out of his troops or squeezing the most from his superiors; nowhere was this better demonstrated than in his drive into the Ukraine in August and September 1941. Here was the repudiation of those who said he was 'no good with men'. Yet although the personal staff officers and ADCs remember their general with deepest admiration and affection – few were blind to his shortcomings. For Guderian's problems were almost as often created by the man as the system or the enemy. His Chiefs of Staff sometimes had difficulty keeping track of him and the orders he gave when separated from them by distance. As Walther Nehring, one of the most efficient of them, said to me, 'His thoughts would race ahead and sometimes he had to be pulled back, and while he was a deep thinker he was also liable to act without thinking'. The same could be said of Rommel's tactical flair – but not his intellect.

And what of the soldiers whose faces lit up in his presence? Well, with this general they knew where they stood. Drive them hard though he did, they responded, recognising him as one among them because he *really* fought at their side in a way few higher commanders ever did. Particularly in time of war (probably more than in peace) the soldiers were touched by his warm humanity, which is the essence of leadership. To him the spur to the most self-sacrificing of all his assaults upon Germany's supreme leadership was the belief that incompetence was ruining both his beloved country and the men of the *Panzertruppe*.

Nehring also helps answer another of Wavell's criteria, that concerning Guderian's energy and driving power in planning a battle. In a German Army which was well supplied with senior officers of outstanding intellect and enormous drive, Guderian won a pre-eminent reputation for seemingly inexhaustible spirits, inventiveness and an utter determination to have his way – if not at once, certainly within the foreseeable future. Reinforcing this tenacity was a much tougher robustness than is sometimes supposed, for while Guderian allowed it to become common know-

ledge that he had a weak heart (to which he drew attention in a hypochondriac style that is unusual among high military commanders who
normally prefer to conceal their defects), there is not one occasion on
which ill-health actually prevented him from completing a task. Each
physical collapse occurred briefly *after* an exhausting series of events or
some quite shattering experience. And at the end, let it be emphasised, it
was not a heart defect which took him to the grave. Nehring says of his
commander's physique and his ability to carry through ideas to their
fulfilment: 'He never showed signs of strain because he was a strong
man – but one who drove himself hard. In time of battle he would find
sleep easy to come by and as a commander he was easy to work
for – wonderful in the way he gave one encouragement, full of banter and
provocation in his efforts to get the best out of you'. And then with great
emphasis, 'He had charisma – much charisma!'

But strategic and tactical ability, skill as a trainer, and reserves of
physique and willpower are qualities such as lesser commanders may
possess without satisfying the demands of high command. There is
another essential facility required – perhaps, in the nature of centralisa-
tion that evolved out of the elaborate signal systems produced by communication officers like Fellgiebel and Praun, the most important facility
of all: it is the ability to deal productively with Government and with
Allies.

In company with Allies Guderian underwent relatively few tests and
none of prolonged severity. In the opening stages of his spell as a commander in the field his victories were won with German troops alone. He
was spared the frustrations of Rommel in trying to prise concessions out
of unwilling Italians; of Manstein making the best of failing Rumanians
and Hungarians, and of Dietl in spurring on the reluctant Finns. Indeed,
when he was Chief of the General Staff in the closing stages of war, there
were few allies left to Germany, and those that remained withdrew
shortly after he took office. But there is nothing to suggest that he was
incapable, through lack of courtliness and understanding, of negotiating
intuitively with other nationalities, for he was a German without racial
prejudice. And it is satisfactory to recall that drinks supplied by the
Japanese Ambassador suitably fortified him prior to a memorably stormy
dispute with Hitler in February 1945.

In debate with Government, however – and for most purposes this
meant with Adolf Hitler – it is much more difficult, because of the dictator's complexity and ambiguity, to draw a positive conclusion. Between
them there seems to have been some sort of mutual understanding,
perhaps a genuine empathy strengthened on Guderian's part by a belief
that the Führer could be the saviour of Germany in desperate days
besides the essential sponsor of the struggling *Panzertruppe*. When the
threat of war was remote Guderian backed a man who, unbeknown to

him, was bent upon confrontations and conflict placed in his hands 'the sharp sword' that made possible a short war – the only sort Germany could successfully sustain. And while this stimulated Guderian's ambition, it also strengthened Hitler's hand against German generals who were divided among themselves over the pace and shape of military reconstruction. The schism within the General Staff ranks was thus not only, in part, of Guderian's making, but of aid to Hitler in his antipathy to the General Staff. The efforts of the highest in command to reduce Guderian's standing prior to September 1939 and their continuing attempts to denigrate him ever after were central to the struggle between State and Army, an intrigue of profound complexity since it reflected the conflicting emotions inherent in a process of rapid institutional change. The instincts of the older, tepid members of the German General Staff turned uneasily against the dynamism of a strongly persuasive character who sought radical change – it was natural that they should do so.

Amid the all-consuming struggle surrounding Guderian on the eve of war it is less remarkable that he was among the last to perceive the evil and menace which Hitler posed. Not only was the truth obscured by Hitler, but antagonism by his military superiors, their hostility through 1939 to 1941, forcibly contributed to Guderian's fatal belief that Hitler should be saved from the incompetence of his own High Command. It is easy to criticise Guderian for persisting in attempts to educate the megalomaniac after he had, at last, in 1942, come to detect the Führer's failings. One has to understand, in this context, Hitler's unassailable position and point out that what hope of change remained in 1943 could only be realised by indirect action from within the system rather than direct action from without. The eventual failure of the active resisters in 1944 consolidates this view. Hitler merely exploited Guderian's loyalty to the utmost and without requital.

It was in his dealings with the Head of State and his underlings – some of them brilliant men – that exposed the essential fissures of Guderian's character without, in the final analysis, entirely fulfilling Wavell's most exacting demands. Guderian, like Wavell, failed to develop a satisfactory working arrangement with his political master. For Wavell, of course, the perils involved were less acute: when he rigorously, though ineffectually, opposed Churchill, he merely hazarded his career. By each act of resistance to Hitler, Guderian risked torture and staked his own life and possibly that of his family too. It is in the light of knowledge that opposition to Hitler, particularly in the closing days of the war, might inflict fatal consequences without doing the slightest good, that Guderian's fundamental political attitude must be examined in the latter years.

Far sighted in army matters though Guderian certainly was as the result of an almost exclusively military education, and politically aware as he showed himself to be at critical moments of his career, it can never convincingly be claimed that he possessed innate political sense and judgement such as equipped politically orientated soldiers like von Schleicher and von Reichenau. Guderian frequently failed to detect the warning signs of oncoming change – could not, as was said of von Reichenau, 'hear the grass grow'. Not that either Schleicher or Reichenau, who helped promote the Nazis, managed to read the future with infallible accuracy, but they did at least recognise the dangers inherent in Nazism and took steps, albeit too late and fallaciously, to curb them. Guderian, on the other hand, tended to swallow the official line, to trust too long – without appreciating the consequences. Ironically, he who formulated radically effective military schemes was prone to accept radically pernicious political notions. His readiness to stand at the side of extremists in the Baltic States in 1919, his support for the Nazi programme in the mid 1930s, his reiteration of Hitler's dogma and diplomatic ploys, bear the marks of superficiality in understanding political motivations and their meaning. Let it be added, however, that he was just one among many in Germany and abroad who were taken in. Yet, while it became habitual for him to challenge those military views which offended his inculcated critical faculties, there is only scanty *contemporary* evidence to indicate his detection and rejection of politically repugnant ideas.

It is erroneous to believe that German officers divorced themselves from the world beyond the barrack gates; the General Staff regularly heard lectures on important issues delivered by qualified speakers. The system failed because so many intellectual personalities had fled the country or abandoned their integrity to Nazi ideology in the interests of personal survival. An unbiased objective dissertation was no longer possible when leading intellectuals from *all* professions fell silent or became warped in their judgement. Their lack of dissent against Nazism in its formative days contributed strongly to Germany's decline into servile unscrupulousness. Guderian, the lower orders of the General Staff, and the rest of the people were exposed to unrefuted evil. He and they became all the more politically vulnerable through receiving bad advice and taking an insufficiently *critical* interest in doctrinaire politics and current affairs. They had been trapped in a characteristic German pursuit, that of the search for an Ideal and a rash haste in implementing it without deep regard for the implications.

It was but a foregone conclusion that, as Chief of Staff in 1944, Guderian stood only the remotest chance of diverting or reversing the political stream which had run so strongly under Hitler's control since 1938, when Hitler had first undermined the authority of the War Minister, the Army Commander-in-Chief and his Chief of Staff. Justly, in reference to these events *after* the war, Guderian wrote: ' . . . younger officers could not conceive that their superiors would accept without a struggle

215

and without proper action a development which those superiors, as they now allege, clearly recognised at the time as disadvantageous and even pernicious. However, this is precisely what did happen, and it happened at a time when it was still possible to offer resistance – in peacetime.'

And yet, in commenting upon the rapid superimposition of an Armed Forces Command (OKW) in time of rearmament and war upon the existing and wasteful system of independent command by each of the three Services, Guderian, in post-war documents, seems not to have fully evaluated the effects of removing a vital, political counterweight. He plays down its political disruptiveness while keen to defend its military advantages. And so when he became the head of a politically devalued organisation (OKH) he felt the draught since he then was deprived of that direct influence over the Head of State which he so badly needed. Therefore, ironically in the winter of 1945, he was compelled to indulge in the very sort of intrigue with politicians that Seeckt frowned upon and Guderian himself, ostensibly in the past, had disapproved. But in the forlorn efforts to manipulate the government and end the war before Germany was overwhelmed, Seecktian rules and principles went overboard. Guderian failed in this attempt as would any other reformer have failed against the entrenched Nazi hierarchy of that time. There was simply nobody left with both the courage and the influence to change Hitler's mind or eject this mentally deranged demagogue and his sycophants. It is, of course, permissable to ask if he could have produced successful resistance in 1938, but this speculation is profitless. To have succeeded where Beck and Brauchitsch and Halder failed, and in so doing satisfied the most exacting of Wavell's requirements, Guderian needed the requisite seniority and prestige – and it was only time and the war which provided these. By then Hitler was treating him, like the rest, with 'scornful disregard'.

It is a travesty of history, though perhaps only a passing phase, that the German people remain scantily aware of the virtues of their generals who were painted black by detractors. The fear of a caste exists and is kept fresh. In 1965 the newspaper *Die Zeit* criticised the proposal by the *Bundeswehr* to name Army barracks after Guderian on the grounds that his character was not emblematic and that he was an unsuitable example because his behaviour was not always exemplary. The old aspersions about his conduct in the summer of 1944 were resurrected with journalistic fervour and, although it was conceded he could not be blamed for taking no part directly in the plot because it was a very difficult matter of conscience, an insinuation of Guderian's unworthiness was but faintly veiled. It is part of the Guderian enigma that he chose not to reveal (not even to his son) his knowledge and tacit assent of the attempt to kill Hitler and that, in maintaining his objection to murder as a political solvent, he deliberately allowed the censure of his people rather than their approbation.

Guderian has been more generously treated abroad though mainly, it must be said, as the author of *Panzer Leader* and as a prophet and architect of a type of warfare which is now orthodox. Whenever tanks and armoured forces win some new victory a reference to the name of Guderian usually crops up. How can he be classified then? A seer? In the strict military sense, the answer can be a qualified 'yes' in that he visualised warfare of the future. A technician? Certainly, since he capitalised upon his vision with professional absorption in his trade to create machinery that worked as near to perfection as is possible in war. A genius? Well, his inspired ability to turn ideas into reality and action by powerfully influencing opinions, feelings, spirit and method can no more be overlooked than he himself could be ignored in person. It was his last Chief of Staff, Thomale, who called him 'Germany's best and most responsible general'. Let a disinterested judgement be that of his interrogators, the sceptical American officers who tackled this formidable general across a table in the prison cages after the war, and whose initial scepticism about an enemy eventually was converted to respect, if not admiration for the man. 'The military career of Heinz Guderian is in itself enough to establish his ability as an organiser, a theorist and an aggressive field commander', it was written. To them he retained 'his exceptional intellectual integrity, his firm and uncompromising attitude, his untactfulness under stress and his alloy of courtliness and acid humour. He is a man who writes what he thinks and who does not alter his opinions to suit his audience.' This judgement, linked with knowledge of the man's staunchness, amply satisfies Wavell in his demands that a general '... must have "character" ' – which, he continued, 'simply means that he knows what he wants and has the courage and determination to get it. He should have a genuine knowledge of humanity, the raw materials of his trade, and, most vital of all, he must have what we call the fighting spirit, the will to win.'

But, in the final analysis, what of the man, the compassionate being who could write such tender letters to his wife and who could feel profound sorrow for Hitler, a man without ' ... friendship with fine men, the pure love for a wife, affection of one's own children'? It is the transmitted warmth of Guderian and his joy in warmth among others which makes him pre-eminent among great generals. Embraced as he was by his professional calling, he performed his duty with sincerity under most hazardous and complicated conditions.

Bibliography

ANON, *The Trial of the Major War Criminals,* International Tribunal, 1949.

BISCHOFF, J., *Die Letzte Front, 1919. Geschichte der Eiserne Division im Baltikum, 1919*

BRUCE, G., *The Warsaw Uprising,* Hart Davis, 1972.

BURKE, R., *The German Panzerwaffe 1920–1939 – A Study in Institutional Change,* NW University, USA, 1969.

DEICHMANN, P., *German Air Force Operations in Support of the Army,* Arno, 1962.

ELLIS, L.F., *The War in France and Flanders, 1939–1940,* HMSO, 1953.

FULLER, J.F.C., *Memoirs of an Unconventional Soldier,* Nicholson and Watson, 1936. *The Decisive Battles of the Western World,* Eyre and Spottiswoode, 1956.

GOEBBELS, J. (Ed. LOCHNOR, L.), *The Goebbels Diaries,* Hamilton, 1948.

GOERLITZ, W., *The German General Staff,* Praeger, 1953.

GUDERIAN, H., *Achtung! Panzer!,* UDV, 1937. *Mit den Panzern in Ost und West,* Volk und Reich Verlag, 1942. *Kann Westeuropa verteitigt werden,* Vowinckel Verlag, 1950. *So Geht es Nicht,* Vowinckel Verlag, 1951. *Panzer Leader,* Joseph, 1953.

HAGEN-SCHULZE, *Freikorps-Republik, 1918–1920,* Boppard, 1969.

HALDER, F., *Kriegstagebuch,* Kohlhammer, 1964.

HORNE, A., *To Lose a Battle,* Macmillan, 1969.

JACOBSON, H.A., *Fall Gelb,* Steiner, 1957.

KENNEDY, R., *The German Campaign in Poland, 1939,* Dept. of US Army, 1956.

KLUCK, A. VON, *The March on Paris,* Arnold, 1923.

LEBER, A., *Der Reichsmarschall im Kriege,* 1950.

LEWIN, R., *Rommel as Military Commander,* Batsford, 1968.

LIDDELL HART, B.H., *The Other Side of the Hill,* Cassell, 1948 (revised ed.1951).

MACKSEY, K., *Armoured Crusader,* Hutchinson, 1967. *Tank Warfare,* Hart Davis, 1972. *The Partisans of Europe,* Hart Davis, 1975.

MANSTEIN, E VON, *Lost Victories,* Methuen, 1958.

NEHRING, W., *Die Geschichte der deutschen Panzerwaffe 1916 bis 1945*, Propylaen, 1969.

REICHSARCHIV, *Der Weltkrieg 1914 bis 1918. Der Marne-Feldzug*, Mittler, 1926.

ROHER, J. AND OTHERS, *Decisive Battles of World War II: The German View*, Deutsch, 1965.

RYAN, C., *The Last Battle*, Collins, 1966.

SCHLABRENDORFF, F. VON, *Offiziere gegen Hitler*, 1946. *The Secret War against Hitler*, Pitmann, 1965.

SEATON, A., *The Russo-German War, 1941–45*, Barker, 1971.

SEECKT, H. VON, *Thoughts of a Soldier*, Benn, 1930.

SPEER, A., *Inside the Third Reich*, Weidenfeld and Nicolson, 1970.

SPEIDEL, H., *Invasion 1944: ein Beitrag zu Rommel und des Reiches Schicksal*, 1949.

STRIK-STRIKFELD, W., *Against Hitler and Stalin, 1941–1945*, Day, 1970.

WARLIMONT, W., *Inside Hitler's Headquarters* Weidenfeld and Nicolson, 1964.

WATT, R., *The Kings Depart*, Simon and Schuster, 1968.

WHEELER-BENNETT, J., *The Nemesis of Power*, Macmillan, 1953.

WINTERBOTHAM, F., *The Ultra Secret*, Weidenfeld and Nicolson, 1974.

Index